FLORA MACDONALD

Also by Hugh Douglas

The Underground Story (Robert Hale)
Crossing the Forth (Robert Hale)
Portrait of the Burns Country (Robert Hale)
Edinburgh, a Children's History (Longman)
Burke and Hare, the True Story (Robert Hale)
Charles Edward Stuart, The Man, The King, The Legend (Robert Hale)
Robert Burns – a Life (Robert Hale)
Burns Supper Companion (Alloway Publishing)
Hogmanay Companion (Neil Wilson Publishing)
The Private Passiosn of Bommie Prince Charlie (Sutton Publishing)
Robert Buns: The Tinder Heart (Sutton Publishing)
Jacobite Spy Wars: Moles, Rogues and Treachery (Sutton Publishing)

FLORA MACDONALD
The Most Loyal Rebel

Hugh Douglas

SUTTON PUBLISHING

First published in the United Kingdom in 1993 by
Alan Sutton Publishing Limited, an imprint of Sutton Publishing Limited
Phoenix Mill · Thrupp · Stroud · Gloucestershire GL5 1RW

This revised paperback edition first published in 1999

A catalogue record for this book is available from the British Library

ISBN 0 7509 2098 X

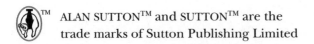 ALAN SUTTON™ and SUTTON™ are the
trade marks of Sutton Publishing Limited

Typeset in 10/13 New Baskerville.
Typesetting and origination by
Sutton Publishing Limited.
Printed and bound in Great Britain by
Biddles Limited, Guidford, Surrey.

To Keeta and John Campbell,

who believed in Flora and in this book

Contents

Author's Note

Flora MacDonald never sought the fame that her contemporaries and history bestowed on her. She seldom spoke of the journey over the sea to Skye with Bonnie Prince Charlie and rarely used her popularity to benefit herself during her hard life. Because of this reticence and the fact that she and her husband lost everything in North Carolina during the American War of Independence, it is difficult to write a conventional biography of her. Little was recorded of the appalling suffering of women and children during that bitter war and its aftermath, when many families experienced greater hardship, deprivation and cruelty than their men who were directly involved in it. Flora endured as much as anyone, but she suffered in silence. As a result, her biographers hitherto have either ignored this period or glossed over it. By examining what was written and said about the Highlanders and other members of Flora's family, it is possible to build a portrait of Flora during her disastrous North Carolina adventure and the terrible winter she spent in Nova Scotia. These 'lost' years showed her at her most noble – facing disaster with bravery which made her as great a heroine as when she was rescuing Prince Charlie. Consequently this book is at once a biography, a social history and a detective story which is a tribute to a clan and one remarkable family within that clan.

Acknowledgements

Eight years is a long time to work on a book and I owe an enormous debt to a large number of people in three countries – I am sorry I cannot name them all. First thanks must be to Keeta Campbell and Gloria Bristow who brought the neglect of Flora to my attention, and to Keeta for discovering many sources without which the book could not have been written. The search for Flora MacDonald covered Britain, the United States of America and Canada, and I have been helped by individuals, organizations, museums and libraries in all three.

IN BRITAIN   Donald F. MacDonald has proved a limitless source of information on his two homelands, the Hebrides and North Carolina. He read the text and made a number of suggestions which have enriched the book. Rob McDonald Parker, International Director, and Margaret Macdonald, Archivist, at the Clan Donald Centre, Armadale, Skye, have given generous help and libraries and museums have provided access to books, manuscripts and information in their keeping. Among these are Edinburgh City Library; the London Library; the British Library; Mitchell Library, Glasgow; Moray District Mobile Library; The National Library of Scotland; Peterborough Central Library; Public Record Office; Scottish Record Office; West Highland Museum, Fort William; Dualchas Skye and Lochaber District Council Museum Service; National Maritime Museum; Royal Marines Museum and Scottish United Services Museum. Alastair Macleod, Genealogist at Inverness Library; William L. Scott, Local History Librarian, Argyll and Bute District; Ian MacDonald, Kintyre; Jamie MacDonald, North Carolina and Edinburgh; Alexander Murdoch; Donald Whyte, Kirkliston; the late John MacInnes, Daliburgh, South Uist; Iain Coates, London, and many others have given valuable assistance. My thanks to all of them.

IN THE USA   Sandy Allen, Raleigh, North Carolina, has helped to research a number of points and Wendy J. Glavis has supplied sources in Pennsylvania. I acknowledge the interest and valuable help of Scott Buie,

Editor of *Argyll Colony Plus*, and Rassie Wicker's daughter, Eloise Knight, Pinehurst, NC; Grace W. Ellis, Cameron, NC; George E. Ammons, Red Springs, NC; and Henry A. MacKinnon Jr, Lumberton, NC, have provided material, and I have had assistance from Alice R. Cotten, Reference Historian, North Carolina Collection, University of North Carolina; Scott W. Loehr, Museum of Cape Fear; Ransom McBride of North Carolina Genealogical Society; Pinny Geffert, Archivist, St Andrews Presbyterian College; Joel T. Loeb, Historical Society of Pennsylvania; as well as Lower Cape Fear Historical Society, Scottish Heritage USA, North Carolina Bureau of Archives and History, Pennsylvania Historical and Museum Commission. Dusty Shultz, Superintendent, Moore's Creek National Battlefield, and staff were especially helpful with photography. My thanks to all of them and and to many others who have shown kindness and encouragement worthy of a Highland community.

IN CANADA   I would like to thank especially John V. Duncanson, Falmouth, Nova Scotia, and Judge Ronald A. MacDonald, Antigonish, for their interest and help. West Hants Historical Society; Mr Justice Ian M. McKeigan, Halifax; Lois K. Kernaghan and Allan C. Dunlop of the Public Archives of Nova Scotia; and Judith Tulloch, History Section, Canadian Parks Service, Halifax, have afforded me assistance. Scott Robson of the Nova Scotia Museum, Judy Dietz of the Art Gallery of Nova Scotia and Bill Nelson of the 84th Foot 2nd Battalion Regimental Associaton have helped with illustrations.

Sue Sharpe typed the manuscript and handled the huge volume of correspondence involved, and my wife, family and friends have encouraged me. My thanks to them all, and thanks and apologies to any others I have omitted – Flora still has many friends on both sides of the Atlantic today.

Clan Donald – The Great Clan

Early in my researches a Nova Scotian of Highland descent wrote, 'You will appreciate that trying to trace a MacDonald in Cape Breton is looking for a needle in a haystack.' I soon came to realize how right he was, not just about Cape Breton, but about North Carolina and the Western Isles of Scotland also – and in the present day as well as in the past. This key to the many members of the great Clan Donald who pass through the pages of this book will help the reader. As to the clan name, I have used the form 'MacDonald', which means 'son of Donald', throughout, unless referring to a present-day member of the clan who prefers another form.

The Hebridean islands in the eighteenth century belonged to many clans or families, but the MacDonalds were the largest. There were two MacDonald chiefs in the islands – Sleat (pronounced 'Slate'), the most powerful, who held much of Skye and North Uist, and Clanranald, who had South Uist, Benbecula and part of mainland Scotland. These chiefs ruled large 'families' who were closely interrelated.

THE CHIEFS

Sir Alexander MacDonald, Chief of Sleat   Seventh Baronet. 1710–46. Owned part of Skye and North Uist. Married Lady Margaret Montgomerie, daughter of Lowland peer, the Earl of Eglinton. Succeeded by his son, James (died 1766). Family had lost their estates following the 1715 Jacobite Rising, but these were returned later. Sleat raised militia companies for King George in the '45.

Sir James MacDonald of Sleat   Eighth Baronet. 1742–66. Succeeded father as Sleat Chief in 1746. Died abroad.

Sir Alexander MacDonald of Sleat   Ninth Baronet. First Baron 1745–95. Succeeded brother, James, in 1766.

Ranald MacDonald, Chief of Clanranald   1692–1766. Owned South Uist, Benbecula and part of mainland. Married Margaret MacLeod of Bernera. The previous chief had died in the 1715 Jacobite Rising, but the

Clanranald MacDonalds hedged their bets in the '45. The Chief did not call out his clansmen, although his son followed Prince Charlie.

FLORA AND ALLAN MACDONALD AND THEIR CHILDREN

Flora MacDonald   1722–90. Daughter of Ranald MacDonald of Milton, South Uist. Accompanied Prince Charlie on his escape over the sea to Skye. Later emigrated to North Carolina.

Allan MacDonald   Died 1792. Husband of Flora. Son of Alexander MacDonald of Kingsburgh, Skye. Factor to Sleat Chief. Fought on British side in American Revolution.

Charles MacDonald   First son of Flora and Allan. 1751–95. Joined East India Company, but went to America at the outbreak of the Revolution and served with the 84th (Royal Highland Emigrants) Regiment of Foot. Later became a captain in the Queen's Rangers. Married Isabella MacDonald of Aird. No family.

Anne MacDonald   Their first daughter. 1754–1834. Married natural son of MacLeod Chief, Alexander MacLeod of Glendale, Skye. Emigrated with parents. Four children.

Alexander MacDonald   Their second son. 1755–81. Captured with his father after Battle of Moore's Creek. Exchanged and continued to serve until he had to return to Britain for health reasons. Lost at sea.

Ranald MacDonald   Their third son. 1756–82. Unmarried. Served with Marines in America and Nova Scotia in American War of Independence. Lost at sea.

James MacDonald   Their fourth son. 1757–1807. Emigrated to North Carolina with parents. At Battle of Moore's Creek Bridge, but escaped and lived with Flora for a time. Joined Tarleton's British Legion. Returned to Skye and settled at Flodigarry with his wife, Emily MacDonald of Heisker and Skeabost. Six children.

John MacDonald Their fifth son. 1759–1831. Left behind in Scotland when parents emigrated. Served in Far East. Married a Mrs Boyle, who died. Married, secondly, Frances Chambers (nine children). Died Exeter and buried in Exeter Cathedral.

Frances MacDonald (Fanny)   Their youngest child. Born 1766. Left behind when parents emigrated to America. Married Donald MacDonald of Cuidreach, son of Flora's half-sister, Annabella. Their family emigrated to Australia.

OTHER MacDONALD CLANSMEN AND WOMEN

Alexander MacDonald of Boisdale, South Uist   Half-brother of Clanranald. One of first to meet Prince Charlie in 1745. Did not come out openly, but supported the Cause.

Alexander MacDonald of Cuidreach, Skye   Married Flora's half-sister, Annabella. Emigrated to North Carolina. Returned to Skye and took over tack (lease of tenancy) of Kingsburgh.

Alexander MacDonald of Kingsburgh, Skye   Sleat's Factor. Related to Sleat Chief. Sheltered Prince Charlie on island. Jailed. His son, Allan, married Flora MacDonald. Died 1772, aged 82.

Alexander MacDonald   Cousin of Allan. Captain in the 84th (Royal Highland Emigrants) Regiment of Foot. Lived on Staten Island.

Alexander MacDonald   Boatman who took Flora and Prince Charlie to Skye.

Father Allan MacDonald   Clanranald clansman. One of Seven Men of Moidart who sailed to Scotland with Prince Charlie in 1745. Prince's chaplain.

Revd Angus MacDonald of South Uist   Flora's grandfather. Married Elizabeth MacDonald of Largie, Argyll. Known as the 'Strong Minister'.

Angus MacDonald of Milton, South Uist   Brother of Flora. Secret Jacobite sympathizer.

Annabella MacDonald   Flora's half-sister. Married Alexander MacDonald of Cuidreach.

Donald MacDonald   Commanded Highlanders in North Carolina in Revolution. Defeated at Moore's Creek Bridge, 1776.

Donald MacDonald of Castleton, Skye   Related to Sleat Chief. Commanded a militia company on the island.

Donald MacDonald   Son of Flora's half-sister, Annabella, and Alexander MacDonald of Cuidreach. Emigrated to North Carolina. Fought on British side in Revolution. Married Flora's daughter, Fanny.

Donald Roy MacDonald   Half-brother of Hugh MacDonald of Baleshare. Wounded at Culloden. Met Prince Charlie on arrival in Skye.

Elizabeth MacDonald of Largie, Argyll   Flora's grandmother. Wife of Revd Angus MacDonald.

Florence MacDonald   Wife of Alexander MacDonald of Kingsburgh. Member of Castleton family. Prince Charlie stayed overnight at her home.

Hugh MacDonald of Armadale   Flora's step-father. Served in French army and became captain of a militia company in 1746. Emigrated to North Carolina. Died about 1780.

Hugh MacDonald of Baleshare   Cousin of Clanranald, and related to both Sleat Chief and Lady Clanranald. Half-brother of Donald Roy. Secret Jacobite sympathizer.

James MacDonald   Half-brother of Flora. In Dutch service.

James MacDonald of Sartle   Nephew of Hugh MacDonald of Armadale. Joined Rising in 1745. His house at Leith was a Jacobite meeting place.

James MacDonald   Son of Cuidreach. Lieutenant in North Carolina Highlanders.

John MacDonald of Kirkibost, North Uist   Factor to his cousin Sir Alexander of Sleat. Commanded militia company, but helped Prince Charlie.

John MacDonald   Boatman who took Flora and Prince Charlie to Skye.

Kenneth MacDonald   Son of Cuidreach. Aide-de-camp to General MacDonald in North Carolina. Captured at Moore's Creek Bridge.

Lady Margaret MacDonald   Wife of Sir Alexander of Sleat. Daughter of Earl of Eglinton. Prince Charlie came to her house in Skye.

Margaret MacDonald, Lady Clanranald (often referred to as Lady Clan)   Wife of Chief. A MacLeod of Bernera. Jacobite sympathizer.

Margaret MacDonald of Kirkibost, North Uist   Wife of John MacDonald. Cousin of Kingsburgh. Arrived in Skye the day before Prince Charlie landed.

Margaret (Peggy) MacDonald   Daughter of Clanranald.

Marion MacDonald   Flora's mother. Daughter of Revd Angus MacDonald. Married Ranald MacDonald of Milton, South Uist, who died. Married, secondly, Hugh MacDonald of Armadale.

Ranald MacDonald of Milton, South Uist   Flora's father. Died 1723.

Ranald MacDonald   Flora's brother. Died accidentally.

Ranald MacDonald   Son of Clanranald, generally known as 'Young Clanranald'. Came out with Prince Charlie in 1745.

Roderick MacDonald   Boatman who took Flora and Prince to Skye.

Roderick MacDonald   Ensign in Clanranald's regiment. Boatman on journey to Skye.

Maps

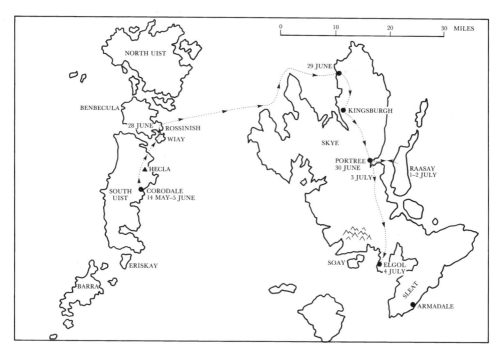

Prince Charles Edward's journey over the sea to Skye

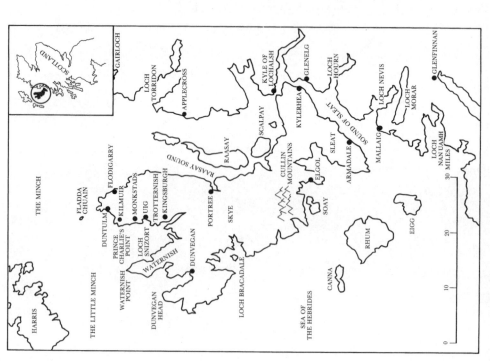

The Isle of Skye

Outer Hebrides (The Long Island)

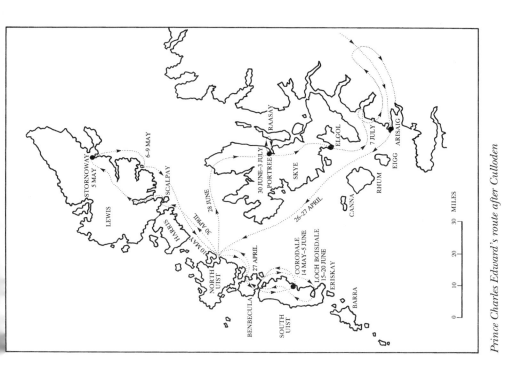

Prince Charles Edward's route after Culloden

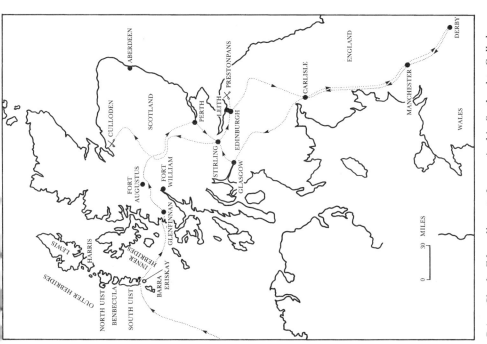

Prince Charles Edward's route from arrival in Scotland to Culloden

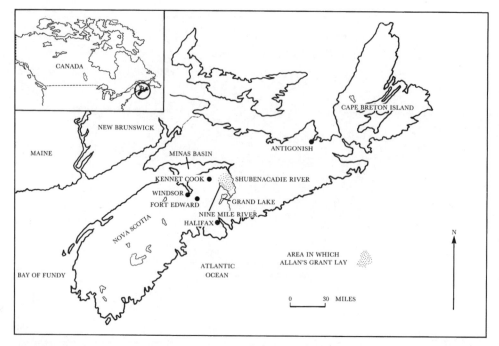

Nova Scotia

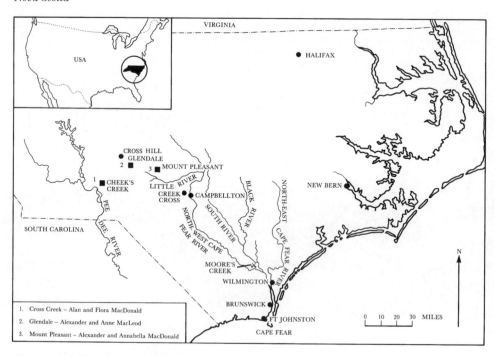

1. Cross Creek – Alan and Flora MacDonald
2. Glendale – Alexander and Anne MacLeod
3. Mount Pleasant – Alexander and Annabella MacDonald

Eastern North Carolina in the 1770s

PART ONE

To Skye and Immortality

CHAPTER ONE

The Lady of the Legend

Speed bonnie boat like a bird on the wing,
  'Onward' the sailors cry;
Carry the lad that's born to be king
  Over the sea to Skye.

Skye Boat Song, Sir Harold Boulton

Sunday 29 June in the year 1746 was no different from any other Sunday in Scotland: the country lay spread-eagled under the blanket of its customary pious Sabbath Day peace. An unbroken mist of silence covered the land from Gretna Green to John o' Groats: from the East Neuk of Fife to the farthermost Hebridean shore. At noon the nation was in church or at dinner – both solemn, cheerless occasions.

The Trotternish Peninsula at the north-western corner of the island of Skye looked as desolate as the drab expanse of sea that extended from its shore to the Outer Isles, without so much as a ship's sail to break the grey monotony. But the sea around Skye was not empty that Sunday. From behind the headland of Waternish a tiny speck emerged, gradually taking on the shape of a boat of the kind used by fishermen in those parts. It made surprising speed as its crew rowed feverishly towards a small, half-hidden bay on the Trotternish coast, pulling on the oars as though their lives depended on it.

Their lives did depend upon it: as did the lives of their three passengers, who were named in the letter of safe conduct which they carried as Flora MacDonald, her cousin, Neil MacEachain, and Flora's Irish maid, Betty Burke. To anyone who gave the maid half a glance, it would have been obvious that Betty Burke was the clumsiest woman imaginable, more like a man in disguise – and ill concealed at that. It was the girl's arrogant manner that betrayed her rather than the clothes she wore. This was a person unaccustomed to playing a menial role, so it was a simple step to conclude that the 'maid' was the fugitive Prince Charles Edward Stuart, a man with a price of £30,000 on his head, in

1

desperate flight from his enemies, the army and navy of King George II of Great Britain.

The journey over the sea to Skye was part of the final act of the 1745 Jacobite Rising: Prince Charlie's rash adventure to win back from Hanoverian George the kingdoms of Scotland and England from which his grandfather had fled more than half a century before, and which his father now claimed. The Prince's father, James Stuart, 'reigned' as King James VIII of Scotland and III of England in a bare little palace in Rome. Elsewhere he was known as the 'Old Pretender' or the 'King over the Water'.

Prince Charlie, the 'Young Pretender', landed in Scotland during the summer of 1745. After some daring marches and incredible victories, his rising came to an end when his army was routed at Culloden on 16 April 1746. His journey over the sea to Skye, the culmination of many adventures and hair's-breadth escapes, may have added no more than a footnote to the history of the '45, but it became a cornerstone of the Prince Charlie legend and made Flora MacDonald a heroine in her lifetime in Europe and America, the two worlds in which she lived.

History and legend present Flora as an unsophisticated young Highland girl innocently caught up in great events, but her picture tells a different story. Flora was twenty-two, maybe just turned twenty-three, that night when her life was overturned, but portraits painted at this time, and soon after, show her to be a mature and confident young woman.[1] The best-known of these, painted by Allan Ramsay, Richard Wilson and W. Robertson, depict a strong, intelligent face, framed in dark brown hair. She is attractive and might even be beautiful but for rather high cheekbones and prominent forehead, nose and chin. Her eyes, like her mouth, smile gently, almost to lend a sense of mischief. One feels that Allan Ramsay's sitter is not telling us all she knows: in the picture she is wearing a tartan plaid and has a white rose of the Jacobite Cause in her hair. Wilson's portraits also echo the Cause, one showing her in a tartan dress and the other depicting the journey to Skye in its background. Robertson also includes a boat, but adds a long Latin inscription, describing Flora as 'a heroine of eternal renown'. One thing is certain from these contemporary portraits – this is not the simple Highland girl that legend has handed down, but a clever, strong-willed young woman who commands attention.

It should hardly be surprising that Flora MacDonald was a worldly young woman, for she was born and bred in one of the most politically sensitive parts of the whole of Scotland, an area where clan and political intrigue boiled together constantly to distil a heady spirit which affected every man, woman and child. She was a member of Clan Donald, the great clan of the western Highlands of Scotland and the Outer and Inner Hebrides, which flank Scotland's north-west coast like a great island milky way far out in the Atlantic Ocean.

The Outer Hebrides stretch in disorder for more than a hundred miles from north to south, starting with the great fat island which begins as Lewis and ends as Harris, continuing through North Uist, Benbecula and South Uist, to a 'tail' of small islands whose very names cast romantic spells: Eriskay, Barra, Vatersay, Sandray, Pabbay, Mingulay and Berneray. From the Butt of Lewis to Barra Head the individual islands lie so closely huddled together, separated by narrow sounds or fords which flood at high tide, that the group is known simply as the Long Island. It would be difficult even to guess at their exact number since many are no more than skerries – fragments of rock, which the winds of time and Atlantic waves have pounded into weird shapes that disappear and re-emerge with every rise and fall of the tide. Like these tidal islands, many of the permanent islands support no human inhabitants but are the homes only of seals, sea birds and spirits of ancient Celtic or Viking gods. Even the larger islands of the Outer Hebrides appear stark and desolate – a stony-faced landscape of undulating moor and low mountains scored and scarred by innumerable lochs. Their coastlines are slashed by hundreds of bays and ragged sea lochs which bore far into the land. Water lies everywhere, for the earth seldom has time to dry out before new rain-sodden Atlantic winds blow in to precipitate new downpours.

The islands that make up the central mass of the Long Island galaxy are North Uist, Benbecula and, largest of the three, South Uist, where Flora was born. Although bigger than its neighbours, South Uist is no more than fifteen miles wide and less than twenty-five long. It is dominated by a range of low mountains running the entire length of the island's eastern side, the highest peaks of which, Beinn Mhor and Hecla, just touch two thousand feet; but even that modest height takes them into cloud for much of the time. This mountain mass makes the island's east coast virtually inaccessible, except from the sea or by a difficult trek across passes through the mountains. South Uist's eastern coast is a remote place, well endowed with safe hiding places.

By contrast, the west of the island is made up of treeless machair (flat, sandy land), strewn wildly with rocks, lochs and peat bogs all the way to the sandy shores of the Atlantic Ocean. Beyond the rocky points and white sands of South Uist's western coast lie only St Kilda and – three thousand miles away – America.

Water is the main natural feature of this wan, grey-green landscape. Winter and summer, water fills every dip and hollow to give it the appearance of a series of islands rather than a single landmass, and, although summer pastures are generous and verdant, in winter the mean grass shows little promise of filling the bellies of the sheep, horses and hardy cattle that graze it hopefully. Nowadays there are hardly any horses but often too many sheep, so that overgrazing is common. The grassy sand-dunes along the coast provide not only grazing but also shelter for animals in all seasons.

A single, narrow road, running from Lochboisdale in the south to Carnan in the north, forms South Uist's spine, marching straight across the peaty bogland and deviating from this determined path only to avoid occasional outcrops of rock, ignoring every other impediment. It strides through bogs and lochs, so that long stretches give the impression of having been built on causeway rather than on dry land. The island road continues on to the next island, Benbecula, across a narrow causeway, where until less than fifty years ago there was only a ford passable on foot at low tide. Beyond Benbecula another causeway carries the road northwards to North Uist, making the drive from Lochboisdale to Lochmaddy a relatively easy one today. Only a couple of generations ago this journey was a very different matter, and in the eighteenth century someone had to have a very serious purpose to consider setting out on it at all.

There are no towns on the two Uists or Benbecula, just a succession of crofts scattered across the countryside as if blown there by the wind, and always set on higher ground above the peat bogs, which isolates them from one another, but exposes them to the eternal Atlantic winds. Here and there a few come together to form a village such as the ferry ports of Lochboisdale and Lochmaddy, and the airport of Balinavanich. It would be a mistake to think that, because the houses stand apart from one another on the Long Island, this is not a single, close-knit community: these people are proud of their kinship and are still bound together in spirit by the long-vanished clan system under which their forefathers lived. Hardship unites people and the unending struggle of tending the sheep and cattle, cultivating their pocket handkerchief holdings of poor land and gathering peats to keep their fires burning has created bonds between islanders such as Lowland townsmen have never known.

Nearer to the Scottish mainland, but separated from the Outer Isles by that often wild and treacherous stretch of water, the Minch and the Sea of the Hebrides, lie the Inner Hebrides, Skye, Mull, Jura, Islay and all their satellite islands. Skye dominates, the misty isle of glorious mountains and sea lochs which probe so far inland that no point on the island is more than five miles from the sea. This fretwork of sea lochs and bold peninsulas has earned it the name 'the winged island'.

Flora's early life was divided between the outer and inner isles, between South Uist, where she grew up, and Skye, where she spent much of her adult life.

Nothing remains of the house at Milton in South Uist in which Flora MacDonald was born in 1722 – no more than a few stones scattered over the thin soil and a cairn as a reminder that this was the birthplace of a heroine. The site lies only a few hundred yards off the main road through the island, yet the cairn is easily missed even when following the route carefully on a map. There is no signpost and it stands on privately owned land, approached by a muddy track, more easily negotiated by the crofter's cows than by visitors. The cairn of stones carries a simple inscription, telling Flora's story:

> Clan Donald raised this cairn of remembrance
> to their Kinswoman Flora MacDonald, daughter
> of Ranald, Son of Angus of Milton, South Uist.
>
> She was born in 1722 near this place and
> spent her early life in the house that
> stood on this foundation. When pursuit was
> drawing near to the Prince in the Long
> Island she greatly aided him by her heroism
> and endurance to gain shelter in the Isle of
> Skye.

Flora would still recognize the countryside around Milton: a drab, treeless landscape in which every dip and hollow is filled with water – puddles, pools, lochans and lochs – and with a range of threatening, low mountain peaks to the east: Ben 'a Mhuillin, Reineval, Sheaval, Trinival and Arnaval. The summits of Beinn Mhor and Hecla stand on the north-eastern skyline and, a mile or so to the west, restless Atlantic waves constantly sound their querulous sigh on Trollaskeir rocks.

Until about seventy years ago a mill stood among the lochs on a small stream which runs into Loch Kildonan, and it was this mill that gave the MacDonalds' land its Gaelic name of *Airidh Mhuillin*, 'the pastureland of the mill'. The present-day Milton covers only about one third of the area of the original township of *Gearraidh-bhailtois*, 'the township of the summer grazing'. By eighteenth-century standards Milton was a fine farm, but the house, even when it was filled with the trappings of a well-off family, could not have looked imposing from the exterior – a low thatched cottage with the smallest of windows, which admitted little light even on the rare sunlit days. Gales sent storms of rain sweeping over the land, so it was hard to keep the three small rooms warm and watertight. Mean as the house was in appearance, in those days it would soon have become obvious to any visitor that the Milton MacDonalds were a family of considerable importance.

The homes of families who were high in the social order of the Islands blended the sophisticated with the primitive. They looked little more than hovels from the outside with low, dark rooms, often choked with peat smoke, and with bare earthen floors that turned to quagmires after periods of rain. Yet these houses frequently contained pieces of good furniture, fine linen and china, and a surprising number of books, for learning has always been greatly prized by the Scottish islanders, to the extent that even today a higher proportion of school-leavers in the Western Isles go into further and higher education than in any other part of Scotland.[2]

The houses of influential families in the Highlands and Islands bore little or no resemblance to the homes of Lowland or English gentry. This strange mixture of refinement and discomfort puzzled visitors from the south. Dr Samuel Johnson told how he stayed at a house where the furnishings and bed linen in his room were of the highest quality, but when he undressed to go to bed, he found himself standing in mud on a waterlogged earthen floor.

Ranald MacDonald of Milton, Flora's father, was a tacksman, and consequently a person of considerable standing on the Long Island. He was related both to the powerful Campbell family of Argyll and to his own clan chief, Ranald MacDonald of Clanranald, who had given him tacks, or leases, of land, a right that lay wholly within the chief's jurisdiction. The clan chief had the power to bestow tacks on his family or others as he thought fit, and those he favoured generally farmed part of their tack for themselves and sublet the remainder to lesser clansmen. Flora's father had held the tack of Balivanich in Benbecula as a young man, and in 1702 he was given Milton in South Uist as well. Tacksmen stood just below the chief himself, so MacDonald of Milton, a distant relative of Clanranald and holder of two tacks, was undoubtedly a man of considerable importance with a number of tenants dependent on him.

Flora's mother, Marion MacDonald, also belonged to a family of proud pedigree, influential in both North and South Uist. Her father, the Reverend Angus MacDonald, the Presbyterian parish minister on South Uist, was the son of Hugh MacDonald of Griminish in North Uist, who could trace his family line directly to the founder of the mighty MacDonalds of Sleat, the 'Lords of the Islands'. The Reverend Angus had begun life as an Episcopalian, but in 1688 at the Glorious Revolution, which deposed clergymen just as it dethroned King James VII of Scotland and II of England, he turned Presbyterian. He became a minister of the Scottish Kirk, first at Killean in Kintyre, a charge which included the small island of Gigha, and later at South Uist. The Reverend Angus was a powerful man in every sense of the word – a forceful preacher, a minister of the highest moral values and a man of tremendous physical strength. No wonder they called him the *ministear laidir*, the 'Strong Minister'. At this time, when the Church of Scotland was filling the remote Highlands and Islands with 'strong' ministers who would root out Catholicism and the Gaelic tongue, the Reverend Angus, for all his strength, had little success – South Uist remained staunchly Roman Catholic and its people, including the Presbyterian MacDonalds of Milton, continued to speak the ancient language of their ancestors.

While living in Kintyre the Strong Minister made a good marriage to a laird's daughter. Just as he could trace his pedigree to the Lord of the Isles, his bride, Elizabeth MacDonald of Largie, could boast royal descent through four centuries of history from Scotland's 'Hero-King' Robert the Bruce and Robert II, the founder of the ill-starred Stewart royal dynasty. Marion, third child of the Reverend Angus and Elizabeth, became second wife of the tacksman of Milton, a man old enough to be her father: indeed, Milton was exactly the same age as his father-in-law. Marion's father and her husband were also cousins, which was not a matter to raise eyebrows in the islands in those days.[3]

The MacDonalds of Milton were wealthy compared with their Uist neighbours because, as kinsmen of Clanranald, they stood high in the clan hierarchy. In the 1720s the clan structure still regulated life in the Islands, which were as yet little touched by the new laws then beginning to be passed by the Government in London to disarm and control the chiefs, or by the building of forts, roads and bridges on the mainland to enable government armies to police the north more easily. Clan chiefs still wielded supreme authority over their clansmen, who in turn regarded them as more important than the King himself. The chief was father, sovereign, landlord, maker of laws and dispenser of justice – parliament, justiciary, judge and jury all in one – and his power was paramount. It was his duty to lead his clansmen in peace and war, and to provide for them, but in return they were bound to follow when he rallied them to battle. It was a simple but rigid system, strictly accepted and honoured without question by both sides.

Throughout Scotland men were usually known by the title of their land, a practice especially necessary in the Highlands and Islands where so many bore the same family name, and often the same Christian name as well. The situation was further complicated by the fact that there could be more than one child with the same Christian name in a family. According to the family tree of a family of MacDonalds in North Carolina, one Skye minister had three daughters all with the same name, and Flora's mother appears to have named a daughter of her second marriage Florence. [4]

As a result, in the Hebrides there were scores of Ranald, Angus, Alexander or Hugh MacDonalds, and consequently Flora's father, Ranald, was known as MacDonald of Milton, or simply Milton, and his son was Young Milton. There were many Flora MacDonalds also, so Ranald and Marion's girl was referred to simply as 'Milton's daughter', even after her father was long dead, and she had left Uist and her family home.

Ranald and Marion MacDonald had two sons, Ranald and Angus, as well as one daughter who was given the Gaelic name *Fionnghal*, or, in her full Gaelic designation, *Fionnghal nighean Raonuill 'ic Aonghais Oig, an Airidh Mhuillinn*, 'Flora, daughter of Ranald, son of Angus, Younger of Milton'.

The Reverend Robert Forbes, later Bishop of Ross and Caithness, who collected Jacobite stories under the title *The Lyon in Mourning*,[5] called her Funnivella, but her name was translated to Flora, and she sometimes signed herself 'Flory'.

In 1723, the year after Flora's birth, her father died, leaving Marion a widow with young children and two well-stocked farms at Balivanich and Milton to look after. Tacks were still hereditary at that time, so Milton and Balivanich were to be inherited by Angus, the elder son, when he came of age. The following year, Flora's grandfather, the Strong Minister, also died suddenly, at Campbeltown, while returning from a visit to his wife's family at Largie.

Although Marion was better off by far than the clansmen around her, she must have found it a hard struggle in those early years of widowhood to manage the tacks and bring up a young family. Life throughout the north and west of Scotland was desperately hard, with whole families of clansmen crowded onto a few acres which had to support them, keeping them poor to the point of starvation. Using the traditional *cas-chrom*, or foot-plough, it could take a man from Christmas until the end of April to turn over sufficient land to sow five bolls of seed, and the few fortunate enough to own a horse-drawn plough of the primitive type then in use fared little better, since it required three men to handle it. Consequently, cultivation of the land was desperately slow, so late sowing made for such late harvests that autumn storms of icy wind and rain often prevented much of the crop from being gathered in at all. Even the best cows gave little milk to provide butter and cheese, so the main diet of the people consisted of a few dairy products, oatmeal gruel, called *brochan* (which was eaten with oat or barley bread), a little fish, kale, and broth made from limpets gathered on the seashore and boiled with milk. Rarely, if ever, did meat grace their dinner table.

Even families of substance, like the Milton MacDonalds, lived simply and considered milk, butter and cheese the choicest fare because they were remote from markets and depended on their own produce, which could be scarce throughout long periods of the year. If that diet sounds spartan but sufficient to sustain reasonable life, it should be remembered that, by late winter, poorer tenants' gruel became thinner by the day, until by spring clansmen barely had the strength to till their poor soil. It was this general debility, rather than indolence, that gave islanders the reputation for being lazy.

Compared with their tenants' holdings, Milton was well stocked with sheep and cattle which were driven to the shielings, or high pastures, on nearby hills each summer. Here herds lived in a primitive hut called a *bothan-airidh*, or shieling-bothy. Women and younger members of the family usually stayed on the shielings in summer to tend the cows and sheep while the men contended with the harvest at the farm.

After four years of struggle following her husband's death, Marion was, quite literally, swept off to the altar by one of her Skye kinsmen, *Uisdean Cam*, or 'One-eyed' Hugh MacDonald, a member of the Sartle branch of the family in Skye. The story that Hugh abducted Marion and carried her off to Skye to marry her is perfectly believable, for he was an heroic character who had lived by his wits for years. His grandfather was the Chief of the Sleat MacDonalds, but as the third son of MacDonald of Sartle, Hugh, was forced to leave Skye and make his own way in the world. We are not sure how Hugh lost his eye: one story said it was by striking a tree branch accidentally while still a boy, and another explains it away as the result of a wound received while serving in the French army. In spite of the handicap, 'One-eyed' Hugh held a commission in King Louis's army, was an expert swordsman and became noted for his great strength. Having returned to the Isles without prospects, 'One-eyed' Hugh saw the opportunity of what the Scots call a good 'downsetting' with the MacDonald widow at Milton in Uist, and took her to Skye and married her.

The date and circumstances of the wooing and marriage of 'One-eyed' Hugh to Marion are not known, although Flora's granddaughter tells a highly coloured tale, well tailored to the romantic Victorian 'Over the Sea to Skye' legend.[6] According to her account, Hugh arrived at Milton by boat one dark night with eight large men and a bagpiper skirling loudly, and carried Marion and her children off while the piper drowned the servants' screams. Even in the Highlands a piper blowing full blast hardly seems a suitable way to kidnap a bride by stealth! It is much more likely that Hugh, as a good Sleat clansman, simply took Marion to Skye to seek his chief's permission to marry her.

Permission granted, they returned to Uist where Hugh settled down dutifully to manage the tacks for his wife and to help raise Marion's boys and Flora. Certainly if Marion was abducted and forced to marry Hugh MacDonald, she and her children bore him no ill will. The couple lived contentedly, and Hugh and his step-children enjoyed the warmest of relationships throughout his life.

It has been claimed that Flora was educated with the chief's children but, since the only daughter of Clanranald was not born until 1739, this seems unlikely. Marion MacDonald would certainly have looked to her chief for support when she was widowed, and Clanranald and his half-brother, Alexander MacDonald of Boisdale, would have responded as clan kinship demanded. A warm affection certainly developed between Flora and 'Lady Clan', as the chief's wife was often called, so that Flora spent a considerable amount of time at the chief's home on the neighbouring island of Benbecula. Up to 1715 Clanranald chiefs had once been near neighbours of the Milton MacDonalds, but their house at Ormiclett was burned down during the '15 Jacobite Rising, on the very day that the old chief of Clanranald was killed at the Battle of Sheriffmuir. His successor built his new home at Nunton, on Benbecula, but that was not far away and the families remained as close as ever. The house at Nunton still stands. It was a farm up until 1923, when it was turned into crofts, and the house and its ancillary buildings are still inhabited.

At Nunton Flora picked up enough social graces to pass herself off in society and make those who met her later in the South marvel that one 'could not discern by her conversation that she spent all her former days in the Highlands'.[7] However little formal schooling Flora may have had, she grew into a cultured, clever girl, able to read, play the *ceolag*, or spinet, dance well and sing sweetly. The main gap in her education was handwriting: she did not write well and had to take lessons later. Flora had a great repertoire of Gaelic songs, which made her popular among her friends, and she grew up to be singularly well informed about the world beyond the Islands, because 'One-eyed' Hugh opened windows onto Europe as he told his family about Highland exiles who were settled there, and the intrigues and plots in which they were constantly embroiled. The chief of these was, of course, the Jacobite Cause. The Cause had flourished in Europe for more than half a century, during which time it had been a nuisance, but little more, to the Government in London. It was all bound up with religion: King James II of England and VII of Scotland was a Roman Catholic, but his heirs, his daughters Mary and Anne, were Protestant, so no one minded too much until 1688 when James's wife bore him a son and the clear intention was to bring the child up as a Catholic. That was when Parliament in London said 'enough', and Mary and her husband, William of Orange, were invited to become joint sovereigns. In exile in France, James might just have been invited back because neither Mary nor Anne had an heir, but James would not compromise his religious beliefs and every opportunity was lost. His son, another James, whose birth in 1688 had triggered the whole Glorious Revolution, proved as unyielding as his father and forfeited his chance to win back his crowns.

By the time Flora was growing up, 'King James over the Water' was an ageing, gloomy, ineffectual man, whose life was littered with missed opportunities: he failed to make his peace with his half-sister, Queen Anne, and when she died and the kingdoms of Scotland and England passed to George of Hanover, he failed to seize the British crown. Invasions, or planned invasions, failed in 1708, 1715 and 1719, largely because of James's lamentable ineffectiveness. But Jacobite hopes rose again when James married and produced a fine young heir, Prince Charles Edward, on the last day of the year 1720. During Flora's childhood James's supporters in Scotland followed the progress of this young prince avidly, and in their hearts they hoped he would grow up to win back his father's crowns. On the predominantly Roman Catholic island of South Uist there was much talk of the day when the King over the Water would come into his own again – talk that led to endless scheming to bring this about.

By and large, the Highlands and Islands were at peace throughout Flora's childhood, but with plenty of talk about plans for a new rising – plans that never came to anything. Underneath an apparently tranquil surface, clan life remained the simmering cauldron it had always been, and in this pot the chiefs stirred a heady Jacobite brew. When gossip from Europe flagged, there was plenty of dissent to be generated nearer home.

The chief on Flora's island of South Uist was Ranald MacDonald, generally known as 'Old Clanranald' to distinguish him from his son, another Ranald. Clanranald was a weak man, so much given to the bottle that in a letter describing a two-day visit to the home of the neighbouring Chief of Sleat it was said that he was not sober for a single hour. 'We had the mortification to be two nights with Clanranald whose senses are entirely departed with the help of whisky', the chief's wife complained.[8]

Clanranald was fortunate to make a good marriage in 1720 to Margaret MacLeod of Bernera, a wife who proved to be a tower of strength to him. In the upside-down Highland world of Jacobitism and religious divides, Clanranald was Roman Catholic, but reluctant to come out for the Pretender, while his wife, a Protestant, was an ardent supporter of the King over the Water.

The southern part of South Uist and Eriskay came under the control of Clanranald's half-brother, Alexander MacDonald of Boisdale, a man out of tune religiously and socially with his clansmen, and who is still remembered with little affection by the islanders. Boisdale was a hard man, astute where his superior chief was naive, and a realist where the Jacobites were concerned: he supported them, but refused to take foolish risks.

At the southern end of the Long Island lay Barra and its dependent islands, which belonged to Roderick MacNeill, another chief who showed great caution about promising to call his clansmen out, yet without the courage to say so. His course was to do nothing until events overtook him.

The northern part of the Long Island – Lewis, Harris and North Uist – belonged to the Clan MacKenzie, the Skye Chief MacLeod of Dunvegan, and MacDonald of Sleat, respectively. Of these, Sir Alexander MacDonald, seventh Baronet of Sleat and a descendant of Somerled, was the most important, and was often referred to as the 'Knight', while MacLeod was known as the 'Laird'. Like Clanranald, the Sleat estates had been forfeited after 1715, but the Government was anxious not to make permanent enemies of such a powerful sept of the clan, so it agreed secretly that

Kenneth MacKenzie of Delvine should be invested with the forfeited estates, covering a large area of Skye as well as North Uist, on the understanding that in due time they should be restored to their rightful owner. Sir Alexander was that rightful owner, and in due time the lands were handed back to him.

Sir Alexander returned from St Andrews University in 1732 and set about rebuilding his clan's fortunes on Skye. His first act was to marry Anne Ogilvie, but she died young, leaving him with a young son who also died. The Knight already held considerable lands on the island, but set about acquiring more as fast as he could, buying up every square yard that came on to the market, a policy which did little for his popularity among his clansmen. He introduced improvements and constructed roads, but a letter from John MacKenzie of Delvine, the lawyer in Edinburgh who acted for many Highland families including MacDonald of Sleat, suggests that he was too lazy to get up in the morning to supervise the work properly. To pay for the roads, Sleat proposed that all islanders should pay tolls to cart their peats, but this stirred up the clergy who thought they should be exempt.

MacKenzie warned the young chief that this was a dangerous practice:

A man who quarrels with the clergy has need to be on his guard and pretty circumspect', MacKenzie wrote, 'for like moalls they work underground and stick at nothing to effectuate their own purpose wherefore in prudence its necessary I'm afraid to overlook their insolence for a season.[9]

How well MacKenzie knew his clergy: they were the first to point the accusing finger at Sleat, supreme though he might be in Skye, when trouble arose.

The Chief felt he could ignore the mean ministers at this time. After all, he was increasing his estates nicely and had built a fine new house at Monkstadt to replace the ancient Sleat stronghold of Duntulm in the far north of the island. The Chief's new home was probably the first house on Skye to have a slated roof instead of thatch, and Sleat lived in it in considerable style with a small army of servants and outdoor workers: gardeners, grooms, blacksmiths, a grieve, a cooper, a tailor, salmon fishers and herdsmen. A kinsman, Alexander MacDonald of Kingsburgh, was his factor, or chamberlain, in the northern part of the island.

Kingsburgh and his elder son, Allan, were both to play an important part in Flora's life, the factor as an accomplice in the plot to help Prince Charlie to escape, and Allan as her husband. Allan was marked for great things from childhood, with the young Chief paying for him to be educated in Edinburgh as part of his training to take over the position of factor when the time came for Kingsburgh to retire.

Apart from the annoyance of 'cackling creditors',[10] who dunned at his door from time to time, Sleat lacked for nothing, except perhaps a wife and that he rectified in 1739. In addition to Monkstadt the Chief had an excellent residence in the Canongate in Edinburgh. In the capital he met and married his second wife, Lady Margaret Montgomerie, daughter of one of Scotland's ancient and distinguished Lowland families, in April 1739. Lady Margaret was one of seven beautiful daughters of Susanna, Countess of Eglinton, reputed to be one of the loveliest women of her day, and in the Islands she must have been regarded as a considerable catch for Sleat.

Lady Margaret Montgomerie was rich, but she was extravagant, headstrong and liked everything her own way. For her, a handsome young Highland chief with vast lands made an ideal husband. She discovered too late that his dislike of Edinburgh matched her hatred for Skye, and that she was expected to spend most of her life buried among those lonely island acres. Lady Margaret grew to loathe life in remote Skye, far from the high society in which she had been enjoying herself, but she made the best of it to begin with and was warmly welcomed by the various branches of the clan.

The Chief's new wife had barely settled in Skye when she learned at first hand of that Highland lawlessness of which she had heard tell so often in Edinburgh, and she discovered that her husband was alleged to be involved, not in one great scandal, but in two.

First, Lady Grange had been abducted from Edinburgh on the instructions of her Jacobite husband and whisked away to the island of St Kilda where she was held prisoner. Gossip implicated both MacLeod of Dunvegan and MacDonald of Sleat in the crime. Worse was to follow. At the end of 1739, or early in 1740, a story reached the Hebrides that a ship had put into the port of Donaghadee in the north of Ireland, with upwards of a hundred men, women and children, who claimed they had been kidnapped from Skye and Harris and were being shipped off to America to be sold as slaves on the Southern plantations. The crime was the work of Norman MacLeod the Younger of Bernera, a relative of Lady Clanranald. Another Norman MacLeod, tacksman of Unish, and William Davison, master of the ship, were also involved. Under pretext of disposing of a cargo of brandy, Davison had put into Loch Bracadale in the Clan MacLeod part of Skye and Finsbay in Harris, and had taken on board a total of forty men, thirty women and twenty children who had been gathered together on a deportation order forged by Unish. He sailed to Donaghadee, his home port, for a refit in preparation for the Atlantic voyage, but while this was being carried out, some of the prisoners escaped and reported the crime.

In Skye many believed that Sleat and MacLeod were implicated – not least those ministers who had objected to Sleat's road tolls and were once again in dispute with the Knight. They now saw the opportunity for revenge. Skye Presbytery accused Sleat of being involved in the 'Ship of the Men' incident, as the crime became known, while others considered him at the very least complacent about what he himself called 'this black scene'.[11]

When the news reached Edinburgh it set up a commotion, and brought the Laird and the Knight so close to prosecution that it took all the skill of lawyer MacKenzie, plus the influence of MacDonald himself and his new wife, to dampen the scandal down. Sleat had incriminated himself by writing, rather unwisely, to MacKenzie that only the year before he and MacLeod had decided that the best method of clearing rogues out of the island was to ship them to the plantations in America. Further correspondence suggested very strongly that Sleat was far from innocent.

In December 1739 MacKenzie wrote to Sleat:

> Ought it or might it not have occurred to you, that there's no such thing allow'd by the British constitution as transporting any man out of the kingdom without his own consent save by the formal sentence of a judge upon conviction for a crime, why so much secrecy to your own hurt – I cannot help entertaining some suspicion that the view of that project was not so much in the contrivance of a design to rid the country of rogues which if gone about in a proper way would be commendable as to put profit in Bernera's son's pocket, tho' I make no doubt it was represented to you in the specious light that you might be more passive to it.[12]

MacKenzie advised Sleat and Lady Margaret to write to Duncan Forbes, Lord President of the Court of Session in Edinburgh, as well as to other influential people, and the Knight and his lady left no stone unturned to clear his name. Lady Margaret asked Lady Pembroke to talk to Sir Robert Walpole, the Prime Minister in London.[13] She was learning how devious her clan kinsmen could be. Sleat himself wrote to the Earl of Morton protesting his innocence, although he admitted that those who did not know him might readily look on him in a false light.[14]

The affair of the Ship of the Men never came to court, but when Charles Edward Stuart arrived six years later it gave the authorities in Edinburgh an additional reason for putting pressure on MacLeod and MacDonald not to call out their clansmen to fight for the Prince. Both the Knight and the Laird stayed at home, not simply because they thought Prince Charlie's rising a lost cause, but partly because they had been well treated by the British Government, who had given Sleat back his lands and let both of them go scot free after the Ship of the Men scandal. It can be argued that the rejection of Prince Charlie by Sleat and MacLeod cost the Prince victory in the '45 for, had they joined the Prince's Cause enthusiastically at the start, other clans might not have hesitated and the Jacobites would have been immensely powerful – probably invincible. It has been suggested that Sleat was a naïve and weak character who was easily influenced, and that MacLeod was ringleader in all these machinations. Perhaps so, but that does not leave Sleat guiltless.

Flora, in her late teens at the time of the Ship of the Men scandal, was living at Milton with her mother, stepfather, brothers and a growing family of half-brothers and half-sisters. Marion and Hugh had at least five children: a son, James, two daughters, Annabella and Florence, and two other sons who died young. Flora lost one of her own brothers, Ranald, as a result of an accident during a visit to Largie. Two versions of the boy's death are given, but there is no known proof to support either. One story suggests that Ranald, who had inherited his grandfather's great physical strength, died as a result of a blood vessel bursting while he was trying to row a boat against a great wind.[15] The second maintains that he and a young cousin were out shooting when both rushed to pick up the same gun: it went off accidentally and Ranald was killed.[16]

Alexander MacGregor, in his highly inaccurate *The Life of Flora MacDonald*, claims that Flora was taken to Edinburgh in the early 1740s to spend three years attending Miss Henderson's school in Stamp Office Close, close to the town house of the Sleat Chief. Here she was introduced to Lady Margaret's beautiful sisters.[17] Although MacGregor's book was based on information given by Flora's daughter, Anne, this is hard to believe. Surely someone in the gossipy city of Edinburgh of that time would have commented on Sleat's wife and her protégée if they had been there for three whole seasons, yet, even after Flora became famous, no one remembered her. Bishop Forbes states categorically that she had never been out of Uist or Skye 'till about a year before the Prince's arrival', when she lived 'in the family of MacDonald of Largie in Argyllshire for the space of ten or eleven months'.[18] Captain Felix O'Neil, who was also involved in the Prince's escape and visited Milton a number of times, confirms this.

If MacGregor is by any remote chance right and Flora did visit Edinburgh, then her stay there must have been brief and she did not play any part in the social life of the capital. Perhaps the Edinburgh visit may be fitted round the reported visit to Largie in 1744 to meet her cousins: she could have stopped off there on the way to Edinburgh, since the easiest route from the Hebrides to the capital in those days was either by boat round the Mull of Kintyre and up the Clyde to Glasgow, then on by coach, or by boat to Argyll, across the Mull of Kintyre and on to Glasgow. Flora's cousins' house at Largie would have been a very convenient stopping-off point on the long and difficult journey.

Whether Flora acquired her education and good manners in the capital or in the drawing rooms of the chiefs' wives of Clanranald and Sleat hardly matters. By 1745 she had become a handsome young woman of twenty-three, 'easy and cheerful, yet she had a certain mixture of gravity in all her behaviour which became her situation exceedingly well, and set her off to great advantage'. In appearance she was 'of low stature, off a fair complexion and well enough shap'd', and she 'talks English (or rather Scots) easily, and not at all through the Earse tone'.[19]

This well-bred young lady, fluent in Gaelic and English, was away from South Uist during the early part of 1745, but returned in June to find the Long Island seething with rumours that the Jacobites were on the move and that Charles Edward Stuart was expected to raise his father's standard among them soon. Like every islander in Uist that summer, Flora felt pangs of dread intensified by a seasoning of excitement at the prospect.

CHAPTER TWO

Meeting at Midnight

There is noe countrey news, but a prodigious bad seasone, and plenty
of redcoat pairties, both very bad articles.

Letter from the Revd John MacDonald,
brother of Kinlochmoidart, to Bishop Forbes[1]

Flora returned to South Uist in June 1745 to an unsettled island and an
uncertain future. She found misery and suffering all around: food was
scarce and harvest prospects poor because rain-soaked gales had once
again blown in from the Atlantic Ocean throughout spring and summer to
turn the land to a quagmire on which no crop could grow. The preceding
year had been exactly the same, causing much of the harvest to be lost.
Many islanders faced the stark prospect of starvation.

In Milton's house people did not suffer hunger pains, but there, too,
uncertainty was all around. Flora's brother, Angus, now of age and ready
to marry, wanted to be master of his own lands, so there was no longer
room for a stepfather at Milton. 'One-eyed' Hugh accepted the situation
and set about finding another living for himself, Marion and their
children.

He turned to his chief, MacDonald of Sleat, who appointed him
factor for the Sleat estates at Armadale at the southern end of the
island of Skye. Later he was also given the lands of Camuscross, but he
was always known as MacDonald of Armadale from the time he
returned to the Winged Island with Marion and their children in
November 1745.

The move to Skye created a major dilemma for Flora: should she
accompany her mother or remain in South Uist, the only home she had
known, and where she was deeply attached to the land and to Lady Clan
and her friends who lived there? She knew that Angus would soon be
bringing a wife to Milton, so the wise thing would be to accompany her
mother. Thus when her brother offered her a home with him, she declined
tactfully and said she would move to Skye.

Flora was fully occupied with preparations for the removal, so she had plenty on her mind that summer and autumn, but even she – far from interested in politics as she was – could not escape being caught up in the momentous events unfolding around her.

In June, when she returned to Uist, the place was alive with rumours and new whispers were borne in on every gust of wind that blew across the island. 'The Jacobites are coming', Long Island gossip said with gathering persistence, and South Uist was likely to be their chosen landing place. It soon became evident also that any new attempted rising on behalf of the King over the Water would divide the clans as never before, so that even individual households within the great clan families were in disagreement over whether to rally to Prince Charlie's standard or to stay at home. Flora must have heard her stepfather and brother talk about the messages that were reaching the island from France and the responses of the chiefs.

The rumours proved well founded. The Pretender's son, Charles Edward Stuart, arrived in July 1745, and he did choose the remoteness of the Long Island, although not actually South Uist. He arrived off Barra Head on the 21st of that month with a single ship, the *Du Teilley*, but had neither arms nor men – only himself and a group of followers so small that they became known as the 'Seven Men of Moidart'. A second ship, which had sailed with him from France, had been badly damaged in a fight with a British warship and forced to turn back.

Charles probably intended to land on South Uist, but instead he put one of his representatives ashore on Barra. The Prince's first disappointment came when he found that the chief, MacNeill of Barra, was away from the island and not to be found – an absence not so much due to chance as to MacNeill's desire to hold back to see what others would do before committing himself. The following day Charles landed on Eriskay, which belonged to Clanranald and was held by the chief's half-brother, Boisdale. He would seek support from Clanranald's South Uist MacDonalds.

Boisdale was sent for and hurried to Eriskay next morning, showing no surprise whatever at the Prince's arrival: he said he had already heard from both MacDonald of Sleat and MacLeod of Dunvegan that Charles was on his way. But he brought the disquieting news that, if the Prince came without an army, few clan chiefs would join him and he should return to France. While Charles argued, the decision on whether to turn tail for France was taken out of his hands. *Du Teilley*, threatened by a British warship, was forced to slip out to sea and head home to France.

Since Milton lay no more than ten miles from Eriskay, on the direct road to Clanranald's home, the news of the Prince's arrival reached Flora's family almost as soon as Boisdale heard it. However, Flora's stepfather was either away on the mainland – in those days they called it the Continent – or perhaps in Skye negotiating his future, for he did not come to Eriskay. Like MacNeill of Barra, Clanranald, too, was absent – another diplomatic disappearance to avoid being committed to calling out his clansmen.

This news appalled the Prince, since he and his envoys had spent the previous autumn writing to the chiefs, and he had with him a petition which he believed offered him eight hundred men each from Clanranald, Sleat and MacLeod. What he did not know was that none of them had actually signed this petition, nor that both Sleat and MacLeod had been to Edinburgh and were under extreme pressure from Lord President Forbes.

Charles sailed to the mainland and landed in Clanranald country at Moidart, where Flora claimed her stepfather was the first clansman to kiss his hand.[2] Flora's stepfather, although secretly committed to the Jacobite Cause, did not dare offer himself to Prince Charlie for fear of upsetting his chief, MacDonald of Sleat, and risking losing the Armadale factorship which he was then busy negotiating. Flora said later that Hugh met the Prince when he happened to be in Moidart at the time of Charles's landing:[3] perhaps so, but it is more than likely that he was directed there by that same 'chance' as brought a great many others to Moidart at that exact moment. Wherever 'One-eyed' Hugh went that summer he remained close to the Jacobite lines of communication. Armadale's wife and stepdaughter were too discreet to give a clue to where Hugh stood in 1745 and, as for themselves, they were too level-headed to be beguiled into jeopardizing Hugh's future by supporting the Cause openly. Flora's brother, although also a secret sympathizer, took his lead from Old Clanranald and stayed at home.

Eventually a few chiefs arrived, including Clanranald's son with eight hundred of his father's men from the mainland, and the Prince was able to raise his standard at Glenfinnan – the Rising was on. Charles Edward struck with incredible speed and success, winning a small victory almost immediately, then outmanoeuvring his enemies to march triumphantly into Edinburgh and proclaim his father King. By the time Martinmas came round, and Hugh moved to Armadale with Marion, their children and Flora, the Prince had routed General Sir John Cope at Prestonpans, held court in Edinburgh for six weeks and was over the Border and away into the heart of England. Following the Prestonpans victory he tried hard to persuade the 'Knight of Sleat' and the 'Laird of Dunvegan' to call out their clansmen, but neither would be wooed even when things looked so favourable for the Prince. Both chiefs were grovelling to the Government so obsequiously that, when a detachment of Lord Lovat's men attacked Forbes's home at Culloden, near Inverness, both rushed to reassure themselves that the Lord President had not been injured. Replying, his lordship referred to MacDonald as 'my dear Knight'. The 'dear Knight' of Sleat had no intention in 1745 of putting his life and estates at risk as his predecessor had done in 1715!

King George's government authorized the raising of twenty independent companies of soldiers among the loyal clans in the north at the very outset of the Rising, but the Chief of Sleat agreed only reluctantly because, as he told the MacLeod Chief, his gentlemen 'felt a certain delicacy' in joining a force that might have to fight their neighbours and relations. Sir Alexander managed to raise two companies before the year was out, and MacLeod of Dunvegan gathered together four others, making a total of six hundred men. It had been hard work: 'I need not tell you the difficulty of recruiting 100 men', the dispirited Sleat told Dunvegan.[4] Flora's stepfather was appointed captain of one Sleat company and John MacDonald of Kirkibost in North Uist captain of the other, with young Allan MacDonald of Kingsburgh as his lieutenant. Kirkibost and Young Kingsburgh were both to be involved in Flora's life later, as indeed were the captain and lieutenant of one of the MacLeod companies, John MacLeod of Talisker and Alexander MacLeod of Balmeanach.

As the militiamen pondered the wisdom of joining the chiefs' companies and drilled for whatever role the Hanoverians planned for them, Charles marched as far south as Derby, but found little support forthcoming from English Jacobites. In the light of this and with the Hanoverian armies closing in on him, there followed much quarrelling among the Scottish leaders over whether to continue to London or retreat to Scotland. At last Charles Edward reluctantly accepted his leaders' decision to turn back and, sulking with bitter disappointment all the way, he rode northwards. There were to be a few more victories, but the end came when the Prince found himself cornered by the Duke of Cumberland near Inverness – by chance close to Lord President Forbes's house at Culloden. There on 16 April 1746 Cumberland's men cut the Jacobite army to pieces: the '45 was over and the whole of the Highlands began to pay the price for the defeat in which many of them had played little or no part.

News that percolated to the Long Island was confused at first, and Clanranald and his wife spent many anxious days worrying about Young Clanranald, who had been wounded in the battle, but managed to escape to Inverness where he was lucky enough to remain undetected. Others were less fortunate, as the victorious Redcoats murdered and pillaged a fiery path through the Highlands, earning for their leader the sobriquet 'Butcher' Cumberland. The hunt was on for anyone who had so much as whispered a word of sympathy for the Jacobites, and many totally innocent people suffered terribly. The real prize, however, was the Prince himself, who escaped from the battlefield and vanished into the wild hills, a fugitive with a price of £30,000 on his head.

When Charles saw no hope of rallying his broken army he made his way to the coast at Morar (by another ironic twist of Jacobite fate) at Loch nan Uamh, where he had first set foot on the mainland only ten months before. This was loyal MacDonald country, of course, and men and women of the Great Clan were to prove staunch friends to the Prince. A boat was borrowed and, during the night of 26/27 April, Donald MacLeod of Galtergill sailed the Prince to the outer islands, landing at Rossinish on Benbecula, which was probably the safest place he could have been at that moment. A plan was devised to sail north to Stornoway on Lewis, and there pass the Prince and his followers off as shipwrecked Orkney sailors who wanted to charter a boat to take them home. Their real destination would, of course, be Norway and then to France. Unfortunately this plan misfired and the Prince had to flee south again to his MacDonald friends on Uist.

'Butcher' Cumberland lost the scent of his quarry, and it was the middle of May before he picked it up again and knew for sure that Charles Edward was on the Long Island. From then on the hunt gathered momentum. There followed six weeks, between mid-May and the end of June, when the Army and the Royal Navy searched without pause. They were supported by clan militiamen who now discovered that Sleat's reservations had been well founded, and that neighbours and relatives were indeed expected to hunt down their own kinsmen. A militia company commanded by 'One-eyed' Hugh of Armadale was among those Skye militia ordered to Uist and Benbecula for the search.

These militia companies, like the regular soldiers and sailors involved, came under the command of Major-General John Campbell of Mamore (later fourth Duke of Argyll), a generous and humane man, but whose orders were implemented by some of the cruellest, most virulent anti-Jacobites in the whole of Scotland. Captain Caroline Scott of the Army and

Captain John Ferguson of the Royal Navy were particularly notorious, carrying torture, murder, fire and destruction through the Highlands and Islands. Throughout the months after Culloden, Scott and Ferguson were dangerous enemies to all Highlanders, disloyal and loyal alike. Nobody was safe.

Ferguson, who hailed from Inverurie in Aberdeenshire, had command of HMS *Furnace*, which was used as a prison ship to hold Jacobites flushed out in the islands, and he was well matched on land by Scott, a southern Scot, who hated Highlanders with all the intensity of the most anti-Jacobite Lowlanders and took little trouble to separate the innocent from the guilty. He actually hanged one of the few Protestants in Barra on a charge of fighting for the Prince, in spite of the testimony of many witnesses that the man was innocent.

The Government's system of gathering information was as brutal as it was efficient. Torture and destruction of property and livestock, as well as threats to their families, made many islanders talk and enabled Campbell to stay remarkably well informed all through the summer – yet he never managed to capture the fugitive Prince. He was hampered by the difficulty of coordinating the Army and Navy searches and by appalling weather in the islands that summer, but most of all by the difficulty of recognizing who were King George's real friends. The role of the chiefs and their senior clansmen was ambiguous to say the least: little has ever been said openly about Clanranald's role in the hunt, but the South Uist MacDonald chief, for all his refusal to raise his clan, undoubtedly made it possible for Charles to evade capture. The moment the Prince arrived in Benbecula, Clanranald hurried to him and brought Neil MacEachain, who spoke Gaelic and French and consequently proved a valuable intermediary. MacEachain is one of the most underestimated members of the cast in the drama of Prince Charlie's escape, probably because he was a quiet, self-effacing man who did not talk grandly about his own achievements. It has been suggested also that he kept silence like the well-trained spy that some believe him to have been. After the '45 Neil returned to France, where he settled, adopted the name MacDonald, and had a son who became one of Napoleon's generals and a Marshal of France.[5]

There were two factions searching for the Prince that summer – with equal lack of success. While the Army and Navy hunted, a series of French vessels came to the islands in the hope of rescuing Charles Edward, but both his enemies and his friends missed him, often by no more than a few breathless minutes. General Campbell was misled into sending his ships to

St Kilda, far out in the Atlantic, before he learned for certain that his quarry was still on the Long Island, and Navy ships were then posted at the northern and southern ends of the Minch to prevent French vessels from entering or leaving. When the general learned with certainty that Charles was being sheltered by the MacDonalds of the Uists and Benbecula, he ordered a systematic search of these islands.

Clanranald took over and hid the Prince at Corodale, a remote, uninhabited glen in South Uist, with no road leading to it and difficult to spot from the sea. In a gamekeeper's hut there, Charles spent three idyllic weeks, which gave him some much needed rest after the terrible mental and physical strain of the retreat from England and Culloden. Here he felt secure for the first time, even as he watched the Royal Navy ships cruising past on their patrols of the Minch. He spent his days shooting and fishing, and in the evenings caroused with Clanranald, Boisdale, Hugh MacDonald of Baleshare (captain of another of the militia companies hunting the Prince) and other sympathetic islanders. It is highly probable that Flora's stepfather and her brother, Angus, visited him as well.

Charles had a good head for alcohol and one carousal, typical of several, continued through the night until all of his guests, even Boisdale, reputedly one of the best drinkers in the whole of Scotland, were under the table. Charles reverently covered the casualties of the night with plaids and sang '*De Profundis*' over them before leaving them to sleep it off. As one remarked afterwards, 'Never have I seen a punch bowl attacked more freely or frankly.' [6]

While the Prince was drinking their menfolk under the table, the women of the islands were busy doing all they could for him too. Lady Clan sent him shirts and a silver cup, and Lady Boisdale gave him food and clothing. Even Lady Margaret of Sleat, whose husband was safely away at Fort Augustus serving with Cumberland's forces, wrote secretly to Charles with a present of fifty guineas, clothing and newspapers. Thanks to the generosity of his island friends and their wives, Charles was now a well-dressed Highlander, with kilt, tartan coat, plaid and brogues, all in excellent condition though well-stained by wear, but his health deteriorated because of the severe mental and physical suffering he had gone through ever since the retreat from Derby.

An air of normality hung over the Outer Hebrides, with people continuing to move between the islands in order to help keep the Prince informed and to conceal his presence. Angus of Milton married Penelope

MacDonald of Belfinlay in Benbecula, and the young couple invited Flora over to the Long Island to visit them. She was at Milton in June, while Angus was away from home, possibly with Charles Edward Stuart at Corodale some of the time.

Prince Charlie's friends knew he could not stay on at Corodale indefinitely because, day by day, the search was intensifying around him. When Caroline Scott began a systematic sweep of the three islands of South Uist, Benbecula and North Uist, the net began to close inexorably: friends of the Prince were arrested, including Boisdale, and the situation became desperate. The Prince had to flee from Corodale, but where could he go? With a few companions he headed south to Loch Boisdale at the southern end of South Uist, only to find himself cornered by militia who were searching there. Trapped at Loch Boisdale, and with Caroline Scott less than a mile away, the Prince's companions decided to scatter. First they destroyed their boat, then boatman Donald MacLeod and Captain John William O'Sullivan, an Irish-born supporter who had come with the Prince all the way from Rome, set off on their own. Charles was particularly upset to lose O'Sullivan, who had accompanied him so far, so loyally and for so long.

Charles decided to retain only two companions with him, Neil MacEachain and Captain Felix O'Neil. The surname O'Neil was the only Irish thing about the captain, since (although his father came from Ireland) he was born in Rome and had served in the Spanish army until he joined General Count Lally's French-Irish Regiment. O'Neil had joined the Prince only towards the end of the campaign, but he had been with him throughout his flight after Culloden. With MacEachain and O'Neil, the Prince struck northwards again into the hills to the east of Milton, desperate to find some means of escape. While Charles lay in the hills only a few miles away, Boisdale was taken aboard Ferguson's ship, his house was ransacked and his wife tied up and left a prisoner in her own home. But this, far from intimidating the islanders, merely served to turn more of them more resolutely against Scott and Ferguson, and generated added sympathy and help for Prince Charles.

A few days later, on 20 June, the Prince met Flora MacDonald for the first time.

To the end of her life Flora was circumspect about her own part in the events of the days that followed and gave the impression that she knew nothing of the plot to save Charles in advance, or the role that had been assigned to her in it. She had certainly met Captain O'Neil at Clanranald's house, and he had hinted then that she might meet the Prince. In a letter written to a friend, Sir John MacPherson, towards the end of her life she said (writing in the third person):

> Colonell O'Neil, who was then along with the Prince, met her at Clan Ranald's house, and, introducing a conversation with her about him, ask'd her what she would give for a sight of the Prince. She reply'd that as she had not that Happyness before, she did not look for it now, but that a sight of him woud make her happy, tho' he was on a hill and she was on another. [7]

Even if she did not know why she had been sent to her brother's shieling, it was more than opportune, to say the least, that she was at the summer hut on Sheaval Hill that night. It is inconceivable that her brother should have allowed her to go there alone without good reason, and stay away overnight during these troubled times when the island was swarming with Scott's notorious soldiers, yet there was Flora all alone at this remote spot called Alisary, just when she was needed.

Neil MacEachain and Felix O'Neil, the only people present apart from Flora and Prince Charlie, each gave a different version of Flora's introduction to the Prince.[8] Felix was attracted to Flora – maybe even in love with her – and on the surface he appears jealous of Neil, who knew Flora well and could converse familiarly with her in Gaelic. When the captain told his story afterwards he failed to mention Neil MacEachain once, and this has been attributed to jealousy. More likely, Felix was simply trying (like a good soldier) to cover Neil's tracks.

Describing Flora's meeting with Charles, O'Neil said:

> I quitted the Prince at some distance from the hut, and went myself with a design of being inform'd if the independent companies were to pass that way next day as we had been informed. The young lady answered in the negative, saying they would not pass till the day after. I then told her I brought a friend to see her. She with some emotion asked if it was the Prince. I answered in the affirmative and instantly brought him in.[9]

MacEachain, who recounted his memoirs in the third person, said:

> Neil left the prince and O'Neil at a little distance off, 'till he went in and wakened her; she got scarcely on the half of her close, when the

prince, with his baggage upon his back, was at the door, and saluted her very kindly; after which she brought to him a part of the best cheer she had, among the rest was a large bowl full of creme, of which he took two or three hearty go-downs, and his fellow-travellers swallowed the rest.[10]

Flora contradicted herself on this point. Not long after the events she said that 'Captain O'Neil brought Miss MacDonald to the place where the Prince was.'[11] She was probably protecting MacEachain at that time, for later she wrote that O'Neil 'sent in a cousine of her own, who had been along with him and the Prince, to awake her'.[12]

MacEachain's version of the encounter makes more sense: Neil MacEachain, as a fellow islander and kinsman, would be far more likely to be the one sent to wake Flora, and the Prince's impetuous bursting in (accompanied by Felix O'Neil) has the ring of truth.

O'Neil then took over. He claimed that it was the Prince himself who told Flora about the plan to take him to Skye in disguise as a maidservant, and asked if she would accompany him. Flora refused 'with the greatest respect and loyalty', because, if discovered, she said, it would ruin the Chief of Sleat.[13] Felix assured her that Sir Alexander could be implicated in no way since he was still on the mainland with Cumberland; then he tried to win her over by assuring her that her 'glorious action' in saving the Prince would bring her honour and immortality. He even offered to marry her when she protested that her own character might be ruined. 'You need not fear your character', he told her, 'for by this you will gain yourself an immortal character. But if you still entertain fears about your character, I shall (by an oath) marry you directly, if you please.'[14]

Flora still would not budge: she could well live without immortality and without Felix O'Neil for a husband. The Prince sized up the situation and told Flora of the 'sense he would always retain of so conspicuous a service'.[15] It was that appeal from Charles that made her change her mind and agree to help. Flora herself merely said they concerted a plan and she agreed to it,[16] and Neil MacEachain must have been trying to flatter her – or perhaps realized that he was writing for posterity – when he wrote that 'she joyfully accepted of the offer without the least hesitation'.[17] Felix's version sounds much more probable.

Flora left immediately for Milton. She arranged to go to Clanranald's house at Nunton to make arrangements for the journey and to prepare the Prince's female disguise, while the Prince, O'Neil and MacEachain tramped back across the hills towards Hecla mountain and the idyllic Corodale, to wait for a message from her. On the following evening, Saturday 21 June, Flora walked north and crossed the ford from South Uist to Creagorry on Benbecula, but here she was arrested by the militia and held prisoner because she had no permit to travel. She was detained overnight. Although the militia who arrested her were MacLeods, by great good fortune her stepfather, Armadale, was captain of the company stationed there and, when he arrived the following morning, he ordered her to be set free.

As she and her stepfather sat with some other gentlemen at breakfast, Flora was horrified to see a party of Armadale's men burst in with Neil MacEachain whom they had captured at Carnan at the southern end of the Benbecula ford. She thought Neil MacEachain was safely in hiding with the Prince on Hecla, but, unknown to her, Charles had grown increasingly anxious throughout Saturday because Flora had neither returned nor sent a message, so that evening he forced poor, exhausted Neil to set out for Nunton to find out what had happened to her. The tide was high when Neil reached Carnan ford, so he was unable to cross immediately, but, worse, the coast was so heavily guarded that he saw no hope of crossing even when the tide ebbed. He was duly picked up by the militia and held until morning, when he was sent to their captain on the north side of the ford. Fortunately the captain at this checkpoint was none other than 'One-eyed' Hugh.

To Neil's whispered questions, asking if everything was ready for the Prince's journey, Flora replied that she had not yet managed to see Lady Clanranald, but assured him she would be on her way to Nunton within half an hour. She told him to return to Hecla and bring the Prince to Rossinish in the north-east corner of Benbecula, where she and the Chief's wife would meet him with provisions for the journey and clothes for his disguise.

Neil wearily struggled south again and found Charles sitting miserably under a great rock where he had left him, sick with worry at the lack of news, and nagged by hunger pains. Charles took Neil by the hand and asked what had happened to Flora. Neil related all that had taken place and, accompanied by Charles and O'Neil, he set out immediately for Rossinish, not knowing how in the world they would ever manage to cross to Benbecula without being seen. They knew they must find a boat since there was no way of travelling by way of the guarded ford, but luck remained on their side, for at Loch Skiport Neil encountered some local fishermen whom he knew. He explained to them that his companions were fugitives from Culloden and, without further question, the fishermen agreed to row the three men over the sound between the two islands. Having reached Benbecula undetected the Prince had to trek across the boggy island until he was exhausted and driven to the very limits of his endurance. They eventually reached Rossinish, where the Prince found shelter with one of Clanranald's tenants. Without Neil MacEachain the journey would have been impossible.

Charles recklessly sent O'Neil to Nunton to find out what was happening there, and the news he brought back was disquieting: the voyage to Skye was off and a new plan was being devised to send Charles to North Uist which had been searched by this time and was considered safe. Although this was passed off by Felix as Flora's idea, it certainly came from someone much more important – most likely Clanranald himself. O'Neil said 'She told me she had engaged a cousin of hers in North Uist to receive him into his house, where she was sure he would be more safe than in the Isle of Sky.'[18]

This 'cousin' was actually Clanranald's cousin, Hugh MacDonald of Baleshare, the militia officer who had already met Charles at Corodale. The Prince now made the journey all the way to Baleshare, only to find (in O'Neil's words) that 'the gentleman absolutely refused to receive us, alleging for a motive he was a vassal to Sir Alexander MacDonald'. Another explanation given was simply that he refused 'from fear of the great dangers attending it'.[19]

The change of plan was much more complicated than O'Neil suggests and the scheme was certainly not called off because of Baleshare's faintheartedness or fear. Baleshare was only to be the first stop on a journey to the isolated island of Fladda-Chuain off the northern point of the Trotternish Peninsula in Skye. Hugh of Baleshare's brother, Donald Roy MacDonald, was at that time in the north of Skye, recovering from wounds he received at Culloden, and was limping or riding around the island to organize things at the Skye end.

Donald Roy had defied his chief's specific order not to join the Prince at the start of the '45, and was accepted into Young Clanranald's regiment. After escaping from Culloden, badly wounded, he was staying with Sir Alexander's doctor close to Monkstadt, in order to have his injured foot treated, so clearly the chief had not been too put out by his clansman's disobedience. Donald Roy had been in correspondence with his brother and had spent much time trying to arrange a hideout for Charles on lonely

Fladda-Chuain, but in the end was unable to do so for a number of reasons, one of which was that this point on the Skye coast was too well guarded. The plan had to be cancelled, but it cost several precious days during which the Prince's suffering became worse. He now had scurvy and sores all over his body, and was barely able to walk. To compound this misery Charles was cold, wet and hungry, without proper shelter or food, and enemy soldiers were encamped everywhere around him. It was all very well for those sitting in the comfort of Nunton to debate the merits of one scheme over another; they did not have to skulk among the waterlogged wastes of Rossinish, or make endless treks across the island as Neil MacEachain and the Prince were compelled to do.

Eventually the rescuers reverted to the original plan and Lady Clan, Flora and other women at Nunton began to sew furiously to make the costume that was to be Charles's disguise. It consisted of a quilted petticoat and a gown of calico material patterned with sprigs of lilac flowers. This was worn with a white apron, and over it all was a dun-coloured cloak 'made after the Irish fashion' with a large hood. It was set off with a cap designed to hide as much of the wearer's face as possible. Stockings, buckled French garters of blue velvet lined with white silk, and shoes completed the disguise.[20]

Understandably, Charles was becoming desperate. O'Neil walked to Nunton with a message urging Flora to hurry things up and stayed to help her. He had scarcely left when Charles became upset by his absence and sent messages demanding that he should return at once, but Felix would not: he waited, determined that there should be no more delays.

At long last, on the morning of Friday 27 June, two young MacDonald officers of the militia arrived to tell the Prince that all was ready, a boat had been found and they were to be members of its crew. Once again a militia uniform was no proof as to which side anyone supported. Charles climbed Rueval Hill, which commands a magnificent view across Benbecula, and sat there watching for Flora and her party, while Neil MacEachain went off to Nunton to hurry them up.

That night he brought O'Neil, Flora, her brother Angus from Milton, Lady Clanranald and Lady Clan's young daughter, Margaret, from Nunton by boat, which was the safest way for them to travel. All sat down to a hearty meal. For once Charles was able to enjoy a 'feast' of 'heart, liver, kidneys etc. of a bullock or sheep,' all roasted on a spit. Charles, who at this time was veering from deep melancholy to brittle high spirits, was at his most courteous, and set Flora on his right and Lady Clan on his left. For a brief moment he felt utterly safe and joined in the conversation and laughter, all troubles forgotten.[21]

Just when they were all at their most relaxed, the meal came to an abrupt and alarming halt. A messenger rushed up with news that General Campbell had landed close to Nunton accompanied by 1,500 men, and the group of merry-making diners panicked.

MacEachain caught the moment vividly:

All run to their boat in the greatest confusion, every one carrying with him whatever part of the baggage came first to his hand, without either regard to sex or quality, they crossed to Lochisguiway [Loch Uiskevagh], and, about five in the morning, landed on the other side, where they had supper.[22]

They could have had little appetite for the cold food at the resumed picnic at that early hour, all the while awaiting news from a messenger who had been sent off to Nunton to find out exactly what was happening. The man returned to confirm that the news was true, adding the unpalatable morsel that Ferguson had actually had the audacity to sleep in Lady Clan's bed. Worse still, Scott was on his way with another large party, and O'Neil estimated that there were more than two thousand Government soldiers on Benbecula at that moment. The net was finally being closed – it was time for Charles to go.

Lady Clan and her daughter hurried home. The chief's wife told Campbell she had been visiting a sick child, and the general announced in a genial voice, which ill disguised the menace behind his words, that he proposed to dine with her, but first would like to know the name of the child. Lady Clanranald gave a name and added as casually as she could that the child was much better. Ferguson did not even pretend to believe her story, but the general stopped him from taking any action.

While the Chief and his wife were undergoing Ferguson's inquisition, the last frantic preparations for the Prince's departure got under way. Flora was given a letter from her stepfather, addressed to her mother, which would be her passport to a safe passage to Skye. This letter was destroyed later for obvious reasons, but Flora agreed that this is what it said:

My dear Marion:
I have sent your daughter from this country lest she should be in any way frightened with the troops lying here. She has got one Bettie Burke, an Irish girl, who, she tells me, is a good spinster. If her

spinning please you, you may keep her till she spin all your lint; or if you have any wool to spin, you may employ her. I have sent Neil MacKechan along with your daughter and Bettie Burk to take care of them. I am, Your dutiful husband,

Hugh MacDonald.[23]

Flora's passport allowed for only three people and named Neil MacEachain, so Captain O'Neil had to be left behind. O'Neil accepted this decision, but Charles begged Flora to allow Felix to come with them. When she refused the Prince made a great fuss, insisting that he would not set foot in the boat without his friend. O'Neil replied that if there was to be any nonsense of that sort he would leave now and go off on his own. In the end the Prince was compelled to agree: O'Neil would remain behind, and they would rendezvous on the island of Raasay between Skye and the mainland in a week or so.

Charles proposed to keep a pistol hidden under the petticoat of his disguise, but Flora would not allow it. She pointed out that, if they were searched, the gun would give him away. 'Indeed, Miss', replied Charles, 'if we shall happen to meet with any that will go so narrowly to work in searching as what you mean, they will certainly discover me at any rate.'[24]

She did allow him to keep his 'crab stick', a 'short heavy cudgel, with which he design'd to do his best to knock down any single person that should attack him', and he had to be content with that. The Prince's pistols were duly handed over to Young Milton, who later gave them to Armadale, and now Milton and O'Neil departed to return to South Uist, leaving only those who were to make the journey.

Flora now produced the clothes that had been made for the Prince and helped him into them. MacEachain described the scene: 'The company being gone, the Prince, stript of his own cloaths was dressed by Miss Flora in his new attire, but could not keep his hands from adjusting his headdress, which he cursed a thousand times.'[25] Under the costume he still wore his breeches and waistcoat.

It began to rain and turned cold, so the men lit a fire to keep warm while they waited to depart. The party was small: only the Prince, Flora, MacEachain and the boat crew, comprising three MacDonald militiamen, Lieutenants John and Roderick MacDonald, and Ensign Roderick MacDonald – on unofficial leave from their companies – Duncan Campbell and John MacMhuirich.

One final alarm sent them running to douse the fire and hide as five wherries loaded with armed men sailed into the loch. Fortunately the soldiers, believed to be from Campbell's landing party, did not notice the small boat and sailed on southward without stopping.[26]

At eight o'clock on the evening of Saturday 28 June the boatmen pushed off from the shore and rowed into the failing light. Charles Stuart had left the Long Island, out of General Campbell's trap, away from the fury of Ferguson and Scott. Enveloped in the Highland gloaming, the heir to the Jacobite King over the Water set sail on the voyage over the sea to Skye.

CHAPTER THREE

'*I owe you a crown*'

Make my compliments to all those to whom I have given trouble.

Secret letter of thanks from Prince Charlie[1]

The rain eased and then ceased altogether by the time the oarsmen rowed the small boat out of Loch Uiskevagh into the open sea. The wherries had vanished too, but the boatmen still had to take great care since the presence of these vessels and the soldiers meant that a naval ship must be nearby. They did not dare raise the sail as they turned northward at the mouth of the loch, flitting among the hundreds of skerries along that coast of Ronay and North Uist for extra protection. This was just as well, for they spotted a man-of-war to the north, but fortunately it failed to see them.

The plan was that when the short summer night closed in – darker than usual that evening because of cloud and rain – they would make a dash across the open sea to reach Skye by morning. As they turned eastward into the exposed waters of the Minch, a wind blew up behind them, a welcome west wind which allowed the boatmen to ship their oars and raise the sail. Taking advantage of this following wind they sailed through the short, pitch-black night, steering without benefit of compass or stars and keeping watch for warships all the time. Suddenly, and without warning, the unpredictable Hebridean wind turned against them by veering to the north-west, causing the sea to roughen until it became so stormy that it swept the small boat wildly into the trough of every wave, only to toss it upwards again on the next crest.

In that exposed stretch of water, which lies between the Outer and Inner Hebrides, there was neither comfort nor shelter from the wind or rain for the passengers, who could only huddle together and try to keep out of the way of the boatmen, as they worked fast to handle the vessel in the rising storm. Flora eventually dozed off into exhausted sleep, with the Prince guarding her carefully 'lest in the darkness any of the men should chance to step upon her'.[2]

When Flora told her story to admirers afterwards, she said, 'Happening to awake with some little bustle in the boat she found the Prince leaning over her with his hands spread about her head. She asked what was the matter? The Prince told her that one of the rowers being obliged to do somewhat about the sail behoved to step over her body . . . and lest he should have done her hurt either by stumbling or trampling upon her in the dark . . . he had been doing his best to preserve his guardian from harm.'[3] The very idea of the Prince protecting Flora sent Jacobite ladies in Edinburgh into frenzied raptures whenever she recounted that story.

Charles was ebullient during the voyage, in spite of all the discomfort, and showed no alarm as the storm grew in intensity towards first light of Sunday morning. He was probably fired by relief at the ending of those taut days when capture had seldom been more than minutes away; and in his high spirits he even sang to Flora. The Cause was clearly on his mind – and how could it have been otherwise? He chose to sing early pro-Stuart songs: 'The 29th of May' and 'The King Shall Enjoy His Own Again':

> For who better may our high sceptre sway
> Than he whose right it is to reign
> Then look for no peace for the wars will never cease
> Till the King shall enjoy his own again

Because they had no compass the sailors steered through the night by instinct and their lifelong knowledge of those seas, but in spite of all that skill they were uncertain of their exact course and argued among themselves. Charles, Flora and Neil watched. The Prince drank some milk, which Lady Clan had given him, straight from the flask, turn and turn about with the boatmen, but insisted that a half bottle of wine which he had left should be shared with Flora.

At dawn the wind died and a mist crept in, leaving the small boat lost on the grey water – an enormous, silent seabird, rising and falling on the gently swelling sea. The boatmen lowered the sail and rowed for a time, then stopped to listen for the sound of the sea breaking on the shore, which they knew must lie close. No sound came and there was not a glimpse of land through the thick mist. The vessel drifted on the current, moving almost imperceptibly. Suddenly, as happens in those parts, a fresh wind blew up without warning to drive the fog before it and reveal cliffs just ahead. The oarsmen identified these through the thinning mist as Waternish Point, a menacing promontory which juts far out into the sea on the north-western tip of Skye. They scanned the line of black cliffs for a break in their sheer face where they might land without being seen, at the same time searching the threadbare grass cap which crowned the cliffs in case any watchers might catch sight of them; but they saw no one. This was hardly surprising since it was the Sabbath morning and all respectable crofters, fishermen and their families would be at church or at home preparing for morning worship. A quick scan of the seaward horizon revealed several warships patrolling, but luckily none sighted their little craft. For the moment they were safe – safely over the sea to Skye.

They headed for the shore, but as they came near the oarsmen suddenly realized they had made a mistake and this was not Waternish at all, but Dunvegan Head, which lies well to the west of Waternish. Worse still, it was Clan MacLeod country, and the loyalty of the MacLeods out on Skye hunting for them was uncertain. The boatmen rowed the small boat fiercely against a strengthening north-westerly wind until they rounded Dunvegan Head and saw the stark, but welcome, black basalt face of Waternish ahead. The cliffs there push seawards, a ship's prow of dark rock topped by grassland, and with streams cascading down the sheer face. Waternish can be a forbidding place even on a midsummer morning, but to the weary sailors that day it was a welcome sight. The wind blew until it was hard at times to tell whether they were making progress or not, and the men became so exhausted that the Prince volunteered to take a turn at the oars. His offer was refused: tired as they were, the islanders would not permit a prince of Scotland's royal house to row them.

What happened next was described by both Flora and Neil and, while the facts of their separate accounts agree broadly, the sequence in which they occurred does not.[4] Since there is no suitable landing place on the east side of Waternish (where Neil says they tried to land), and an excellent one can be found at a little bay called Ardmore on the west, it would seem that Flora's version is the correct one.

They decided to rest at Ardmore, but to their horror they discovered two militiamen on the beach, the first positioned in one of three boats that lay beached on the sand, and the other standing close by. At once the Prince's oarsmen began to row furiously away, ignoring a shout to stop from one of the soldiers. The man in the boat fired on them, but missed, and they were soon out of range. As the second soldier made for some buildings, where the fugitives presumed the men's companions were based, they rowed out of the bay and round the little headland.

'The poor men, almost ready to breathe out their last, at length made the point of Watersay', wrote Neil MacEachain,[5] but soon they were too exhausted to continue, so they manoeuvred the vessel into a narrow cleft in the rockface, where they would be sheltered both from the wind and from being seen by pursuers. Having stayed there for an hour or so, they 'revived their drooping spirits with a plentiful repas of bread and butter', washed down with fresh water from one of the many waterfalls that tumble down Waternish cliff face.[6]

By that time there was no sign of pursuit and the weather had calmed again, so they continued into the mouth of Loch Snizort and set course across the loch towards the Trotternish Peninsula. At its mouth Loch Snizort is so broad that it has the appearance of a wide bay rather than a sea loch, with the little scatter of the Ascrib Islands providing the only cover from watchers on either shore. The oarsmen made for a small beach, which is still called Prince Charles's Point, a little north of Totescore above Uig Bay, and there they landed at about two o'clock in the afternoon. In Neil's words they were 'within a cannon shot'[7] of Monkstadt, home of the Chief of Sleat – within cannon's fire, but out of sight over the crest of a low hill.

Sunday was probably chosen deliberately by the Prince's helpers in the Long Island as the best day to arrive in Skye, since most people, including officers and soldiers of the militia, would be in church and the coast would be at its least well guarded. The boatmen had arrived at Rossinish on the Friday and said they were ready, yet it was Saturday evening before they left. Flora and Lady Clan could have hurried operations to get the Prince off the island immediately, but made no effort to do so. It can only be assumed therefore that they planned to leave on Saturday night in order to reach Skye on Sunday. The ruse worked. This part of the coast was normally well guarded, as is proved by the fact that the wife of John MacDonald of Kirkibost in North Uist was stopped by the militia and questioned closely when she landed from the Long Island only the day before, yet nobody intercepted the Prince's boat.

Flora and Neil decided to leave Prince Charlie alone in the care of the boatmen, while they walked over the small knoll that hid Monkstadt House from the sea to ask for Lady Margaret MacDonald's assistance. Before setting out they instructed the oarsmen neither to stir nor to allow the Prince to leave the boat. They explained to the men exactly how they were to deal with any soldiers or local people who might become curious about the strange female: they were to answer that she was 'Miss McDonald's maid, and to curse her for a lazy jade, what was she good for, since she did not attend her Mrs'.[8]

Still uneasy in their minds, Flora and Neil hurried to the Chief's house to discover that Sir Alexander had been at home, but had left for the mainland only the day before. His wife was at Monkstadt with the factor, Alexander MacDonald of Kingsburgh, Lieutenant Alexander MacLeod of Balmeanach, the officer in charge of the militia standing guard over this stretch of coast, and Mrs MacDonald of Kirkibost, the lady who had arrived the previous day. MacLeod was not liked by anyone: he was considered to be a 'sneaking little gentleman',[9] not to be trusted. It was he who had acted as intermediary between MacLeod of Dunvegan and that wily old jack-in-the-box Lord Lovat, when Lovat tried to 'support' both sides but eventually ended up on the scaffold for doing so.

Flora did not panic on hearing that the militia officer was in the house; she calmly sent a message to Lady Margaret to say that she had called on her way home to Armadale and would like to pay her respects. Lady Margaret hurriedly excused herself and left her guests who had just sat down to dinner. When Flora told her that the Prince had arrived at Monkstadt, the Chief's wife became very agitated and furiously tried to think of some way of smuggling the Prince safely into the house without MacLeod or one of his men seeing him.

The first person Lady Margaret thought of sending for was Donald Roy MacDonald, who had been in touch with her about the plan to conceal Charles on the isolated island of Fladda-Chuain. While she waited, Flora agreed to join Lieutenant MacLeod in the dining room and engage the militia officer in conversation, and in the meantime Lady Margaret took the factor outside under some pretext to consult him.

Flora bravely sat in the room and talked affably with MacLeod, answering his searching questions about reports of the Prince's movements on the Long Island. Her calmness and straightforward replies lulled any suspicion the officer might have had, so that he had no inkling of the drama being enacted outside the house.

The Chief's wife's great fear was that discovery of the Prince at Monkstadt would mean ruin for her husband and herself, yet she felt compelled to offer him shelter. Kingsburgh would have none of it – if Betty Burke came into the house one of the servants might suspect that she was a man in disguise, and it would require only the slightest hint of that to be passed on to a member of the militia to give the game away. Charles must not be brought to Monkstadt, not on any account, Kingsburgh insisted.

While Flora continued to keep MacLeod occupied, Lady Margaret paced the garden in a state of great agitation, arguing with Kingsburgh and waiting for Donald Roy, who soon rode up: it did not take long since he had been waiting to respond at a moment's notice when news of Prince Charlie's arrival reached him. Lady Margaret rushed to meet Donald Roy, crying, 'O Donald Roy we are ruined for ever,' and poured out the story of Charles's arrival accompanied by Armadale's stepdaughter. The three began at once to discuss what should be done.[10]

Their first consideration was Charles's immediate safety, so Neil MacEachain was sent to guide the Prince to a spot behind a hill, just off the Uig road a mile from Monkstadt, where he could wait until one of them came for him. After Neil left, Kingsburgh raised the Fladda-Chuain idea again, but eventually proposed that the Prince should be taken by boat round the northern promontory of Trotternish to Raasay, an island on the eastern side of Skye. Lady Margaret thought that too risky, since there was a strong militia unit stationed at Bornesketaig near the tip of the peninsula which would certainly intercept any vessel that passed. Perhaps she was terrified, as indeed most islanders were, of John MacLeod of Talisker, an officer with a notorious reputation who had command of the militia there, and in fact was the commanding officer of the young lieutenant who was at that moment sharing dinner with Flora in Lady Margaret's house. In the end they decided that the safest place for the Prince to spend the night would be Kingsburgh's house, from where he could travel 'fourteen long Highland miles' overland to Portree, cross to Raasay and move on to MacKenzie of Seaforth country on the mainland. Donald Roy left immediately for Totrome, near Portree, where he thought he might find Rona, son of the laird of Raasay, to check whether that island would be safe.

Flora gamely played her part in the plot by keeping the militia lieutenant occupied with light chat and answers to his questions about the Prince's whereabouts in the Long Island, and she carried all this off so successfully that Kingsburgh and Lady Margaret were able to join them without MacLeod's having the slightest suspicion of the real reason for the factor's absence. MacLeod assumed that they had been discussing urgent estate business and accepted Kingsburgh's excuse that he had to leave shortly afterwards. While Flora was detaining MacLeod and the others were busy plotting at Monkstadt, Neil had plenty on his mind down by the shore. He found Prince Charlie where they had left him and set off to take him to the chosen safe place at the back of the hill on the road to Uig, telling him to carry a bundle of light clothes in order to add authenticity to the Betty Burke disguise. But a prince is a prince even in adversity and not given to carrying his own baggage, so Betty Burke – true to the reputation she had been given – soon threw the bundle down and told Neil to carry it himself or leave it where it was. Neil complained, but Charles said flatly that he had carried the baggage long enough and that was that. There was more drama when they reached the meeting place: the Prince suddenly asked if Neil had brought his case of knives from the boat. Neil had not.

'Then you must return and look for them', Charles ordered.

Neil remonstrated that it was unsafe to leave him alone on an open hillside so close to the road. 'Shall I for the sakes of all the knives in the universe leave you here all alone?'.

'There will be no fears of me', the Prince replied. 'Do you what you are ordered, for I must absolutely have it, so no more words.'

Neil protested again in vain, but when he saw the familiar signs of Charles about to fly into one of his passions, he obeyed.[11] And that is why Kingsburgh found the Prince sitting all alone on a rock close to a flock of sheep, whose running to and fro on the hillside had shown Kingsburgh where to look for the Prince. Neil was right – any passer-by could have discovered the Prince – but Charles was unconcerned; he had his 'crab stick' cudgel ready to defend himself so he felt safe. When Neil returned he found the Prince enjoying wine and food, which Kingsburgh had brought, and chatting contentedly to the factor as he ate. An hour before sunset Kingsburgh and the Prince set off, with Neil at a discreet distance, to walk to Kingsburgh House on the shore of Loch Snizort a few miles south of Uig.

Word was sent to the boatmen, ordering them to return to Uist which was considered, for some unfathomable reason, the safest place for them, and Flora was invited to stay at Monkstadt overnight. She refused, although she knew it would have been much safer to stay with Lady Margaret than to travel with Charles through this part of North Skye, which was more heavily populated than Uist, crawling with militiamen and consequently far more dangerous. It was a brave decision, but Flora had committed herself to help the Prince escape and she was determined to remain with him as long as she was needed. Charles was still travelling as her maid, Betty Burke. Flora carried a letter of safe passage from her stepfather, the best protection they could have, so she felt she was needed to play her part if they should be stopped. Flora did not hesitate: if Charles Edward was to stay at Kingsburgh House, she would go there too.

She made her apologies to Lady Margaret, telling her (for the sake of Lieutenant MacLeod) that in these unsettled times she was anxious to be on her way home to see her mother. Accompanied by Mrs MacDonald of Kirkibost and Mrs MacDonald's maid, Flora rode south on horseback, listening with alarm to remarks of local people on their way home from evening church service about the strange figure of a woman who accompanied Kingsburgh. These passers-by criticized the way the woman walked and the improper manner in which she held her skirts high as she passed through a shallow ford. Neil was horrified at the Prince's carelessness, too, and once cried out, 'For God's sake, Sir, take care what you are doing.' Charles just laughed and thanked him for his solicitude.[12]

When Flora and Kirkibost's wife caught up with the Prince, Mrs MacDonald's curiosity got the better of her and she could not stop staring at Charles. Then her maid also began to look closely and comment on how awkwardly the Irish maid wore her clothes and what large strides she took. Flora hurried the girl and her mistress on, but after that Kingsburgh decided to leave the road and cut across the hill to Kingsburgh House, safely away from curious eyes of returning churchgoers and the many militiamen who were on the road.

Flora, Neil, the Prince and Kingsburgh arrived at Kingsburgh House almost simultaneously to find that everyone there had gone to bed – Mrs MacDonald, her daughter, Anne, and her son-in-law, Ranald MacAlister of Skirinish. MacAlister was a militia officer and no mention is made of him in anyone's version of the events that followed. He vanished from the house immediately, probably because it was thought that the less he saw or heard the better. He was never referred to in connection with the Prince's stay at Kingsburgh.

A servant woke Mrs MacDonald to tell her that the master had returned with company.[13]

'What company?', asked Kingsburgh's wife.

'Milton's daughter, I believe, and some company with her', the maid told her.

Mrs MacDonald was tired. 'Milton's daughter is very welcome to come here with any company she pleases to bring', she replied. 'But you'll give my service to her, and tell her to make free with anything in the house; for I am very sleepy and cannot see her this night.'

Soon Anne MacAlister came to her, saying, 'O mother, my father has brought in a very odd, muckle, ill-shapen-up wife as ever I saw! I never saw the like of her, and he has gone into the hall with her.'

Kingsburgh himself appeared at this point and ordered his wife to dress and prepare some supper for his visitors, but he refused to tell her who they were. The factor's wife asked no more questions, but sent Anne to fetch her keys from the hall. The girl soon returned, afraid to enter the room because there was an 'odd muckle trallup' there 'making lang wide steps'. Mrs MacDonald went to fetch the keys herself, but soon retreated and begged her husband to go instead; he refused, so she had to steel herself to enter the room. As she did so the strange female rose and kissed her hand, and she realized that this was some 'distressed gentleman', a Jacobite fugitive probably, but she had no thought that it might be the Prince himself.

Back to her husband she rushed. 'Why, my dear', he told her calmly, 'it is the Prince. You have the honour to have him in your house.'

Her first thought was that they would be all be hanged if the Prince were to be caught in Kingsburgh House, but her husband replied lightly that one dies only once and, if they died for this, then it would be in a good cause. Patiently he added 'Pray, make no delay; go, get some supper.'

Wailing in true housewifely fashion that she had nothing in the house fit to feed a Prince, she rushed off to the kitchen and produced a meal of 'roasted eggs, some collops (slices of meat), plenty of bread and butter', to which they all sat down together. Flora makes no mention of her part in all these proceedings, but presumably she helped with the kitchen preparations and joined them to eat. Neil MacEachain's account breaks off just before the Kingsburgh episode, but he also must have been at the supper table. Kingsburgh had insisted that his wife sit with them too because the Prince demanded that she should do so. Only Anne MacAlister did not eat: in order to prevent the servants from seeing Betty Burke, she served the meal herself (according to her own account) and would not eat with them in spite of several pleas from the Prince. When supper was finished the royal guest poured himself a large glass of brandy and drank to the happiness of his host and hostess before the women retired to bed, leaving Kingsburgh, Neil and the Prince to sit far into the night, smoking and drinking punch. Eventually MacDonald and MacEachain helped Charles to wash and he went to bed, to sleep between clean sheets for the first time since Culloden.

Charles slept more soundly than all the others. Mrs MacDonald was up early to go to Flora's room to ask all about the escape from Uist. Flora told her everything, including the part Lady Clan played in providing the disguise. Mrs MacDonald then asked what had become of the boat and its crew and Flora explained that they had been sent back to South Uist. Kingsburgh's wife was horrified. She said that they would be seized by the militia and forced to tell all that they knew: 'I wish you had sunk the boat and kept the boatmen in Sky where they could have been concealed . . . all will be wrong by their returning to South Uist.'

Flora reassured her: 'I hope not for we took care to depone them before they parted from us.'

'Alas, your deponing of them will not signifie a farthing', Kingsburgh's wife sighed, 'for if once the military get hold of them they will terrifie them out of their senses and make them forget their oath.'

This raised new fears in Flora's mind, which nagged her until she had to go to Kingsburgh and plead with him to rouse the Prince and get him on his way. MacDonald hesitated, but at last Flora prevailed upon him and he went into Charles's room to wake him. However, he found his guest so soundly asleep that he did not have the heart to disturb him, so he slipped out of the room and told Flora he had decided to let Charles sleep on.[14]

Mrs MacDonald took a notion that she would like a lock of the Prince's hair as a memento, and Bishop Forbes relates an elaborate tale of how she persuaded Flora to ask for it. Forbes tells that Flora at first refused to go to the Prince's room to ask for the lock, but Kingsburgh's wife insisted.

'What then', said Mrs MacDonald, 'no harm will happen to you. He is too good to harm you or any person. You must instantly go in and get me the lock.'

Then, says Forbes:

> Mrs MacDonald, taking hold of Miss with one hand, knocked at the door of the room with the other. The Prince called, 'Who is there?' Mrs MacDonald, opening the door, said, 'Sir, it is I, and I am importuneing Miss Flora to come in and get a lock of your hair to me, and she refuses to do it.'
>
> 'Pray', said the Prince, 'desire Miss MacDonald to come in. What should make her afraid to come where I am?' When Miss came in he begged her to sit down on a chair at the bedside, then laying his arms about her waist, and his head upon her lap, he desired her to cut out the lock with her own hands in token of future and more substantial favours.[15]

Flora kept one half of the lock and gave the other to Mrs MacDonald, Forbes added. Flora does not mention this incident in her account, and Anne MacAlister claims that it was she who cut the lock after the Prince awoke on the afternoon of Monday 30 June. As Flora and Neil MacEachain left for Portree quite early in the day, probably before the Prince was awake, to make arrangements for the Prince's arrival there, it is much more likely that Anne's account is the correct one.

Anne's husband, Ranald MacAlister, was of a similar size to the Prince, so one of his suits was produced for Charles to wear to continue his journey. The Prince could not put his new suit on immediately in case one of the Kingsburgh servants saw him: his hosts insisted that he should leave wearing the Betty Burke disguise in which he had arrived. He was told to change once he was out of sight of Kingsburgh. There was much merriment while Charles dressed as Betty Burke again, helped by Anne MacAlister, who commented that he was so useless at dressing himself that he could not even put in a pin without help.[16]

Charles delayed departure as long as he dared, but at last, late in the afternoon, he said his farewells and set out to walk to Portree, accompanied only by a boy named MacQueen as guide. It was a miserable journey for Charlie, across boggy tracks in pouring rain, without companionship since the boy probably spoke only Gaelic. Charles knew he would soon be leaving the MacDonalds who had cared for him so assiduously throughout his time in the Long Island and in Skye, and about that he was badly distressed.

As soon as the Prince left, Mrs MacDonald and her daughter took the sheets from his bed, folded them carefully and laid them away unwashed. Kingsburgh's wife asked her daughter to see that she was buried in one of them. The second sheet was given to Flora, who also asked for it to be used as her shroud. The Betty Burke dress was retrieved and Mrs MacDonald had it made into a bed cover while Flora was given the apron. Most of the other clothes were destroyed.

At Portree the travellers found Flora and Neil waiting with Donald Roy MacDonald, who had made arrangements to have a small boat ready to ferry Charles to Raasay. They met at Charles MacNab's inn, a small building on the site of the present-day Royal Hotel, but it was very late in the evening and, since it had rained all the way from Kingsburgh, Charles and young MacQueen were soaking wet and cold. Yet the Prince still thought of others. When Donald Roy commiserated with him about the terrible rainstorm, Charles replied, 'I am more sorry that our Lady [his name for Flora] should be abused with the rain.'[17]

Inside the inn the fugitive stood miserably, rain running off his clothes on to the floor because he had had no plaid to protect him on the walk from Kingsburgh. Before he sat down he demanded a dram and downed it.

Donald Roy gave the Prince his own kilt and a dry shirt, but Charles refused to change because Flora was present. He had shown no reticence about dressing in front of a woman at Kingsburgh, so it does seem strange that he should hesitate now. Perhaps he was embarrassed, as a prince of royal blood, to undress in a public place rather than because Flora was there.

Donald Roy and Neil told him this was no time to stand on ceremony and pressed him to put on a dry shirt. Food was now brought in – roasted fish, bread, butter and cheese – giving him an excuse to delay changing for a little longer. Donald Roy made a joke of it, which the Prince appreciated, but Charles still had his way: he would eat first and change later.

MacNab's was a whisky house, so apart from whisky there was only water to drink, and that was in 'an ugly cog', the dish the landlord kept to bail water out of his boat. When Charlie hesitated, Donald Roy, fearing someone might become suspicious of this fastidious stranger, took the cup, handed it to Charles and whispered to him to drink without any more fuss. 'You are right', said the Prince and took a hearty draught. He then began to put his new clothes on.[18]

Charles would gladly have stayed at the inn all night rather than go out again into the rain which was still coming down in torrents, but Donald Roy would have none of it, so the Prince bought some tobacco and prepared to leave. Charles begged Donald Roy to go with him, because he would feel safer with a MacDonald at his side.

Donald Roy refused, but took the opportunity to put in a good word for his chief. 'Though Sir Alexander and his following did not join your royal highness', he said, 'yet you see you have been very safe amongst them: for though they did not repair to your standard they wish you very well.'[19] And if Charles needed money he assured him that Lady Margaret would supply it. Charles had plenty of money for the present. In fact he had been flashing golden guineas in the inn to the alarm of Donald Roy only a little earlier.

It was now time to say farewell to Flora, but first he must settle his financial debt to her. Donald Roy related that the Prince turned to Flora and said, 'I believe, Madam, I owe you a crown of borrowed money.' She told him it was only half a crown, which accordingly he paid her with thanks. He then kissed her hand and told her, 'For all that has happened I hope, Madam, we shall meet in St James's yet.'[20]

It was the early hours of Tuesday 1 July, just eleven days since she had first met the fugitive Prince, and for three of these he had been in her constant care. Without her assistance he could never have escaped from the trap that was on the point of snapping shut on him on the Long Island. There was to be no meeting again at St James's or anywhere else: Flora never saw Prince Charlie again, but she did not forget him.

Charles had some food with him and, taking a piece of sugar out of his pocket a little later, he handed it to Donald Roy, saying prophetically, 'Pray, MacDonald, take this piece of sugar to *our Lady*, for I am afraid she will get no sugar where she is going.' Donald Roy tried to decline the sugar, but Charles was insistent, so Donald Roy slipped it to Malcolm MacLeod, whispering to him to keep it for the Prince's use later.[21]

Charles begged Donald Roy to tell no one, not even Flora, where he had gone. He was adamant about this: 'Tell nobody, no, not *our Lady*, which way I am gone, for it is right that my course should not be known.'[22]

After a final attempt to persuade Donald Roy to accompany him, Charles departed with a promise that Donald Roy would meet Young Raasay the following Thursday, 3 July, and rejoin the Prince on the island. So Charles left, satisfied that they would soon be reunited.

A dozen different feelings must have crowded Flora's mind as she watched the small boat disappear into the stormy night: relief that her part in Prince Charlie's escape was over; satisfaction that it had been accomplished so easily and so successfully; compassion for the man who had arrived with such high hopes a year before and now was skulking like a common thief; unease that this matter was not over yet because the militiamen were still hunting him; fear for his future, for her clansmen and friends, and for herself. She may have been too exhausted from the physical and mental strain of the past days to examine the motives for her action in helping to rescue the Jacobite Pretender's son, but she knew one thing even then: if she were asked to do it again she would. Highland honour demanded that one should help a fellow man in distress. Charles Edward Stuart had come to her in dire need of help, so she had given it to him.

Tomorrow would be time enough to think about the consequences. A weary Flora and Neil stayed in Portree overnight, and the following day MacEachain escorted her south to Armadale (either by boat or overland: we are not sure how they travelled). Her mother was surprised to see her, but accepted her daughter's explanation that she had returned from the Long Island because of 'things being in a hurry and confusion in South Uist, with such a number of military folks, she was uneasy till she got out of it'.[23]

That same day Donald Roy headed back to Monkstadt to report to Kingsburgh and Lady Margaret that the Prince was safely off the island, and there he also met Lieutenant MacLeod who was an old friend. MacLeod asked him to stay overnight, to which Donald Roy agreed gladly because it gave him the chance to pump the militia officer and his men to discover what the searching forces knew of the Prince's movements. Donald Roy stayed at MacLeod's headquarters and actually shared the lieutenant's bed that night, and he had a long talk with the sentries who were still guarding the sea approaches to the island. When he set off for Portree again to rendezvous with the Prince, Donald Roy felt easy in his mind that the militia knew nothing of the arrival of the Prince in Skye or his stay at Kingsburgh. He took with him a letter from Lady Margaret for the Prince, but missed meeting Charles because the fugitive had found Raasay so devastated by the Hanoverians that he could not stay there. Charles had returned to Skye almost immediately and made for MacKinnon country in the south-west of the island. Donald Roy had to be content with a brief letter which said simply:

> Sir, – I have parted (I thank God) as intended. Make my compliments to all those to whom I have given trouble. – I am, Sir, your humble servant
>
> James Thomson[24]

This was Charles Stuart's last word of thanks to those who had taken part in his escape, and Donald Roy hurried south to Armadale to show it to Flora.

During that fateful first week of July much was happening in the Hebrides to mislead and divert government forces, especially the Navy which wasted days hunting the French vessel *Le Hardi Mendiant*, then sailing among the Outer Hebridean islands in its own desperate search to find the Prince and spirit him off to safety in France. *Le Hardi Mendiant* made contact with O'Sullivan who, in the meantime, had met up with Felix O'Neil and learned that Charles was in Skye. It was agreed, therefore, that O'Neil should dash to Skye, find Charles and rendezvous with the Frenchman at Lochmaddy some days later. Felix could not pick up the Prince's scent on Skye, which was perhaps as well because he returned to Lochmaddy to find that *Le Hardi Mendiant* had sailed. Flora was angry about this and blamed O'Sullivan's cowardice. She told Bishop Forbes later that:

the timorous Sullivan, having a fair wind, and not having courage to stay until O'Neil's return, being resolved to take care of Number One, obliged the captain to set sail directly, lest he should be taken and should lose his precious life.[25]

This uncharacteristically acid comment confirms that Flora cared for Felix and was greatly upset by his betrayal.

The diversion of *Le Hardi Mendiant* and the best efforts of clan militia could only delay discovery of the Prince's escape: within ten days General Campbell had all the information he needed. As Kingsburgh's wife prophesied to Flora, it was a mistake to send the boatmen back to the outer isles because they were arrested almost as soon as they set foot on Uist and one of them confessed under threat of torture. In the meantime the general made several other excellent catches: Clanranald and his wife were held, then the old boatman, Donald MacLeod of Galtergill, and Felix O'Neil, who had waited at Lochmaddy until he was convinced *Le Hardi Mendiant* had gone, before taking to the water-filled wilds of Benbecula only to be arrested at Rossinish.

The boatman told everything he knew about Kingsburgh and Flora, and every detail of the Prince's disguise down to the last lilac sprig on Betty Burke's dress. By 9 July General Campbell and Captain Ferguson were sure they knew enough to sail HMS *Furnace* into Loch Snizort and anchor close to Monkstadt.

Lady Margaret feigned innocence and the general believed her:

Lady Margaret was surprised when she knew of our errand, told us most frankly upon our inquiry that Miss MacDonald had dined at her house on Sunday the 29th, that though she pressed her to stay all night, yet she could not prevail and that she had a man, and a maidservant with her. I think her ladyship did not know the maid's quality.[26]

Her ladyship had certainly proved a very plausible liar.

HMS *Furnace* then sailed down the coast to Kingsburgh. Captain Ferguson was cunning enough not to rush straight to the house and arrest the Sleat factor. First he had one of the Kingsburgh dairymaids brought aboard his ship and quickly persuaded her to tell him all about the Prince's visit down to the details of the cutting of the lock of hair for a keepsake. That had been too good a morsel for the maids at Kingsburgh House to miss.

It was now time to go ashore. According to the story, as it was related afterwards and no doubt lost nothing in the telling, Kingsburgh's wife was a match for the hated captain. How Jacobite hearts rejoiced as it was recounted! When Ferguson informed Mrs MacDonald that he had come to question her about some lodgers she had lately had in her house, and 'desired her to be distinct in her answers', she replied, 'If Captain Ferguson is to be my judge, then God have mercy upon my soul.'

Taken aback, Ferguson asked why she spoke in such a way.

'Why, Sir', she retorted, 'the world belies you if you be not a very cruel, hard-hearted man.'

'People should not believe all the world says', he answered lamely, then turned back to Kingsburgh to ask in which room Miss MacDonald and 'the person along with her in woman's clothes' had slept.

'I know in what room Miss MacDonald herself lay', Kingsburgh replied, 'but where servants are laid when in my house, I know nothing of that matter, I never enquire anything about it. My wife is the properest person to inform you about that.'

Ferguson now turned back to Mrs MacDonald and asked whether she had 'laid the young Pretender and Miss MacDonald in one bed'. She refused to let the man cow her. 'Sir', she replied, 'whom you mean by the young Pretender I shall not pretend to guess; but I can assure you it is not the fashion in the Isle of Sky to lay the mistress and the maid in the same bed together.'

Ferguson demanded to be shown where the visitors had slept and noted that it seemed strange that the maid had been given the better room. When he left he took Kingsburgh and Anne MacAlister with him as prisoners.[27]

According to General Campbell's secretary, David Campbell, the Sleat factor later gave considerable information 'upon promise of secrecy that the Prince had gone to Raasay, left there on 3 July, and came back to Skye with one MacLeod who lives eleven miles from here'.[28]

Kingsburgh admitted the involvement of Flora, and it is hard to see how he could have done otherwise since it was already well known. It does seem a pity, however, that he felt able to give such detailed information about others. In his statement to Campbell he betrayed both the MacLeods of Raasay and the MacKinnons of Skye by telling the general, 'The second or third of July the young Chevalier came from Raasay with Malcolm MacLeod who left him in John MacKinnon's house in Arn in MacKinnon country.'[29]

Clearly Kingsburgh was more prepared to protect his own clansmen than members of the other clans on the island.

At Armadale Flora, Donald Roy and Neil were unaware of any of this, but the trap was now about to be sprung on them too. Ferguson sailed south and anchored close to Armadale on the 11th of the month.

A message was sent to Flora to inform her that Donald MacDonald of Castleton, near Armadale, wanted her to come to his house to meet Roderick MacDonald, a lawyer, who had some questions to put to her on behalf of MacLeod of Talisker. Donald Roy tried hard to persuade her that this was a trap, but Flora insisted she must obey so, before she left, he made her hand over her stepfather's letter of safe passage which he destroyed, along with the one signed 'James Thomson' and another from Lady Margaret to Charles that he had been unable to deliver. Whatever happened, no incriminating written evidence must be found at Armadale.

On Saturday 12 July Flora set out for Castleton, but never reached her destination: on the road she was intercepted, arrested and was soon a prisoner aboard HMS *Furnace*. Flora told in 1747 how she met her stepfather on the road just before she was arrested, but that is hard to believe because 'One-eyed' Hugh would certainly never have permitted Flora to walk into so obvious a trap.[30]

The wily Donald Roy, having failed to save Flora, did not wait to be arrested. He took to the hills, armed with only a pistol and dirk, and was never caught. He hid out for a whole year in several different caves, supplied with food from Lady Margaret, and whiled away the time writing Latin poetry which, needless to say, was highly praised by fireside Jacobites in Edinburgh. Among his verses were a lament for Culloden and an ode to his wounded foot. When all the hue and cry died down and an amnesty was declared at last in 1747, Donald Roy reappeared as quietly as he had disappeared.

Neil, the supposedly quiet, retiring man in the shadows throughout the escape, vanished into the heather, too, only to re-emerge in time to join the Prince and sail with him for France on 19 September.

For Flora a voyage of a very different nature lay ahead in Ferguson's ship HMS *Furnace*.

CHAPTER FOUR

Flora – Innocent or Guilty?

He insisted that he was in no danger of being taken especialy while he was among McDonalds

Hugh MacDonald of Baleshare[1]

When Captain Ferguson ordered HMS *Furnace* to sail from Armadale with Flora on board, he could look landward and feel smugly sure that he and his master, General Campbell, had now virtually cleared the Long Island and Skye of the perpetrators of the plot which had enabled Charles Stuart to slip out of the net. Kingsburgh was on his way to Fort Augustus, where important prisoners were taken for interrogation, and those held on the Long Island, now included the most influential members of the Clanranald family, the chief himself, his wife, Boisdale and Felix O'Neil, the foreigner with an Irish name, but who claimed to hold a French army commission. The boatmen who had rowed the Prince across the Minch were in custody, too, and they had incriminated many more.

Only the Pretender himself still eluded them and he had gone to earth; but soon they would pick up his scent again. John Ferguson had every reason to preen himself on a good job well on the way to being completed.

Ferguson was correct in believing that he and his colleagues held most of those who had actually effected the escape, but he could not know then that they had missed some of the most important conspirators, including the man who had masterminded the escape. He was never caught, and it is difficult from the mass of oral and written evidence that exists even to link him with it for certain.

Under questioning, the more important prisoners were circumspect in what they said, and even after the Rising had become history and it was safe to talk, few gave much away.

Flora was discreet to the point of being misleading. She never incriminated her stepfather, or the principal MacDonalds in Uist, and remained silent about Neil MacEachain until she thought it safe to refer to him. O'Neil, too, gave such contradictory versions of his story that he has been accused of being a congenital liar. He veered from boastfulness to wary half-truths, presumably to protect others as well as himself. It has been assumed that pique at being left behind on the Long Island when the Prince sailed on the voyage to Skye, or jealousy over Neil's familiarity with Flora, led him to omit all mention of MacEachain in his accounts. It is much more likely that Felix, a highly trained soldier, knew more than we do, even today, about Neil's importance as a spy and Jacobite organizer.

There were very good reasons for holding silence, both at the time and later. MacEachain's role in all the Jacobite machinations is mysterious. We know that South Uist was considered by many in France to be the queen bee's nest in the Jacobite hive, and Neil, a South Uist man with knowledge of France and the ability to speak French, was in a good position to be the link between the Cause and the island. Felix would know about that and would want to protect MacEachain if only for the sake of the Cause.

After 1746 it was still prudent to keep silent because Charles did not regard Culloden as the end of the Cause. To him it was just a setback – one defeat to be set against half a dozen victories – and he spent years afterwards scheming and contriving to return to Scotland.

In 1746 there were many in Scotland who expected the Prince to return, so while this situation endured – however faltering that flickering candle of their hope might be – individual Jacobites would say nothing to compromise their own position or that of other supporters when Charles came again. Flora's stepfather in particular kept silent ever afterwards. Like Donald Roy he went to ground when the hue and cry arose after the arrests started and was not seen again until it was safe to re-emerge. He went secretly to Skye where he had all the connections to enable him to move swiftly and silently, and always to find friends who would shelter him. Hugh of Armadale had other advantages which helped to protect him while he hid: he kept his weapons and, like Flora's grandfather, was renowned for his great strength, so that few would have been 'desirous of the task to lay hands on him; for he never quit with his arms when he was skulking, and the people in Sky stood in awe of him'.[2]

The Government did itself a great disservice when it persuaded the island chiefs to raise militia companies to help with the search of the Highlands and Islands. Clansmen, even from clans whose chiefs refused to rise in 1745, were, to say the least, unreliable. They may have worn their clan chief's militia uniform, but their loyalty was first to their chief and then to the great island community. Many clansmen who stayed at home or joined the militia in 1745 retained strong Jacobite sympathies.

The Government knew this and never really trusted the chiefs, even those who were fighting on its side. When Cumberland first met Sleat at Fort Augustus, he said half-jokingly to Sir Alexander, 'Is this the great Rebel of the Isles?'

'No, my Lord Duke', the chief replied coldly, 'had I been the Rebel of the Isles, your Royal Highness would never have crossed the Spey.'[3]

Sir Alexander was safely in Fort Augustus during much of the plotting, so no one could point an accusing finger at him. Clanranald, on the other hand, was constantly on and off the Long Island and had been in touch with the Prince from the moment he first arrived there after Culloden, on 27 April. He was certainly aware of what was going on because the final days before Flora left for Skye with the Prince were a frenzy of activity at the chief's house at Nunton, with messengers coming and going, and Lady Clan, Flora and the womenfolk sewing like fury to make Betty Burke's costume.

Boisdale, too, was involved right up to the moment of his arrest, and Neil MacEachain attests to the fact that Charles 'kept [up] a private correspondence with Boystile about leaving the country, as it appeared impossible for him to conceal himself any longer from those cursed villains who left not a stone unturned to find him out'.[4]

Boisdale, he claimed, used every endeavour to have Charles conveyed to the mainland, but all the chief's scheming fell apart when he was taken prisoner and put aboard HMS *Baltimore*. Lady Boisdale took over and kept the Prince informed as best she could until her house was ransacked, and she, her daughter and her servants were left bound hand and foot. It was at that point that Charles's men panicked at Loch Boisdale and decided to separate and leave the Prince to head into the mountains, accompanied only by Felix O'Neil and Neil MacEachain.

There was a good reason for turning northwards. Boisdale's plan to spirit Prince Charlie out of the outer islands had involved people there. One of these was Hugh MacDonald of Baleshare who had actually visited Charles at Corodale along with Boisdale. Baleshare later told how the Prince, when in danger of being hemmed in by General Campbell's forces, wrote to him and asked for advice. Baleshare was reluctant to suggest anything in case it might lead to capture, but in the end he admitted:

> I was obliged to say something. My advice was this, that as he lay in view of the chanell, if the chanell was clear of ships he shoud go of in the afternoon to give him a long night, to keep closs by the land of

Sky, that he might have the opportunity of running ashore in case of the wors, and desir'd him he shou'd go to Kulin hills in Sky, where he cou'd get to the Laird of M'Kinon, who woud see him safely landed on the mainland. He told me it was impossible for him to recollect the whole thing without I gave the direction in write. He had his writeing instruments about him, and writt the direction as above; but advis'd him if he shoud not get to M'Kinon, that he shoud without loss of time go in to Sir James M'Donald's country of Slet, and apply to Donald M'Donald of Castletoun, to Hugh M'Donald of Armidell, to Alexander M'Donald of Kingsborow, to Archibald M'Donald of Tarsquivag, and Rory M'Donald of Camiscross, all cadets of Sir James M'Donald's family. Any of the above, I was confident, woud see him safely to the mainland.[5]

By good fortune one of these men was actually on the Long Island at that moment and he had the further advantage of strong family connections on both sides of the Minch. Hugh MacDonald of Armadale – 'One-eyed' Hugh who had married the MacDonald widow from Milton and had lived in South Uist until eight months earlier – was now back in the Outer Isles in command of one of the militia companies at the key crossing between South Uist and Benbecula. He had never admitted to being a Jacobite, but he had served in the French army and had been the first man to greet the Prince on the Scottish mainland. He was now in a perfect position to help. His stepson, young Milton, was also a secret Jacobite sympathizer, who knew Neil MacEachain well.

There is no evidence to prove that 'One-eyed' Hugh saw the Prince at Corodale but, if he did not, then he must have been the only man of importance who did not hunt, eat, drink and talk long into the night with Charles. O'Neil passes the actual disguise idea off as the Prince's own, but that sounds far fetched – how could a prince who had been reared in the rare atmosphere of a small royal court in Rome, narrower than a monastic order, ever think of such a thing? O'Neil may well have heard it first from the Prince's lips and thought it to have been Charles's own idea, or he may simply have been trying to make his master appear more heroic.

The idea has the hallmarks of being inspired locally, dreamed up by someone who knew the area and the people, but it contains one ingredient that points straight to Armadale. Hugh's stepdaughter was at that time staying with her brother at Milton and was one of the few people who had a good excuse for travelling from Uist to Skye. Hugh was the person most likely to think of that, so he must be given principal credit, or the blame, for evolving the plan.

Flora herself attributed it to her stepfather and made it clear that the Prince was in on it from a very early stage, but she only did so at the very end of her life when Charles Stuart and the Cause were history:

> The Prince himself then spoke to her, being previously perfectly well known to the situation of the country, and told her she wou'd be quite safe in udertaking what he wanted, as her step-father, Hugh Macdonald of Armadale, was commanding officer there, a gentleman he knew himself, and waited on him personally when he landed first on the mainland, and was sure he wish'd him well, and that he would give her a pass in to Sky.[6]

Neil MacEachain confirms her story. He wrote:

> When Captain Scott landed in South-Wist [Uist], Hugh MacDonald, who lay in Benbicula then with his party, sent one of the country gentlemen in whom he could repose a great deal of trust, to tell the prince privately that, as it seemed now impossible for him to conceal himself any longer in the country, if he would venter to be advised by him, though an enemy in appearance yet a sure friend in his heart, he would fall upon a scheme to convey him to the Isle of Skay, where he was sure to be protected by Lady Margaret MacDonald.[7]

'An enemy in appearance yet a sure friend' points us straight to Hugh MacDonald of Armadale, who was wearing the uniform of the clan militia yet had been the first to greet Charles Edward Stuart when he landed on the mainland of Scotland.

General Campbell certainly was convinced that Armadale was the mastermind behind the plan, so he, a man at all times lenient with Jacobites, turned all his fury on Hugh.

As early as 24 July Campbell realized that Armadale was a ringleader and was furious at having been duped by him. On that day he told the Earl of Cromartie 'this villain met me in South Uist and had the impudence to advise me against making so close a search and that if I should for some days a little desist he made no doubt of my success'. The general was doubly aggrieved because he had suspected Hugh. 'I suspected him at the time and have given it in charge to the officers in Skye, to apprehend him, plainly telling them, that if he was not taken, I should have reason to suspect them likewise.'[8] But Hugh had already taken to the hills and was never caught.

Captain John Hay of the Ayr Custom House yacht, who was helping with the search, said, 'General Campbell complained to me more than once that MacDonald of Armadale was the man that had misled him when searching for the Young Pretender.' Hay never failed to be surprised that Hugh was not taken into custody because 'he had done very much, and far more than ever it was in the power of Miss MacDonald to do'.[9]

Ronald MacLeod, the Bailie of Benbecula who gave evidence against Hugh, boatman Donald MacLeod of Galtergill and Malcolm MacLeod all claimed that Hugh was the grand contriver in laying and executing the scheme.

Neil MacEachain is quite specific about Armadale's involvment. He states that he broke the news to Flora about her stepfather's proposal. Clearly Neil, in his nightly wanderings around the island talking to friends, had learned of the plan from Armadale or perhaps from Young Milton and agreed to take the Prince to the shieling hut to explain it to Flora.

Every clue pointed to 'One-eyed' Hugh, but there was no proof when General Campbell needed it.

Hugh planned the escape with all the military precision one would expect of a trained army officer, and there can be no doubt that its whole success depended on expert organization. Every detail was worked out, and, subject only to occasional interference from the enemy, it was implemented in the same efficient way. E.M. Barron, the author of *Prince Charlie's Pilot*, said that Hugh told the Prince of the plan on the morning of 21 June and that Charles went to Flora at the hut on the summer pasture that night. He wrote, 'We hardly need Neil MacEachain's assurance that the scheme pleased the Prince mightily and he seemed very impatient to put it in execution.'[10]

Flora held the key to success, yet it appears that she was the last to have been made fully aware of the plan. From her talk with O'Neil, and all the comings and goings at the Clanranald house, she must have guessed sthe plan, but she was clearly taken aback when MacEachain turned up at the shieling in the middle of the night with O'Neil and the Prince, and told her about the scheme. She had to be persuaded to agree to become involved – blandishments and Felix's offer of marriage failed to move her, but a sense of duty finally won her over. We know nothing of what took place between Flora and her stepfather at the Benbecula crossing, but she was able to whisper confidently to Neil that she would be on her way to Nunton within half an hour, so perhaps Armadale had already explained to her that morning that he was involved. If not, then Lady Clan would do so shortly afterwards.

While Armadale was organizing the escape and ensuring that the militia were never in the right place at the right time to capture the Prince, Neil MacEachain had charge of the royal fugitive. His presence was providential, for his local knowledge of terrain, people and Gaelic language were vital to the plot's success. This was never better demonstrated than when Prince Charlie had to cross from South Uist to Benbecula by way of the heavily guarded sound. They met a party of fishermen whom Neil, being a local, knew and was able to persuade to ferry the Prince over in their boat.

Neil's task must have seemed depressingly difficult at times: soothing the Prince, who was sick and a nervous wreck much of the time, and coping with touchy, arrogant Felix O'Neil. He carried off his part in the exploit with courage and good humour. For example, when Neil's fishermen friends landed them, as they thought, on Benbecula, and the Prince lay down, exhausted, to sleep. Unfortunately, they were on a tidal island, so that by the time the Prince awoke the tide had come in and cut them off. Charles lost control, 'started up like a madman and walked to the island at such a rate as if he had a mind to fly over to the other side'. He raged, he stormed and he cursed the boatmen until Neil volunteered to swim over and bring a boat to rescue him. Neil began to strip off his clothes, but fortunately the tide receded and in less than three-quarters of an hour 'they passed over without wetting the soles of their shoes'.[11]

Poor Neil had much to contend with, as he often related in his story, telling how he 'was straggling every day about the neighbouring towns [farmsteads] for intelligence, and . . . never missed to come in seasonable time with what news he gathered among the people'.[12] He was known all over the island, was obviously trusted and well liked, yet he held back from trusting his fellow islanders fully. Money was a great persuader and the £30,000 reward offered for the Prince was a fortune beyond anyone's dreams.

Much has been made of the fact that no one betrayed Prince Charlie for that alluring sum, but there must have been some who were sorely tempted. How else could the Hanoverians have remained always so well informed, often only a few minutes or miles behind the fugitive? Someone somewhere in the Highlands that summer was talking, so it was fortunate for Charles Stuart that he had enough friends to enable him to keep ahead of his enemies. Neil MacEachain must have been well aware of the danger of betrayal, which is why he kept hurrying Charles on, 'fearing the fickleness and inconsistency of the common people, who might perhaps be perverted from their fidelity to discover him to his enemies, in hopes of a great reward'.[13]

Charles came within minutes of capture time and again, but he always managed to elude the militia. Great good fortune existed alongside all the misfortune that dogged the Prince's steps during that miserable summer of 1746, or was it simply that the militiamen were sometimes diverted by friends within the companies? These men and their officers certainly appear to have been free to come and go from their posts at will to carry messages, to act as lookouts, to warn the Prince of the searchers' next movements or even to row him to Skye.

One could never be absolutely sure, however, and great caution was essential at all times. Donald MacLeod of Galtergill gave it as his view that the militia were the worst enemy of all because they knew the country so well and could find anyone hiding in it. Donald was in a position to know, since he suffered the indignity of being taken by a militiaman and fellow islander, Allan MacDonald of Knock.

Hugh MacDonald of Baleshare and John MacDonald of Kirkibost, the Chief of Sleat's cousin, also played a part in setting up the escape and were an important link to those who were to take Charles into their care on Skye, where the Prince had a friend in the highest place – within the home of the Chief of Sleat. For all the chief's hunting with the Hanoverian hounds at Fort Augustus, his wife and his clansmen were willing to run with the Royal Stuart hare on the islands. Baleshare hints that the chief privately gave orders for Charles Edward to be protected because, 'as it did not lay his way to do him [the Prince] good, he had no inclination to do him hurt'.[14] Donald Roy underlined this view too, telling Charles 'Though Sir Alexander and his following did not join your royal highness, yet you see you have been very safe amongst them'.[15]

Certainly opinion was more favourably disposed towards the MacDonald chief than it was to the MacLeods. As another commentator put it, 'Though Sir Alexander MacDonald did not join his royal highness they were sure to meet with greater favour among the worst of his men than among the cold MacLeods.'[16]

Sleat's wife certainly was in a position to do Charles good, and she did so, using Baleshare as an intermediary. Lady Margaret had been sending gifts to Charles while he was in hiding at Corodale. Money, newspapers and her husband's best shirts were all delivered to him secretly. Baleshare's brother, Donald Roy, was also living near Monkstadt, having his Culloden wounds treated by the Chief's doctor, and he too was working on the abortive scheme to take the Prince to Fladda-Chuain, so Lady Margaret clearly was privy to what was being organized on the Long Island. The only thing she did not know was precisely when to expect her visitor – until Saturday 28 June, that is.

On that day the wife of John MacDonald of Kirkibost arrived at Monkstadt with an alarming tale, recounted by Neil, about being 'so strictly examined by a party [of militia] on the point of Waternish (taking her to be the Prince in disguise), that she was at all pains imaginable to keep off the soldiers' hands from examining her too closely'.[17] Mrs MacDonald knew that the Prince was on his way and had come to warn Lady Margaret – Flora admitted this only when it was safe enough to do so. 'Lady Margaret knew her [Flora's] errand well enough by one Mrs MacDonald, *who had gone a little before to apprize her of it'*, Flora said in a narrative which was passed on to Bishop Forbes.[18] If Mrs MacDonald knew of the Prince's journey, she also knew of his disguise, and all the play about the soldiers' strict examination to make sure she was not a man in disguise suggests that. The wife of a cousin of Sir Alexander, who was an officer in the militia, Mrs MacDonald, was the perfect emissary to carry advance warning of the Prince's arrival. Donald Roy MacDonald gave confirmation of Kirkibost's wife's part in the escape by telling Bishop Forbes that it was she who brought the message from Lady Margaret summoning him to Monkstadt after Charles's arrival.[19]

There can be little doubt that Charles Edward Stuart was expected in Skye: the only uncertainty was when. Why then did the escape, so carefully planned and executed in the Outer Isles, become frantic and disorganized the moment he reached Skye? Lady Margaret must carry much of the blame for, although she had sent presents to the Prince and assisted with the plot earlier, she went to pieces as soon as he arrived at her door. The reason was probably a sudden realization of the enormity of her crime when faced with its reality. The risk was even greater because a lieutenant of the militia was sitting in her dining room and his men were all around the area. Lady Margaret simply panicked and ran around like an ant whose nest has been disturbed, unable to decide what to do. Fortunately there were others to retrieve the situation: Kingsburgh, Donald Roy and Flora. It is hardly surprising that ever afterwards she was unable to face Flora, who remained so calm and efficient.

But what about the militia? Why should they have examined Mrs MacDonald 'so strictly' if they were unaware of the plot? Did they know of the Betty Burke disguise? And were they trying to ensure that they did not arrest the Prince while at the same time appearing to do their duty thoroughly? Why did Lieutenant MacLeod fail to carry out his duties the following day when Flora arrived? And was the whole drama at Monkstadt, with Flora talking small talk to MacLeod while Lady Margaret fluttered around Kingsburgh and Donald Roy, a great charade? These are all questions that need answers if one is to be sure of the militia's real allegiance, but there are no certain answers! Certainly Alexander MacLeod would have been hugely embarrassed to have been responsible for capturing Charles Stuart at the Sleat Chief's house, where he was a warmly welcomed guest. He was normally an extremely conscientious man, so it appears unthinkable that he would ever have failed to carry out his duties to the letter. By good fortune, or careful planning, the Prince arrived on a Sunday, about the middle of the day, when MacLeod could say with hand on heart that he had been to church and was dining with the chief's wife (and he was also able to assist Lady Margaret's alibi at the same time). His men had been lax at that exact moment and he could be reprimanded for that, but a rebuke was preferable to having the 'Young Chevalier' on his conscience. On the surface, however, it appeared that MacLeod of Balmeanach for once was simply negligent.

Who was behind the plot to rescue the heir to the 'King over the Water'? This role can be traced to Boisdale first, then to Armadale, helped by Clanranald, Baleshare, Kirkibost, their respective wives and a host of largely unnamed and unidentifiable militiamen who wore the uniform of the Hanoverians but served the Stuarts. Neil MacEachain was the link between these characters in the drama and he had Prince Charlie's day-to-day care in his hands during the period leading up to the escape. On Skye Donald Roy was probably the person who knew most. Lady Margaret may or may not have had the Prince wished upon her – the last thing she wanted was his actual presence in her house because she could never be completely sure that one of her clansmen might not give him away inadvertently. She managed to keep him out of Monkstadt house and let her factor commit the crime of harbouring the Prince under his roof. Kingsburgh and his family were innocent of being involved in the organization of the escape. Kingsburgh happened to be in the right place at the right time, and Highland honour compelled him to shelter the fugitive.

But what of Flora? Flora MacDonald had heroism thrust upon her. She was the least guilty of all, since she clearly did not know in advance what was afoot until all the arrangements had been made and the midnight callers arrived at the shieling on Sheaval. She was thunderstruck and reacted, as one might expect, by refusing flatly to become involved.

What changed her mind? She certainly did not agree willingly, as Neil MacEachain suggests, and Felix O'Neil's blustering flattery left her unmoved, although one suspects that she had a sneaking admiration for the swarthy Irish-Spanish officer, but never contemplated marriage to him. Felix's offer to take her as his wife could have been accepted there and then in the hut on Sheaval, because this form of irregular marriage by exchanged vows was recognized in Scottish Law until 1 July 1940.

The Prince's appeal to her honour won her over. As a Highland lady she could not refuse to assist a stranger in need. And when she learned that her stepfather was the mastermind behind the plot and wished her to take part, she could not turn back.

In one sense Flora was guilty. She could have made her exit from the plot as soon as she had delivered the Prince to Skye – that was all she had been asked to do – but she chose not to. She stayed on to accompany him to Kingsburgh and assist with the arrangements at Portree, which went well beyond the demands of Highland honour.

Flora MacDonald has always been assumed to have been a non-Jacobite, accidentally caught up in the Cause, but her position must be considered against the clan background. She never betrayed any affection for either side, Hanoverian or Jacobite, it is true, and throughout her life showed no interest in politics of any shade, but in the Hebrides she was surrounded by relatives and kinsmen who either supported the Stuarts openly, or at the very least had room in their hearts for them even if their heads held them back from rallying to the Prince's standard. We know nothing of her mother's views, but her brother and stepfather both gave covert support to the Prince and were privy to all that was going on. Thus Flora lived her early life against a pro-Stuart background, but a very prudent one, not given to showing feelings publicly, and cautious about making comments that might compromise them.

Her clan chief, Clanranald, and Lady Clan were Jacobite sympathizers, and, although the old Chief did not rise in 1745, his son did. Young Clanranald was wounded at Culloden and was in hiding, so there must have been much anxiety and speculation about him in Uist and Benbecula during the time that Prince Charlie was hiding there. As he was a near contemporary of Flora's, she must have known him well and been moved by his loyalty and bravery. Flora MacDonald may not have been an active Jacobite, but she was an involved one.

Flora's role in Prince Charlie's escape over the sea to Skye confirms her sympathy for Scotland's ancient royal house. Although she may not have volunteered to help Charles Edward, she willingly lent him all the aid she could when he needed it. All in all, however, Flora bore less guilt than the others who were party to the plot, as she lay in HMS *Furnace*, waiting to be questioned by that barbarous captain whose cruelty rang round the islands. She looked forward with fear.

CHAPTER FIVE

Confessions and Accusations

Yet, when the rage of battle ceased,
The victor's rage was not appeased;
The naked and forlorn must feel
Devouring flames and murd'ring steel.

Tobias Smollet's poem, 'The Tears of Scotland'

It was a bewildered and frightened Flora MacDonald who sailed along the east coast of Skye in HMS *Furnace*, surprised by the speed with which the searchers had caught up with her and terrified of what lay ahead. For weeks past the islands had abounded with reports of the brutality with which the captain of HMS *Furnace* and other members of King George's forces were treating every known Jacobite: pillaging and burning houses, killing cattle, and murdering men, women and children without mercy or even discrimination as to whether they had been supporters of the King over the Water or not. Although Flora had seen little actual devastation on the Long Island or in Skye, Donald Roy was in a position to tell her about their cruelty. She had heard about Boisdale's arrest and the ransacking of his house, and she knew that worse had taken place elsewhere. No one was safe, neither the culpable nor the innocent, and Flora was all too conscious at that moment of her own guilt.

Even before she was brought to face the terrible Ferguson, Flora was able to observe what was happening to others around her. To be a prisoner aboard HMS *Furnace* was not comfortable: the vessel was a single-decked sloop converted from a bomb-ketch, which had already seen service exploring the North West Passage before it was directed to the Scottish Highlands in August 1745 after Prince Charlie landed, and if HMS *Furnace* was damnably uncomfortable for her crew, it was hell for the prisoners. Captives were kept below deck in the hold, sleeping wherever they could on coils of rope, boards or the ship's ballast, without blankets. Each had only half a seaman's ration served in 'foul nasty buckets'.[1] Ferguson had stolen many articles from the houses he had raided, but the most useful item among these was an instrument of torture known as the Barisdale, after MacDonald of Barisdale who had invented it to extort confessions from cattle thieves. The Barisdale held the prisoner immobile while it slowly pressed him forward on to a great spike aimed at his throat. It was a vicious contrivance, but just what Ferguson needed to obtain confessions when his cat o' nine tails failed. Sometimes he subjected his prisoners to both.

Only a couple of days after Flora's capture, Ferguson picked up another dozen and a half men together with the most up-to-date information on the Prince's movements, because among these new prisoners were old John MacKinnon of MacKinnon, Captain John MacKinnon of Elgol, Captain Malcolm MacLeod of Brea, who had accompanied the Prince to Raasay and back, and boatmen who had taken Charles to the mainland from Skye just the week before. Donald Roy had been premature in rejoicing that nothing was known of the Prince's movements or who had helped him. He had not reckoned with the trail that led from the Long Island to Kingsburgh and the factor's confession. Nor did he know that Lieutenant MacLeod's superior officer, MacLeod of Talisker, furious at being so utterly outwitted, was now rounding these people up – even members of his own clan – with fiery zeal.

Ferguson was in his element: torture began even before the prisoners were taken on board HMS *Furnace*. He ordered John MacInnes, one of the Prince's boatmen, 'to be stripped naked, tied to a tree, and whipped with the cat and nine tails till the blood gushed out at both his sides'.[2] Writing nearly a century later, the minister of Strath recalled the death many years earlier of an old man called John MacInnes who had ferried the Prince to the mainland and who, to his dying day, carried the marks of Ferguson's cat o' nine tails.[3]

Ferguson at first threatened to put John MacKinnon in irons, and also to flog him if he did not reveal the Prince's whereabouts. The captain was 'swearing bloodily that when he got him on board, Barisdale and the cat and nine tails should make him squeak'.[4] Once on board HMS *Furnace*, however, MacKinnon was brought before General Campbell, who questioned him in a much more humane way.

Felix O'Neil had been threatened earlier with Ferguson's tortures to 'make him squeak' when he was first taken prisoner on the Long Island. O'Neil claimed prisoner of war status because he held a French army commission, but the captain of HMS *Furnace* refused to believe him. Felix wrote, 'I was . . . brought to Captain Ferguson, who used me with all the barbarity of a pirate, stripped me, and had ordered me to be put into a rack and whipped by his hangman, because I would not confess where I thought the Prince was.'[5]

As Felix was about to be flogged a Lieutenant MacCaghen of the Scots Fusiliers intervened and drew his sword. He 'threatened Captain Ferguson that he'd sacrifice himself and his detachment rather than to see an officer used after such an infamous manner'.[6] O'Neil was not flogged, but was relieved of his money, watch and valuables, and questioned by General Campbell, who remained suspicious of his claim to be a French officer. The general was uncharacteristically reluctant to show the foreigner with the Irish name the leniency he displayed so readily towards others. It was said he would gladly have seen O'Neil hanged.

On 21 July after a brief foray northwards to Gairloch in search of more prisoners, HMS *Furnace* anchored in Applecross, a bay surrounded by the high peaks of Wester Ross which provided a sheltered anchorage. The bay looked across to the island of Raasay, which Ferguson had devastated only weeks before, destroying every house and killing all the livestock on the island. It was a convenient point for warships to gather and from which to transfer important prisoners to Fort Augustus for questioning, while others were trans-shipped for transportation to gaols in the South. By now Flora had a number of friends and acquaintances on board the sloop, but there was little opportunity for her to discover exactly who lay in that ghastly hold. As a woman and a key figure in the escape, she was kept apart, not out of kindness on Ferguson's part, but because General Campbell did not want to give his prisoners the opportunity to agree their stories before they came before him to be interrogated.

She and Kingsburgh, who had already been questioned at Monkstadt, were now brought before Campbell of Mamore for further questioning on board HMS *Furnace* at Applecross.[7] Both revealed considerable detail of the escape, naming some names but withholding others. Unfortunately they had not had any opportunity to agree their stories, so Kingsburgh included the names of Flora, MacLeod of Raasay and Neil MacEachain in his, but withheld Donald Roy's, while Flora incriminated Neil and Donald Roy, but was very careful to make Kingsburgh appear as innocent as possible. It is likely that both felt that the authorities already knew the identity of most of the culprits anyway, so they believed there was little point in concealing names now.

When he began his inquisition of Kingsburgh, General Campbell already knew much about the voyage over the sea to Skye since one of the boatmen had been captured and had confessed, just as Mrs MacDonald of Kingsburgh had feared.[8] At Applecross Kingsburgh amplified his earlier statement, saying that MacEachain had accompanied the Prince from Kingsburgh House to Portree and Flora had left him there when he sailed to Raasay. He made no mention of Donald Roy in the hope of saving his MacDonald clansman. Kingsburgh had fewer scruples about members of other clans: it was then that he told of the Prince's return to Skye, accompanied by Malcolm MacLeod, and how John MacKinnon had sheltered him.[9]

In his cups Kingsburgh was known to be fond of singing a song which began:

> Green sleeves and pudding pies,
> Tell me where my mistress lies.

Talisker, who was present at the Monkstadt interrogation, knew this and remarked slyly to the old man, 'Had she green sleeves?'[10] Kingsburgh ignored the jibe, but Lady Margaret was furious with Talisker for his impertinence and arrogance towards her factor when he was in such danger. This and other actions of Talisker, including alleged cruelties and the arrest of Captain Malcolm MacLeod on Raasay by a party which included some of the captain's blood relations, accounted for the fact that, after the turmoil died down, Talisker left Skye to serve in the Dutch army for several years. He eventually returned to the island where he was accepted as a very respectable man.

Kingsburgh's honesty did much to save him. He was given the choice of staying with Campbell, or of accompanying Sleat to Fort Augustus where the chief could plead his cause with the Duke of Cumberland. He chose the latter course, but even though the chief, General Campbell and Lord President Forbes were all anxious to help, it did Kingsburgh no good. The Duke of Cumberland, in a rage about how foolish the escape had made him look, was not one bit pleased to learn that Kingsburgh had not arrived at Fort Augustus in manacles. He wrote tartly to reprimand General Campbell, and had the factor put in irons immediately.[11]

Although Campbell questioned Flora in minute detail aboard HMS *Furnace*, she kept her composure and faced up to him with great courage, giving the impression of being open and utterly honest. She was not overawed by the general's rank, and certainly was not browbeaten by him. As a fellow Highlander he admired and respected Flora. How was he to know that behind the frank face of the Highland girl lay a clever brain, which was able to beguile him into believing what she wanted him to believe?

The general did not realize that Flora's deposition at Applecross, like the versions of her story as she recounted them later, appeared full and honest on the surface, yet were as interesting for what they concealed as for what they revealed.[12] The statement was taken down by someone who knew neither Flora nor the islands, for it describes her as 'Miss MacDonald, daughter-in-law of McDonald of Milton in Sky', whereas she was the daughter of MacDonald of Milton which is in South Uist. It also states that she left her father-in-law's house at Armadale six weeks prior to the Prince's escape to go to Uist, a mistake for her stepfather's house.

These opening inaccuracies apart, the statement gives a plausible enough account of what actually happened, carefully avoiding mention of Neil MacEachain in its first part and lifting a little of the guilt from Lady Clan. 'Miss MacDonald says that after this she went and stayed with Lady Clanranald at her House, communicated the scheme to her, and desired that she would furnish cloaths for the Young Pretender as hers would be too little', it states.

O'Neil, she claimed, came frequently to Clanranald's house to keep her informed of the arrangements for the voyage, and at the same time to 'hasten her to get her affairs in Readiness for going off'. She gave details of these arrangements, the voyage to Skye and their arrival at Monkstadt, carefully avoiding incriminating Lady Margaret and making no mention of Kingsburgh. To ensure this she took upon herself responsibility for sending for Donald Roy, but now brought Neil into the plot. Clearly someone had to be sacrificed and, so far as she knew, Neil and Donald were both in hiding so could safely be named. Her statement continued:

Miss MacDonald and Mr MacAchran landed, leaving the Young Pretender in the boat. They went to Sir Alexander MacDonald's house and from thence Miss MacDonald sent for one Donald MacDonald, who had been in the Rebellion but had delivered up his arms some time ago. She employed this Person to procure a boat to carry the Young Pretender to Raasay, after acquainting him with their late voyage and where she had left the Young Pretender. Miss MacDonald stayed and dined with Lady Margaret MacDonald, but MacDonald and MacAchran returned to the Boat to inform what was done.'

Her effort to save Kingsburgh was valiant, but not likely to be believed by the general who already knew many of the details of the stay at Kingsburgh House:

After dinner Miss MacDonald set out for Portree, it being resolved that they should lodge there that night; but on the Road overtook the Young Pretender and MacAchran. They had been joined by MacDonald of Kingsbury. She told them she must call at Kingsbury's House and desired they would go there also. Here Miss MacDonald was taken sick, and therefore with the other two was desired to stay all night, which they agreed to. She had a room to herself, but the Young Pretender and MacAchran lay in the same room. At this time he appeared in Woman's cloaths, his face being partly concealed by a Hood or Cloak.'

Flora tried to make General Campbell believe that no one at Kingsburgh questioned the identity of the strange woman. She told him the servants thought he was another Jacobite fugitive, MacLeod of Bernera, in disguise. That was too much for the general to swallow: 'Being pressed to declare what she knew and believed of Kingsbury's Knowledge of his Guest, owns that she believes he must suspect it was the Young Pretender.' Her deposition went on to say that they set out for Portree next day and she requested the Prince to change his clothes on the way because the clumsy manner in which he wore his maid's outfit simply made him more conspicuous:

> Miss got to Portree about 12 at night, where she found Donald MacDonald, who had been sent before to procure a Boat. The Young Pretender and MacAchran arrived about an hour after. Here he took some Refreshement, changed a Guinea, paid the reckoning, took his leave of Miss MacDonald, and went out with Donald MacDonald, but who, after seeing him to the Boat, returned. She believes he went to Raasay, but cannot tell what became of him since.

This last part, at least, was true and enabled Flora to end on a genuinely honest note, which impressed Campbell. He was greatly taken with her apparent straightforwardness and, although she still had to be held prisoner, he ordered that she should be treated with respect.

John MacKinnon of Elgol was lucky to be brought before General Campbell in HMS *Furnace*, because Mamore did not press the question of disloyalty to the Government as Ferguson would have done. When asked why he had not handed Charles over, Elgol said he could not have betrayed the man whom he had served, whose food he had shared and whose pay he had received, when that man was in the greatest difficulty. 'Had I done it', he finished, 'I dare say your excellency would have looked upon me as a monster of a wretch.'

Turning to Campbell of Skipness and MacLeod of Talisker, who were also present, the general said, 'Gentlemen, let us lay to heart what Captain MacKinnon has just now said, and let us determine from honour and conscience, and then surely we must applaud his conduct.' He ordered Ferguson, who had listened to all of this with unconcealed disapproval, to pour him a drink and one for MacKinnon, and watched while the 'Black Captain' sourly handed the glass to MacKinnon, whom Campbell ordered to remain seated while Ferguson stood – an insulting rebuff to Ferguson.[13]

Among those who were on board HMS *Furnace*, at one time or another while Flora was on the ship, were Kingsburgh, Felix O'Neil, Father Allan MacDonald, Donald MacLeod of Galtergill and Malcolm MacLeod. Flora said little about meeting any of them, but Felix told later of seeing Flora and giving her advice. A few of those who spoke to Bishop Forbes about their discussions with Flora also made reference to a meeting between the two. Felix and Flora very likely did meet, but that would have been after the arrival of HMS *Furnace* at Applecross.

Flora told some of those who came to see her later that she had had the good fortune to encounter the dashing Spanish-Irish captain, and said she had slapped his cheek playfully and told him, 'To that black face do I owe all my misfortune.' The Captain smiled and replied, 'Why, Madam, what you call your misfortune is truly your greatest honour. And if you be careful to demean yourself agreeably to the character you have already acquired, you will in the event find it to be your happiness.'[14] This suggests that Flora had already been questioned by General Campbell when she met O'Neil, and that he was warning her to stick by the story she had already given and which had been accepted by Campbell.

Flora was still afraid, though, and believed that her captors planned to take her to London, which she dreaded because, by this time, word was trickling through of the trials, executions and cruelties being perpetrated there and elsewhere in the South. Felix talked lightly and reassuringly. He told her he could foretell what lay ahead for her:

If you are carried to London I can venture to assure you it will be for your interest and happiness; and instead of being afraid of this you ought to wish for it. There you will meet with much respect and very good and great friends for what you have done.

But he warned again that she must not be frightened into saying anything that might change her captors' opinion of her. 'Never once pretend', he told her, '. . . to repent or be ashamed of what you have done . . . I do not think that the Government can be so very barbarous and cruel as to bring you to trial for your life.'[15]

Of course the stories of what Flora said Felix had told her lost nothing in the retelling. They were relayed by ardent Jacobite women to Bishop Forbes, who was collecting every scrap of information about the Cause and using it to show the Jacobites in the best possible light. Nevertheless a certain warmth does shine through all the exaggeration and embellishment, so that one is aware at least of admiration and possibly affection between Flora and Felix. She was never in love with the captain and did not hesitate to reject the one offer of marriage that he made, but she obviously liked and admired him. After all, he was a dashing officer who had led a similar life to her stepfather with whom she had grown up, so she could see much to admire in Felix. Those very qualities that led the solid islanders to criticize O'Neil and call him a braggart and a liar may well have made Flora's heart beat just a fraction faster.

It is often said that, without Neil MacEachain as a guide and interpreter, Felix could not have managed to move about the islands without being captured. Yet, after the Prince sailed to Skye and *Le Hardi Mendiant* arrived, the Spanish-Irish officer, who had only been in the country a few months and spoke no Gaelic, managed to get himself from the Long Island to Skye and Raasay, and back again, and was only caught because the French ship let him down by not waiting for the promised rendezvous. Perhaps 'One-eyed' Hugh was behind Felix's voyage from the Long Island too.

Today many Hebridean islanders tend to dismiss O'Neil as an arrogant man, much inferior to Neil MacEachain, but the facts suggest an efficient, resourceful officer, well able to fend for himself in hostile territory, and with a carefree, pleasant nature that certainly impressed Flora MacDonald.

O'Neil told people who came to see him in Edinburgh Castle that he went to the greatest lengths, 'the same pains as a parent would be with a child to lay down rules to Miss MacDonald for her future behaviour under the misfortune of being a prisoner'.[16] As a soldier, aware of the risks, it may well be that he discussed these with Flora, even before she set out on the voyage to Skye and advised her on how she should respond to questions. He said that it gave him infinite pleasure to hear 'that she had sacredly observed the advices he had given her'.[17]

Much was happening elsewhere while Flora lay miserably in HMS *Furnace*. The search for the Prince continued unabated, but still without success. More prisoners were being brought in and more information was being wrung from them by torture and threat. Again the net was tightening as the Royal Navy cut off sea escape routes and the Army formed a single cordon on the mainland all the way from Loch Hourn to the head of Loch Eil in Invernessshire, cutting off Knoydart and Morar where the Prince was believed to be. From hill to hill the Prince moved cannily, not daring even to light a fire to cook food. The fugitives pushed on northwards until, on the night of 20 July, they lay on a hill from which they could see a chain of lights from campfires which pinpointed the line of enemy positions. In the early hours of the following morning they passed between two of these fires and Charles Stuart was again out of the net.

It was all extremely frustrating for the Duke of Cumberland, who was anxious to leave this cold, God-forsaken country which he hated and where he did not trust even avowedly loyal Scotsmen. How could he tell who was loyal anyway? There was little intelligence to be had anywhere, he complained, and he felt himself more in enemy territory here than when he had been warring against the French in Flanders.

Even the Scottish leaders were not to be trusted. Only weeks after Culloden, the Duke of Cumberland, who hated all Scots (even Lord President Forbes, who did so much to save King George's throne) said he thought the Lord President was far too lenient and referred to him thereafter as 'that old woman who talked to me about humanity'.[18]

Cumberland's soldiers loved him dearly, and built him the nearest house to a palace that they could at Fort Augustus to replace the barracks that had been burned down by the rebels. From there the 'Butcher' organized the devastation of the Highlands and whiled away the long days by offering his officers prizes for running races on small Galloway ponies. Women joined in these 'sports', often wearing 'no cloaths but their shirts' as they raced on foot, or on horseback dressed in soldiers' coats and falling off as their horses turned, to create a splendid diversion for the Duke and his men.

General 'Hangman' Hawley wagered twenty guineas in a race against Colonel Howard, and the 'Hangman' won by about four inches. It made life bearable for the army, but in between they enjoyed other entertainments, which included the destruction of the fabric of life in the Highlands and Islands.[19]

In the hope of capturing the Prince, Cumberland stayed on at Fort Augustus for a fortnight longer than he had intended and left for the South only on 18 July. Although he did not take news of the Prince's capture with him, London gave him a rapturous welcome when he arrived there on the afternoon of the 25th. It was the Culloden victory celebration all over again. All the bells of the City rang, gun salutes boomed for hours, and at night there were bonfires and illuminations everywhere. A thanksgiving service was held in St Paul's and 'Hail the Conquering Hero' was sung for the first time. For weeks the celebrations continued – ballets, patriotic plays preceded by dashing loyal prologues and dances – and every shop displayed his portrait with the legend *Ecce Homo* beneath it. An inoffensive little flower was dedicated to him and named Sweet William. Indeed, the only sour notes were struck by his elder brother, Frederick, Prince of Wales, who could not stand him, and a City of London Alderman, who on hearing that Cumberland was to be appointed liveryman of one of the City companies, said 'Then let it be of the Butchers.'[20]

Tyburn Gate, London's traditional place of execution, was renamed Cumberland Gate, an appropriate tribute to the man who turned his Culloden victory into a Highland massacre. The first of the prisoners who had been taken to London for trial suffered the gruesome ritual death of being hanged, drawn and quartered at the very time when Cumberland arrived.

At Fort Augustus Cumberland was succeeded by the Earl of Albemarle, who disliked Scotland and the people who were supposed to be helping him to subdue the rebels every bit as heartily as his predecessor had. He never trusted Sleat either, so the chief was unable to achieve any leniency for his factor. Kingsburgh had been brought to Fort Augustus, where his money and belongings were taken away and he was held in irons, in spite of all the efforts of Sir Alexander to help him – which was more than either Sleat or Lady Margaret did for Flora. In all the time she was held in prison, neither Sir Alexander nor his wife put pen to paper to ask anyone to help her.

While Kingsburgh lay in prison at Fort Augustus during that July, an officer came to him one evening to ask if he would recognize the head of the Young Pretender if he saw it. MacDonald answered that he would, but only if it were attached to the body.

'What if the head be not upon the body?', the officer asked.

'In that case, Sir, I will not pretend to know anything about it.'[21]

There was a head to be identified at Fort Augustus and it proves beyond any doubt that Charles Stuart would never have been taken alive, for the last thing the London Government wanted was for another Stuart to die a martyr on the scaffold. The ghost of Mary Stuart haunted – and still haunts – relations between Scotland and England, and the executioners of Charles I have never been forgiven. Execution of a third Stuart could even have spelt disaster for the union between Scotland and England.

The head, which was never brought to Kingsburgh for identification, belonged to a young Jacobite called Roderick MacKenzie who was similar in age and looks to Charles. He had been cornered near Fort Augustus, and on being asked if he was the Prince, replied – in the hope of misleading the searchers – that he was. He was immediately murdered as Charles himself would have been had he been captured by anyone other than Ferguson of HMS *Furnace*. Ferguson was once asked whether he would have killed the Prince if he had caught him. He replied, 'No, (by God) . . . I would have preserved him as the apple of mine eye, for I would not take any man's word, no not the Duke of Cumberland's for £30,000 sterling.'[22]

A little later Kingsburgh was released by mistake for another prisoner of the same name – one of the advantages of there being so many Alexander MacDonalds in the Highlands – but instead of heading straight for Skye, the factor loyally called on his chief to ask what orders he wished him to take back to the island. The chief was astounded to see the factor, but ordered a bed to be made up for him in his own room. At about eleven o'clock, just as Kingsburgh was about to undress, an officer knocked at the door and ordered him to come to see Lord Albemarle at once. A dozen soldiers with fixed bayonets waited outside to escort him, but they had gone only a few steps when Albemarle himself appeared, bellowing excitedly, 'Have you got the villain? Have you got the villain?'

Kingsburgh assured the earl that he was not rushing to leave, but Albemarle, still in a towering rage, shouted, 'It is well, Sir, you are not gone; I had rather by God have given anything before this mistake had happened. Go, throw the dog into irons.'[23] Kingsburgh was thus manacled again. Albemarle's rage cooled, and a few days later Kingsburgh found himself in better quarters, and even enjoying food and wine from his lordship's table. But he was not released.

Sir Alexander and Lady Margaret showed great personal concern for Kingsburgh and worked hard to obtain the factor's freedom. On 24 July the Chief's wife wrote to Lord President Forbes on Kingsburgh's behalf.[24] It was a carefully written letter, but her ladyship's memory was highly selective in recollecting the details of Prince Charlie's visit to her factor's house. It did nothing to help Flora other than describe her as 'a foolish girl, with whom the disturber of this Kingdom landed at this place'. Lady Margaret wrote:

I can not but look upon myself and family as peculiarly favoured by Heaven, in drawing that unlucky visitant quickly away from the place of his landing that there was no room for considering Him as a Person in Disguise; far less knowing anything of it.

She pleaded eloquently for Kingsburgh, as well she might since it was she who had landed him in his plight:

I must at the same time, not only look upon myself but the whole Country as greatly suffering from the hurt it is likely he has done to the Man into whose House he intruded himself that night; I mean Kingsborrow; a Man well known for his singular honesty, integrity and prudence, in all occurrences of Life, before that unhappy night, a Man of such consequence and so well liked in his country that if the Pretender's Son had done no other hurt to it but the ruining of this single Man, it could not but render him odious to their Posterity.

Unfortunately Sir Alexander was away at Fort Augustus and could not consult his wife before he put pen to paper on the factor's behalf five days after his wife wrote to the Lord President. As a result his letter to Forbes contained more detail of the Prince's visit and actually incriminated his wife:[25]

When the Young Pretender made his unhappy visit to Skye, from South Uist, in a small boat, he landed near my house, in woman's clothes, by way of being maid-servant to one Florence MacDonald, a Girl of Clanranald's family, now a prisoner with General Campbell. Miss MacDonald went and made a visit to Lady Margaret, dined with her, and put her into the utmost distress by telling her of the Cargo that she had brought from Uist. She called on Kinsborrow who was at Mugstot [Monkstadt] accidentally and they had a very confused consultation together; and it was agreed to hurry him off the Country as far as possible.

Although Sleat made much of the fact that Charles was 'eat up by scab', miserably wet and played on Kingsburgh's feelings, Lord President Forbes must have realized when he received these two letters together that the Chief's wife and Kingsburgh were both involved, and doubtless he agreed with the Duke of Cumberland's response to Sleat's pleas. For as long as he remained at Fort Augustus the royal duke had no time for 'the great rebel' or his whinging pleas for his clansman. Sir Alexander wrote miserably:

> He stopped my mouth by saying that this man had neglected the greatest piece of service that he could have done, and if he was to be pardoned, you have too much good sense to think this the proper time as it would encourage others to follow his example.

The letters of the chief and Lady Margaret did Kingsburgh no good. On 28 July he was sent from Fort Augustus to Edinburgh, guarded by a party of Kingston's Horse, and arrived in the city on 2 August to the sound of trumpets and kettledrums, so that everyone would be made aware that an important rebel was passing through the streets of the capital on his way to Edinburgh Castle.

The Chief continued to do what he could for his factor, pleading with MacKenzie of Delvine to do all in his power for 'Sandy', as he called Kingsburgh. The day after Kingsburgh left Fort Augustus, Sir Alexander sent another letter to MacKenzie in Edinburgh to give him the news and asking the lawyer 'to be as useful to Sandy as possible'.[26] In the same letter he said, 'You see it is possible this will cost me a London jaunt.' Lady Margaret had also sent the lawyer a letter on 24 July giving her own carefully slanted version of the Prince's visit and laying the blame squarely on poor Flora:

> Milton's sister from South Uist, who I never saw, but once, thought fit to bring the Young Pretender from that country in disguise. She had not just assurance enough to bring him to this house but came herself and dined here among a crowd which lukyly for me was here that day.[27]

In Lady Margaret's vivid imagination, Lieutenant MacLeod, Mrs MacDonald of Kirkibost and Kingsburgh constituted a crowd! Lady Margaret emphasized her own innocence by repeating that the Prince had not entered her house. 'Flora', she added, 'sent her servant Betty immediately upon her landing along with a fellow she had with her to Kingsborough where they intruded themselves that night.'

The chief's lady had not finished with Flora yet. She told Delvine, with what sounds like bitter dislike, 'The gipsy that brought that unwelcome guest to this country is taken up and on board the Furnace.'

The 'gipsy' lying fearfully in HMS *Furnace* was given favours, too, but no thanks to the Chief of Sleat or Lady Margaret; she had to earn these for herself. At Applecross she had won over General Campbell with her calm and straightforward answers to his questions, and with her quiet composure as a prisoner under threat of trial for treason, so that Campbell instructed Commodore Thomas Smith, the officer in charge of the Navy ships, that she was to be treated with respect. From then on Flora's situation improved. As HMS *Furnace* cruised close to Armadale, Smith, who could be harsh enough with his captives, allowed her to go ashore and say farewell to her mother. She was taken to Armadale under escort but was forbidden to speak Gaelic while she was in her mother's house. When she returned to the ship she brought with her, probably at her mother's insistence, a girl called Kate MacDonald, who had 'generously offered to run all risques with the captive lady'.[28] Kate accompanied Flora to Edinburgh and helped her in her prison ship. After that she vanished from Flora's story and nothing more was heard of her.

There is a tradition in the Scottish Highlands that Flora was held in Dunstaffnage Castle just north of Oban, where the governor, Neil Campbell, one of her own kinsmen, and his wife, treated her as a special prisoner. Alexander MacGregor, in his *The Life of Flora MacDonald*, quotes a letter from General Campbell to the Governor of Dunstaffnage, dated 1 August, asking him to 'receive a very pretty young rebel' within a few days. The general had been convinced of Flora's innocence since he added: 'Her zeal, and the persuasion of those who ought to have given her better advice, have drawn her into a most unhappy scrape, by assisting the Young Pretender to make his escape.' He added a postscript: 'I suppose you have heard of Miss Flora MacDonald?' Of course he had: Flora's fame had already spread through the Highlands.[29]

After a few days' stay at the castle, during which 'her society was courted by all the respectable families in the neighbourhood', another letter arrived from the general ordering Flora to be handed over to the bearer, John MacLeod, and for an officer of the garrison to accompany her. MacGregor, in his customary fanciful manner, relates that the governor's lady had tears in her eyes as she handed Flora into the boat. The sails, he said, were immediately set, and before a stiff breeze the frail craft glided swiftly down Loch Etive, towards the Sound of Mull and soon disappeared.

Fantastic as all that may sound, it would make sense for Flora to have been put ashore while the general awaited instructions from the south as to what was to be done with her. The hunt for the Prince in the west was beginning to be scaled down now that rumours were circulating that he had escaped the Hanoverian net on the mainland – as indeed he had on the night of 20 July. On the 28th and 29th, Lord Albemarle wrote to tell Commodore Smith that the Prince was at Loch Broom, so the ships *Serpent*, *Tryton* and *Greyhound* were sent there to cut off his escape. Believing that Charles might make for Caithness or even Orkney, the commodore also ordered ships to look out for him there.

With the certainty that Charles was no longer in the Hebrides, it was decided to send most of the fleet back to Leith with the prisoners, but to make careful enquiries during the journey in case Charles Edward had fled to the East Coast in an attempt to pick up a ship for France. While the Royal Navy vessels prepared to sail round the northernmost point of the Scottish mainland between John o' Groats and the Orkney Islands, Charles lay safely hidden in the Inverness-shire hills waiting for word of a French ship that would take him back to France.

The main body of prisoners was to remain in ships such as HMS *Furnace* and the *Happy Janet*, but Flora and those being taken south as witnesses were to be given special treatment and put aboard Commodore Smith's own ship, HMS *Eltham*, for the long journey. On 15 August General Campbell left HMS *Eltham* and two days later the warship exchanged messages with the sloop *Two Sisters* bound 'from Dunstaffnage Sound to Inveraray with General Campbell's baggage on board'. This is likely to have been the moment when Flora was brought from Dunstaffnage and put aboard HMS *Eltham*, since the convoy of naval ships headed northwards shortly afterwards, round Cape Wrath, through the Pentland Firth, then on to Kinnaird Head on the north-east corner of Aberdeenshire and down the east coast towards Edinburgh's seaport, Leith. While HMS *Eltham* dawdled, perhaps trying to pick up information about the Prince's movements, HMS *Furnace* raced ahead and was lying off Leith by Thursday 4 September.

HMS *Bridgewater* and HMS *Scarborough* arrived about the same time, and the *Happy Janet* brought more prisoners who were transferred to HMS *Furnace* on the 10th. Two days later, on the 13th, HMS *Furnace* left for London with her complement of captives. It had a lively turn of speed: on 13 September it was close to Inchkeith Island in the River Forth; by the 16th, when HMS *Eltham* moored in Leith Roads, it was off Great Yarmouth, and two days later reached Gravesend. On 3 October it discharged its prisoners to Tilbury Fort.

HMS *Eltham* did not linger at Leith either: on 19 September, only three days after the arrival of HMS *Furnace*, Commodore Smith transferred to HMS *Bridgewater*. Two days later she took on board a new tiller rope, six hogsheads of brandy and fifteen tons of coal, then twenty soldiers fired a salute and she was ready to weigh anchor. The last duty was to send to HMS *Bridgewater* twenty-three crown witnesses and Flora MacDonald. The following day HMS *Eltham* sailed.

The weather in the Firth of Forth was miserably wet throughout September, with gales lashing HMS *Bridgewater* as it lay there. For Flora, who had no reason to like boats, it was extremely disagreeable. In her misery she could not have conceived that this was to be her prison for two long months.

The only consolation she had was that the brutal Ferguson had sailed out of her life. The captain was soon promoted for his barbarous efficiency to be captain of HMS *Nightingale*, a new Royal Navy frigate. He went to India and, while returning as a passenger from there in 1773, became involved in a quarrel with a Captain Roache, as a result of which he was stabbed to death. The event, duly recorded in the *Scots Magazine*, caused little sorrow among any of his victims who were still around to read it.[30]

CHAPTER SIX

The Envied Prisoner

I could wipe your shoes with pleasure, and think it my honour so to do, when I reflect that you had the honour to have the Prince for your handmaid. We all envy you greatly.

Jacobite admirer of Flora[1]

Flora was well treated in both of her floating prisons, HMS *Eltham* and HMS *Bridgewater*. Commodore Smith went far beyond the orders he had been given by General Campbell: in the words of Bishop Forbes he 'behaved like a father to her',[2] and gave her excellent advice on how to cope with her dangerous situation, while Captain Knowler of HMS *Bridgewater* 'used her with the utmost decency and politeness.'[3] She was accorded many privileges, but these stopped short of being allowed ashore, so she was never able to visit any friends or to see Kingsburgh and O'Neil in their prison cells in Edinburgh Castle.

Kingsburgh had already been in the castle for a month by the time Flora reached Leith, and found it a huge improvement on Fort Augustus, which had been primitive in the extreme. At first he had very congenial company, but soon he was placed in solitary confinement, which the ageing Sleat factor found most disagreeable.[4] He was not even allowed visits from his wife, until he fell ill and Mrs MacDonald was allowed to sit with him during the day. Felix O'Neil's status as a foreign officer was accepted and, by comparison with Kingsburgh, life for him as a prisoner of war was easier. He was allowed plenty of visitors to whom he told his story and boasted of the help he had given Flora.

Flora's life, too, was easy, with as many visitors allowed aboard HMS *Bridgewater* as wished to see her. The officers were generous and were even known to go ashore sometimes to bring friends to her, yet they tried always to shield her from the merely curious. Commodore Smith even bought her 'a handsome sute of riding cloaths, with plain mounting, and some fine linen riding shirts'. This was hardly the most appropriate present for someone who was unlikely to be riding anywhere in the foreseeable future, but perhaps the kind naval commander intended by his gift to give her the best present he could – hope. Her servant, Kate, a bewildered and confused Highland girl in this strange place where she did not even understand the language, was given a gown and linen with which to make herself some shirts.[5]

Leith, like Edinburgh, was filled with Jacobite ladies who came aboard HMS *Bridgewater* to bask in the Jacobite sunshine of the young woman who had saved the Prince, then went ashore and reported every word to the Episcopalian clergyman, Robert Forbes, who was still deeply immersed in his task of collecting Jacobite stories. That autumn Flora formed the focus of much adulation, and her lack of comment on her visitors gives us the clearest indication of how she felt in her heart about them. They simpered sickeningly around her, then returned to the security of their drawing rooms leaving her with only Kate for company, to reflect on her future, which might well mean removal to London, trial and death.

It was not easy to be a heroine, but Flora carried off the part with dignity. Forbes unwittingly summed up the patronizing tortures the poor woman suffered from these tea-table Jacobites when he wrote: 'Her behaviour in company was so easy, modest and well-adjusted that every visitant was much surprized'. All the more unexpected, Forbes opined, since she had never been out of the islands until about a year before the Prince arrived in 1745:

> One could not discern by her conversation that she had spent all her former days in the Highlands; for she talks English (or rather Scots) easily, and not at all through the Earse tone. She has a sweet voice and sings well; and no lady, Edinburgh bred, can acquit herself better at the tea table.[6]

In looks Flora was described at this time as 'of a low stature, of a fair complexion and well enough shap'd'.[7] Her cheerfulness was mixed with gravity, as well it might have been in the face of the seriousness of her position and all the unwanted hero-worship around her.

The focus of Flora's Jacobite admirers was Lady Bruce, widow of Sir William Bruce of Kinross, whose home at the Citadel of Leith was a great centre for supporters of the Cause.[8] The Reverend Robert Forbes lived there until his marriage and it was at the citadel that he interviewed many of the veterans and victims of the Rising. Lady Bruce was seventy-six years of age at this time, but as vigorous as ever in her enthusiasm for the Stuarts, welcoming every supporter of the Cause and giving generous financial assistance to any who needed it.

This old woman, ever practical in her help, brought some linen and cambric, needles, a thimble and thread, so that Flora and Kate could sew clothes for themselves to while the time away usefully.

Others brought Flora gifts of clothes, and Rachel Houston, who was later to marry Robert Forbes, gave her a two-volume Bible because the only piece of reading matter Flora had in her cabin was a prayer book.

These Jacobite women sometimes danced in the cabin, but Flora refused to join in, giving them what sounds like a very specious excuse:

> that at present her dancing days were done, and she would not readily entertain a thought of that diversion till she should be assured of her Prince's safety, and perhaps not till she should be bless'd with the happiness of seeing him again.'[9]

Flora could not have thought at that time that there was any chance of her ever seeing Charles Edward Stuart again. It was more likely that an astute Flora was giving the good Jacobites of the Leith Citadel circle the answers she knew they wanted to hear. They could not listen to Flora's story often enough, hanging on every word: when Flora told, or retold, how the Prince protected her from being trampled on by the sailors during the voyage to Skye, one of them simpered:

> O Miss, what a happy creature are you who had that dear Prince to lull you asleep, and to take such care of you with his hands spread about your head, when you was sleeping! You are surely the happiest woman in the world![10]

Lady Mary Cochrane, the Countess of Dundonald's daughter, must have taken Flora aback when, stranded on board HMS *Bridgewater* by a sudden storm, she whispered that she would stay on the ship all night with pleasure if she might have the honour of sharing a bed with 'that person who had been so happy as to be guardian to her Prince'.[11] She was allowed to sleep in Flora's cabin, and to share the heroine's bed.

Flora's visitors chattered incessantly about the Prince, and rumours circled the Citadel, thick as Leith seagulls, speculating on Charles's whereabouts. Suddenly, towards the end of September, the trail went cold in the Highlands. No one there knew yet, but two French ships, *L'Heureux* and *Le Prince de Conti*, had managed to sail into the unguarded Loch nan Uamh. Charles went aboard *L'Heureux* on the evening of 19 September and, by another of those ironic twists that fill Jacobite history, at that same loch where he had landed on the mainland fourteen months before. In the small hours the two ships slipped out of the loch, the islands of Eigg and Muck on the starboard bow and Coll to port as dawn rose. Past Barra Head they sailed, then set course into the safety of the Atlantic, away from British warships, before turning south for the long voyage round Ireland to France. As Prince Charlie was taking his last look at the Hebrides, Flora, who had saved him, was being moved from *HMS Eltham* to *HMS Bridgewater*, a prisoner with little hope.

Searchers and supporters alike were puzzled by the disappearance of the Prince and put their own interpretations on what had happened. The Jacobite ladies of Leith were full of woe because they believed he had been captured, and they transmitted their despair to Flora.

Again Forbes reported the heroine's reaction as his informants wanted to hear it. She would not be cheered up by her visitors and spoke with tears in her eyes: 'Alas, I am afraid that now all is in vain that I have done.'[12]

The Prince's supporters were greatly relieved when Hanoverian searchers arrived without warning at Lady Bruce's home on the morning of Sunday 28 September to comb the house and search every paper in it. News of the Prince's sailing from Loch nan Uamh had reached the authorities in the capital several days before, so they were trying to find evidence to link the Edinburgh Jacobites to the escape, rather than information about the actual departure. However, Lady Bruce and her circle were oblivious of this, and they were overjoyed to think that their hero was still free.[13]

After the Prince left, weeks passed drearily for Flora in the confined space of HMS *Bridgewater*, despite the efforts of the crew, and of Lady Bruce and her band at the Citadel. Squalls of rain continued to wash over the ship, keeping it in motion even while it lay at anchor and causing Flora extreme discomfort wherever she was – in her cabin or on deck. Not a single report has survived of a visit from anyone from the Islands who travelled to the capital at that time. Perhaps they were being very circumspect or were taking their cue from Lady Margaret, who had turned distinctly cold towards Flora. It was understandable that the chief's wife should wish to distance herself from the 'crime' in order to maintain her own innocence, but she could have done so without turning on Flora who, heaven knows, was the least culpable of all of them!

Flora was allowed to write letters, but none has survived apart from a reference to a note she sent home, asking that the French garters of the Betty

Burke disguise, which Charles had given her, should be looked after. Her half-brother, James, brought the garters to her as he passed through Leith on his way to Holland to take up service in the Dutch army, but Flora had sailed from Leith by then, so he left them in the secure hands of Lady Bruce.

When word spread that Flora was to be taken to London, a large crowd gathered at Leith to cheer her on her way – small enough comfort because, as far as she knew, they were cheering her on the first step towards trial and whatever punishment the Government chose to mete out to her.[14] She left Leith on 27 October and arrived at the Nore a couple of weeks later, but as Captain Knowler waited for instructions she had to be patient on board HMS *Bridgewater* without visits from Jacobite friends or news of what was happening at home.[15] And the news from home, had she but known it, was shattering.

In the autumn Sleat decided to make the 'jaunt' to London he had talked of to join Cumberland and plead for Kingsburgh. His wife was opposed to the idea because it would take him away from the island where she now hated to be alone. 'I suppose the knight has hinted to you he has some thought of going this winter to London', she told lawyer MacKenzie at the beginning of September, 'as you already know his own company is the only bribe I have ever had to make this remote corner tolerable.'[16] Ever since Kingsburgh was moved to Edinburgh, the chief, determined to 'leave no stone unturn'd to save him',[17] believed he would have to travel to London to plead for the factor, but he was held back by the fact that times were so bad that he could not afford the trip, and his wife was pleading with him to stay or at least take her to Edinburgh. He dithered about going south, pouring out his worries to the ever-sympathetic MacKenzie:

I devis'd seeing you about the beginning of October in my way to London [but] I must now and consequently forever remain where I am. Lady Mgt can't live in this countrey when I leave it and she can live nowhere without her children. It will be obvious to you that the finances won't bear my London journey and her family liveing at Edinburgh.'[18]

Although Skye had suffered less than most other parts of the Highlands and Islands after Culloden, life was precarious even for the Chief. Lady Margaret told lawyer MacKenzie on 1 September that 'whole familys here are in the utmost want of the common necessarys of life. Kingsboro's family and others were at the point of starving.'[19]

In spite of his own fears and his wife's opposition, the Chief set out on 18 November while Flora lay in HMS *Bridgewater* at the Nore. He was accompanied by Kingsburgh's son, Allan, who hoped that the Chief would obtain a regular army commission for him now that the militia's work was finished. No sooner had they crossed from Skye at Kylerhea to the mainland than Sir Alexander became ill suddenly and had to take to his bed at Glenelg Barracks the following day, complaining of feeling cold and shivering. Next morning he had a stitch in his right side and the doctor bled him five times. On the 22nd he was well enough to dress and enjoyed a game of cards, but the following morning, as he prepared to leave, he sat down on the side of his bed, gave a great moan and died. Allan hurried back to Monkstadt with the devastating news, and wrote to Lord President Forbes immediately to tell him 'your Lordship lost a firm friend and alas we have lost our happiness on earth'.[20]

Others were less stricken by the Chief's death and a vicious little quatrain soon circulated about him:

> If Heav'n be pleas'd when sinners cease to sin;
> If Hell be pleas'd when sinners enter in;
> If Earth be pleas'd, to lose a truckling knave;
> Then all are pleas'd – MacDonald's in his grave.[21]

This was most unfair to the chief, who had done all he could to mediate on behalf of members of other clans as well as Kingsburgh. He did not have an easy time at Fort Augustus during the Rising and the months following it. On 19 August 1746 he told MacKenzie in Edinburgh:

My sojourn at Ft Augustus was very agreeable in some Respects as I met with great Civility, nay kindness from the better sort of People there but I was teased out of my Life by the folks whose Goods were drove into that Place. I had the comfort to recover the Cattle of many a poor family upon representing their innocence, nay I saved Spots of Country from Ruin by getting the Inhabitants to submit cheerfully.[22]

The Earl of Albemarle showed little grief: only a month before he had been complaining bitterly to the Duke of Newcastle about the intelligence he was receiving from Sleat, and when he wrote to inform the duke of the chief's death his letter began: 'Since I had the honour of writing to your Grace, nothing has happened.' Nothing had happened – only the death of one of the most important men in the Highlands! Of the actual death he had no sorrow to spare, only a brief remark about the chief's children: 'Sir Alexander MacDonald died suddenly within these few days at Bernera; as he has left some children very young, I hope he may have directed proper people to take care of their education.'[23]

Sleat could be spared by both sides, which seems unfair. For all his faults he had done much for the clan and for the island. Against his instincts he helped the Government in 1745, and now he paid the price for weakness and for trying to placate both sides. Lady Margaret was devastated.

At the Nore Flora knew nothing of this. Captain Knowler was at a loss to know what to do with her and asked urgently for instructions as to where she should be held until the Admiralty decided on her final destination. On 30 November he sent a letter, probably to Commodore Smith, saying

> Miss Flora MacDonald is arrived here with me and as she esteems you her best friend [s]he has in the world should be much obliged if you'd be pleased to let her know what is to become of her. I have wrote to the Admiralty about her but as it may be some time before it may be settled, as their Lordships will first sen'd to the Secretary of State we may possibly go into the Dock before that time and she be send on board the *Royal Sovereign* which would not be very agreable to her. Therefore I should be glad [if] there could be an order got for her being sent up to London as soon as possible. Miss joyns me in Respects.[24]

Aboard the *Royal Sovereign*, as in other transport ships, prisoners were held in the most squalid and dangerously unhygienic conditions. These ships were feared, not merely for the overcrowding, starvation and ill-treatment to which the prisoners were subjected, but for the disease that raged through them unchecked, especially typhus. Hundreds of prisoners were held in floating gaols during the latter half of 1746, first because the authorities had no space for them in gaols ashore, and second because, when illness broke out, those in charge were terrified that landing the sick might start epidemics in prisons on land. It was a vicious circle – the longer the captives were held in insanitary ships' holds, the more contagion spread, and the greater the epidemics grew, the less likely the sick or the well were to be put ashore. In spite of orders to ease the problem, men were left to die, regardless of age, injuries or standing in their clans. The mighty lay shoulder to shoulder with the poor, teenagers alongside the aged, and death took his pick indiscriminately. When a medical officer was sent to inspect the *Pamela*, one of the most notorious of all the transports, he reported that the uncleanliness of the hold was 'surpassing imagination and too nautious to describe, so that, together with the malignant fever raging amongst them, and another odious distemper peculiar to Scotchmen, may terminate in a more dreadful disease.'[25]

Throughout the latter months of 1746 and in early 1747 a regular Sunday outing for Londoners was to be rowed down the Thames to Tilbury to gaze at the prison ships. Such excursions made a diversion from watching the army practise the bayonet manoeuvre that had won the day at Culloden, attending public executions of criminals at Cumberland Gate or witnessing the hanging of army deserters in Hyde Park.

Both Commodore Smith and General Campbell made special pleas for Flora. Albemarle wrote to the Duke of Newcastle on 27 October, the day she left Leith, to request special treatment for her. He wrote:

Her behaviour has been such during her confinement, that Commodore Smith and General Campbell begs of your Grace, that when she arrives she may rather be put into the hands of a messinger than into any common prison, this favour the poor girl deserves, her modest behaviour having gained her many friends.[26]

Flora was now accepted to be 'a poor girl' rather than the wicked rebel she had been considered when first captured.

The 'messinger's house' to which Albemarle referred meant the home of one of a number of messengers at arms in London, the men who acted as couriers between Whitehall and the King's representatives in Scotland and elsewhere, carrying information and escorting people, mainly crown prisoners and witnesses, to London. Influential prisoners, who presented no risk to the Government and could afford to pay for their keep, were held in these messengers' houses which were virtually private prisons. The messengers could charge whatever they liked and many made a good thing out of it. They treated their captives badly, but even the worst messengers' houses were preferable to Newgate Prison, Southwark New Gaol and the Tower of London.

Flora had to be moved before orders arrived, so she spent a few miserable days aboard the *Royal Sovereign* until orders came through that she was to be sent to messenger William Dick's house. There is a tradition, without foundation, that she was held in the Tower before she was ordered to Messenger Dick's house, but if this was the case she can only have been there a few days.

Flora was luckier than some who ended up in messengers' houses. The young wife of the old Laird of MacKinnon was crowded with others into an attic, which was described as an unheated cockloft with a rotten floor and a hole in the roof to provide the only light.[27] Messenger Dick's was reckoned to be one of the better houses although, like all the other messengers, Dick lined his pockets well from his 'guests'.

At Dick's house Flora found excellent and congenial company from South Uist: Clanranald was there, as well as Boisdale, but Lady Clan had been separated from her husband and was with another messenger. Flora had a number of other interesting prisoners for company, among them several Skye and Raasay men: Captain Malcolm MacLeod, who had taken the Prince to Raasay; Captain John MacKinnon of Elgol; and boatman Donald MacLeod of Galtergill. MacNeill of Barra, held only on suspicion, and John MacLean of Iona, who had piloted a ship with Spanish money for the Prince to Barra, were in Dick's house too. Two other prisoners of importance detained with Flora were John and Aeneas MacDonald, whose brother, Ranald of Kinlochmoidart, had been captured early on in Prince Charlie's campaign and executed at Carlisle at about the time Flora was sent south. Aeneas was the Paris banker who had helped to finance the Rising.

At various times during Flora's stay at Dick's house the messenger was also 'host' to John Gordon, son of Gordon of Glenbucket; Katherine McDougall, sister of the notorious John Murray of Broughton; a Jesuit priest John Farquharson of Strathglass; and three army ensigns, George Ramsay, Christopher Taylor and Roderick MacDonald, probably one of the boatmen on the voyage over the sea to Skye.

Messenger Dick also held a number of witnesses who must have made uncomfortable companions for Flora: men like Lachlan McMhurrich and Kenneth MacDonald, who gave evidence against Lady Clanranald and the MacKinnon Chief; Charles MacEachain, a South Uist man who turned King's evidence against MacDonald of Garrifleuch; and Richard Morrison, Prince Charlie's barber and wigmaker, who had been convicted and reprieved and was now in London to give information about the Prince. Flora made a lasting friendship with an enthusiastic young Jacobite physician from York called John Burton, a fellow detainee at Dick's house. Burton had set out to kiss Prince Charles's hand when he heard the Jacobites were marching into England the year before, but was arrested and brought to London where he was held until March 1747. If Dr Burton could not kiss his Prince's hand, he found very acceptable substitutes in the heroine of the crossing to Skye, and others who were imprisoned for helping to save the Stuart heir.

Burton listened avidly to everything he heard about the Cause and took down a long statement from Aeneas MacDonald, which he passed on to Forbes to be incorporated into the *Lyon in Mourning*. He and Flora became attached to one another and it is thanks to this friendship that we have so much detail of the journey to Skye. Forbes incorporated information given in London either to Dr Burton or to John Walkinshaw – Forbes himself was not sure which. Burton later met Flora in Edinburgh, when she told him her story.[28]

By the time Flora reached London the worst of the anti-Jacobite feeling had subsided, but it was not extinguished by any means. At the time of Flora's arrest and initial questioning the first captives were being brought to London and put on trial. Their executions followed at Kennington Common, with the victims' heads displayed on Temple Bar in London, at Manchester and Carlisle as a grisly warning to others.

At the end of July, just before Flora began her journey south, the first peers, Lords Kilmarnock, Cromartie and Balmerino were tried and sentenced to death. Cromartie was eventually pardoned, but the other two were beheaded at the Tower of London on 18 August. When Flora was taken to Messenger Dick's house on 6 December, the news was on everyone's lips that a third peer, Lord Derwentwater, was about to be beheaded. Two days later a frightened Flora learned of Derwentwater's execution. She lived in constant fear, waiting every day to be summoned again for questioning or to stand trial. Far from home, and now without her servant Kate who appears to have been left behind in Edinburgh, Flora found little to comfort her even among the few friends who now surrounded her.

In 1747, as the days began to lengthen, London waited with ill-concealed impatience for the next great trial, that of Lord Lovat. On 9 March it began and, with Murray of Broughton as star witness, the outcome was easy to predict: Lovat was found guilty and went to the execution block on 9 April.

A week later London was lit up by a blaze of bonfires, fireworks and illuminations as the capital celebrated the first anniversary of Culloden with almost as much rejoicing as it had shown immediately after the battle. Behind closed doors the Jacobites toasted the King over the Water.

Although one peer, the Earl of Traquair, still awaited trial in the Tower, and London's gaols and the prison ships were still full, the anniversary celebration of Culloden seemed to purge the English capital of the worst of its venom against the Jacobites. It now became possible to talk more openly about the Cause in the Jacobites' traditional meeting place, the Cocoa Tree coffee house, and once again Lady Primrose, widow of the third Viscount Primrose, was able to entertain supporters of the Cause openly at her house in Essex Street, off the Strand.

Prisoners in the messengers' houses, including Flora, were freer to move around, attended by their 'gaolers', so Flora was invited to Essex Street. She was a great celebrity in London during the spring of 1747, partly because of a publication called *Alexis, or The Young Adventurer*, which had appeared towards the end of the previous year.

Alexis was described as a novel, but it was no more than a pamphlet, thirty-three pages long. The plot, place and characters were utterly transparent but, just in case anyone failed to understand, a key to the characters explained them. The story told how Alexis, 'a shepherd of the first rank', came to rescue the lower shepherds from the depths of their misery, but was defeated in battle at Lachrymania and forced to hide among the islands until he was led to safety by a beautiful girl called Heroica, with the help of Honorious, her stepfather, and Fidelius of Regicia. Alexis was Prince Charlie, of course, Heroica was Flora, Honorius was Armadale and Fidelius of Regicia was Kingsburgh. Neil MacEachain figured in the tale as Veracious, the Sleat Chief as Deceptus, Lady Clanranald as Clarinda, Lieutenant MacLeod as Constantius, and there was a character Sa-gui-ius, 'Some Butchering Fellow'. There was no need to identify him.

The *Alexis* story ended at a point before the Prince left the mainland for France in September 1746, suggesting that it was written while Charles was in hiding during August. It contained touches of comic genius, with Skye called Aetheria and Scotland Robustia. The MacLeods were the Erronei, so the author clearly believed the clan had been wrong to refuse to support Charles. The language they all spoke was called Yalk.

Alexis was published anonymously, so that no one has ever been absolutely certain as to the author's identity, but Bishop Forbes believed that, from the facts given, it could only have been the work of Neil MacEachain or Kingsburgh himself. The factor, a man of sixty, had plenty of courage but showed no spark of literary interest, so he is unlikely to have been the author of such a work: which leaves Neil, the educated young man anxious to help his Prince, and with time on his hands. Neil was in hiding at the time *Alexis* was written, so could well have had both the time and the opportunity. While Donald Roy was composing his Latin poems, perhaps Neil was writing *Alexis*.

The following year another pamphlet appeared, obviously with the aim of exonerating Flora, although it was clearly the work of a loyal Hanoverian supporter. The author was 'J. Drummond' and the work was entitled *The Female Rebels, 1747. Being Some Remarkable Incidents of the Lives, Character and Families of the Titular Duke and Duchess of Perth, the Lord and Lady Ogilvie and of Miss Flora MacDonald.* The pamphlet shed little new light on Flora, but spoke warmly of the calmness with which she was facing the danger of her situation, for it was written during her stay at Messenger Dick's. Clearly Flora was making the best of impressions on her enemies as well as among her friends: Drummond wrote that she was 'of graceful person, good complexion and peculiar sweetness mixed with majesty in her countenance'. She surely bore the worry and hardship of her life as a prisoner well, since the author flattered her by describing her as a young lady of about twenty: she was in fact nearer twenty-five.

If Flora's enemies were able to be so gracious to her, then it is hardly surprising that she drove her friends to raptures of delight. Frederick, Prince of Wales, received her in order to annoy his father and 'Butcher' brother, whom he disliked intensely, as much as to honour the rescuer of the Stuart Pretender's son. When Frederick asked why she had dared to help his father's enemies, she replied boldly 'that she would have done the same thing for him had she found him in distress'. According to Alexander MacGregor 'The Prince was so struck with this reply and her artless manner, that he afterwards interested himself to procure for her every comfort.'[29]

Lady Primrose became Flora's best friend and, in order to help to pay the excessive lodging charges of Messenger Dick, she raised a subscription, which soon totalled £1,500 – a very large sum indeed in those days.

Thus life for Flora was exceedingly comfortable and, as the weeks passed, it became clear that she was unlikely to be put on trial, at least not on any capital charge, so she became more relaxed. Life was pleasant, with visits to friends, accompanied by Messenger Dick's daughters, and Aeneas MacDonald even planned 'a jaunt to Windsor' for her. Alas, just as they were about to leave on this outing, an order came through to commit the banker to Newgate Gaol – a sharp reminder that danger had not totally receded for any of them.[30] Aeneas was put on trial towards the end of the year, was found guilty and sentenced to death. He was pardoned eventually and released, but because he did not have enough money to pay his messenger 'gaoler' he was not set free until December 1749.

Flora continued to be showered with kindness. Portraits were made of her and she was given presents in kind over and above the £1,500 subscription. It was at this time that Richard Wilson painted her, portrayals that suggest that Flora had coped well with months of confinement on board ship and in the messenger's house. Apart from looking a little pale, she displays no outward signs of her ordeal but appears serene and confident. She had maintained contact with the naval officers who had been her gaolers on board ship, and gave a painting to Nigel Gresley, an officer of HMS *Bridgewater*, in thanks for all he had done for her.

Flora accepted all the attention that was given to her, but 'could never understand how such a simple act of humanity should produce so much excitement, or confer upon her, what she considered, such unmerited celebrity'.[31]

At long last, on Saturday 4 July 1747, a year all but a week from the day she was arrested on the road near Armadale and bundled aboard HMS *Furnace*, an amnesty was declared. John MacDonald of Kinlochmoidart, old Donald MacLeod and Ensign Roderick MacDonald had already been released on 10 June, but now Clanranald and his wife, Lady MacKinnon and Malcolm MacLeod were all freed. For some unexplained reason the order to release Flora was delayed for several days more. On the day the main body of prisoners was released in London, Kingsburgh was set free in Edinburgh. As he remarked ruefully, he had suffered a year in gaol for one night's hospitality.

The general amnesty did not cover all the people in Messenger Dick's house: Aeneas MacDonald moved back from Newgate but was still held along with the two ensigns, who were transported together in August the following year. A large number of other prisoners, some of them leaders of the Rising but many of no importance whatever, continued to be held. In London Lord Traquair still lay in the Tower untried, and in fact never was brought to trial: he was eventually released in October 1748. MacKinnon of MacKinnon, who had helped the Prince in Skye, remained at Messenger Munie's for a further year and a half until he petitioned that he was old and destitute. The process of release continued slowly and transportation of men across the Atlantic continued until spring of 1749.

Flora stayed on in London for a few days after her release, apparently with Lady Primrose, until she could arrange to return to Scotland by post-chaise, the fastest mode of transport, apart from riding really hard on horseback, available for the four-hundred-mile journey. She was escorted by Malcolm MacLeod and, since they could hardly conceal their Highland identity, they chose to travel as brother and sister, Mr and Miss Robertson. This they hoped would enable them to avoid being recognized on the way. It was a wise precaution for, even then – more than fifteen months after Culloden – a Scotsman was not safe on an English road.

MacLeod enjoyed his journey with the heroine of Prince Charlie's escape, forever afterwards telling anyone who would listen (including James Boswell and Dr Samuel Johnson): 'I went to London to be hanged and returned in a post-chaise with Miss Flora MacDonald.'[32] 'Mr and Miss Robertson' left London on Monday 27 July 1747 and, after a brief stop at York to visit Dr Burton, reached Edinburgh the following Sunday evening, 2 August. Flora was at last not only free, but back in her home country.

CHAPTER SEVEN

Home to a Husband

I heartily wish my worthy Flory as happy as it is possible to be on this side of the grave.

Letter from Dr John Burton to Reverend Robert Forbes[1]

Flora's early biographer, Alexander MacGregor, described in florid detail her home-coming to the islands: a heroine among her clanspeople who fawned over her and fêted her, and Flora, he said, was equally delighted to be back among them. She was welcomed by her mother, her brother, and the chiefs of Sleat and Clanranald, and she made a great tour which took in South Uist, Benbecula, Scalpa, Raasay and many places on Skye. Cumberland's triumphant arrival in London was lacklustre alongside Flora MacDonald's welcome home to the Hebrides. It was the stuff of legend. But it was totally untrue.

Flora stopped at Edinburgh and made no plans to continue the journey to Skye, a strange thing to do when one would have expected her to be anxious to return home as quickly as possible. It was not as if she had lots of family or friends in the capital. By the time she climbed down from the post-chaise in Edinburgh, even Kingsburgh, her fellow conspirator in the escape, had been freed and had left for Skye to help Lady Margaret manage the estates for the new chief, her five-year-old son, Sir James.

The Jacobites certainly did not detain her in the capital. She now had less time for them than ever, although they still made a fuss of her and went out of their way to befriend her. But she did not look for, or accept, adulation of the kind that had been bestowed on her while she was a prisoner aboard HMS *Bridgewater*. Forbes dearly wanted to hear more of Flora's story, preferably from her own lips, and it was not for want of trying that he did not manage to talk to her face to face until January of the following year. Flora MacDonald was clearly avoiding him and chose to hide herself away in the city.

It was as if Flora felt unable to face returning to the Hebrides which held such traumatic memories: she had left the islands a girl and was now a mature woman, aware that her life had altered irrevocably but not sure how to cope with the change. There was little cheer in the news she heard from home: her stepfather was still in hiding and no one knew what life would be like under the new chief, which in effect meant life under Lady Margaret's rule. Lady Margaret was still devastated by her husband's death and, since he died on a journey south to plead for Kingsburgh, she blamed the Jacobites for it. Much of her anger focused on Flora because it was she who had brought the Prince to Monkstadt.

One positive thing Flora did in Edinburgh was to attempt to improve her handwriting by taking lessons from David Beatt, a schoolmaster with Jacobite sympathies.[2] Beatt claimed that Flora waited several weeks specially for him to return to Edinburgh so that he might tutor her. In September 1747 he wrote to James Burnet of Barns in Peeblesshire:

> As I have entered with Miss Flory McDonald, who waited five weeks for my return to Town, and who needs very much to be advanced in her writing, confines me to daily attendance, and must do so till she is brought to some length in it, which obliges me to keep the Town close.[3]

Much as she needed to improve her handwriting, that could not have been Flora's sole, or indeed principal, reason for staying on in the capital – a minister or dominie could easily have been found in Skye to give her lessons.

Malcolm MacLeod, Flora's travelling companion in the post-chaise from London, also remained in Edinburgh for a while, and was much more easily persuaded to talk with Forbes because he was 'poorly provided for in money matters,' a situation that Forbes and his friends were happy to remedy. On 13 August MacLeod dined at Lady Bruce's house and was given 'six guineas and a crown'.[4] That same day Forbes asked James MacDonald of Sartle, a Skye man whose house was a popular meeting place for islanders who had been out in the Rising, to 'lay himself out to get me a meeting with Donald MacLeod, Miss Flora MacDonald, and any others if they came in his reach'.[5]

Flora was proving elusive, so Dr Burton travelled to Edinburgh in November 'purposely to make enquiry about matters relating to the Prince's affairs'. Forbes knew that Flora was particularly well disposed towards the York doctor and that Burton would persuade her to talk if anyone could. Burton met the heroine again in Edinburgh and talked her through the details of the escape and her involvement.[6] A copy of her account was passed to Forbes, together with her replies to a number of questions which Forbes had specially requested Burton to put to her. To the first of these, asking how Flora met O'Neil, she replied that Felix had come to Milton several times when he 'used to scour about' the island while Charles was hiding there.

Forbes asked next if Armadale ever met the Prince privately while Charles was in hiding. 'No', she said, 'Armadale happening to be on the Continent when the Prince first landed, he was the first person to take the Pretender's hand and kiss it. Armadale never saw the Prince again.' Her stepfather had been in hiding for more than a year and she was determined to avoid incriminating him. The third question, concerning the contents of the letter granting her safe conduct to Skye with Betty Burke, was dealt with tartly by saying that she had already covered that in her journal. Again she was protecting 'One-eyed' Hugh.

Next Forbes wanted to know which songs the royal fugitive sang on the crossing to Skye. She confirmed that these were 'The King Shall Enjoy His Own Again' and 'The Twenty-Ninth of May'. The fifth question was whether Lady Clan had supplied some bottles of milk and if the Prince 'put the bottle to his head' and drank along with the boatmen. Yes, he drank the milk 'Jock-fellow-like' from the bottle, but he kept a small amount of wine he had with him for Flora 'lest she should faint with the cold and other inconveniences of a night passage'.

Dr Burton added one last question of his own: how long was it after the Prince's departure from Kingsburgh House that Ferguson came to question the factor? Six or seven days, Flora replied, by which time Charles was on the mainland.

Early in the New Year of 1748, Forbes himself managed at long last to meet Flora. Her half-brother, James, who had brought Betty Burke's garters to Edinburgh, again passed through on his way home to Skye to recruit for the Dutch army and called on Forbes on Friday 22 January. There he collected letters for Baleshare, Malcolm MacLeod and Kingsburgh from Forbes, and the following day Flora came to meet the Jacobite chronicler for the first time, accompanied by Donald Roy. During this meeting, which took place at Lady Bruce's house, Forbes questioned her further about the Prince's arrival in Skye, and she was much more forthcoming now, mentioning that Lady Margaret had been told of the Prince's impending arrival and about her ladyship's panic, 'going often out and in as one in great anxiety'. Flora saw no need to protect the Chief's wife anymore.[7]

She had a second meeting with Forbes, again at Lady Bruce's house, on Saturday 22 March, and at this confirmed the text of the Betty Burke letter and added a sentence about Neil MacEachain which had been omitted previously. At this meeting she also told Forbes that it was her brother, Milton, who had taken the Prince's pistols at Rossinish and given them to Armadale.[8]

About this time Flora met Neil in Edinburgh, although she was too discreet to refer to this directly: the fact just emerged in a letter Neil sent to her from Paris a year later.[9] As rumours of another French invasion were current in 1748, Neil could well have been in the Scots capital secretly acting as Price Charlie's go-between to Scottish Jacobites.

At long last – nearly nine months after her release – Flora decided to return home. She set out on 19 April 1748 accompanied as far as Argyll by a friend, Peggy Callander. From this journey Forbes picked up another gem for his collection of Jacobite memorabilia, and to pass on to Dr Burton: 'In crossing [on] a ferry to Argyleshire she had almost been drown'd, the boat having struck upon a rock; but (under God) a clever Highlander saved her.' Flora arrived home safely at the beginning of July and 'waited upon her mother and the worthy Armadale'. She had been away for two years.[10]

MacGregor wrote that Sir Alexander of Sleat (who had been dead eighteen months) welcomed her with a great feast which lasted four days! He also lists countless visits, receptions and celebrations – far too numerous to have been possible in the short time Flora spent on the island.[11] Yet it would be wrong to dismiss all of MacGregor's claims since his *Life of Flora* was based largely on information obtained from her daughter. Probably many of the events did take place, but not in 1748: some may have been part of another celebration, and others related to her marriage two years later.

MacGregor's version of the home-coming suggests there were people Flora was not pleased to see. When she met Major Allan MacDonald of Knock, the officer who had trapped old Donald MacLeod of Galtergill by a trick, he took her hand, only to be told:

> I give you my hand, but not entirely with my heart. I wish to show all courtesy to the profession which you have disgraced by a low and base stratagem, utterly unworthy of the conduct of a soldier, a Highlander, and a gentleman![12]

The words sound Victorian rather than Flora's, but they expressed what Flora felt after listening to Galtergill's account of his capture as he related it when they were prisoners together in Messenger Dick's house. Knock was despised in Skye because of the breaches of the rules of kinship and Highland honour by which he captured Galtergill and others.

MacGregor also relates that Flora was taken ill at Monkstadt and Lady Margaret in great anxiety sent to Dunvegan for her husband (deceased!), but that Flora recovered to enjoy a four-day-long banquet attended by all the important families. This has all the characteristics of a wedding celebration.[13]

The reality was, in all probability, that Flora's welcome in Skye was not as warm as one might have expected. Her own family and the Kingsburghs, who were always fond of her, were delighted to see her, of course, but other islanders were jealous or felt resentment against her. After all, she had been singularly favoured to be treated so leniently when others, who had committed far lesser crimes or no misdemeanour at all, had lost property, been tortured or even put to death. For all Flora's discretion during questioning, she had betrayed a few islanders, and her reward for all this was to be lionized by both friends and enemies, and handed a large fortune in cash. While the rest of the Highlands suffered, Flora MacDonald flourished, they felt. She may have heard hints of this in Edinburgh and stayed away from the island as a result.

The Skye to which she returned was a very different place from the island she had left: it had scarcely been touched by the devastation that was spread through the rest of the Highlands and Islands by the Hanoverians after Culloden, yet it was undergoing changes more subtle and more fundamental than those inflicted by occupying soldiers. The Chief of Sleat was dead and the traditional clan system had passed on with him. The whole basis of island life was changing so radically that, even if Flora herself had not altered and fellow islanders had not been suspicious of her, it would have been impossible for her to slip back into the life she had known prior to 1745.

But Flora had changed. A year's imprisonment, interrogation and fear had made her harder, and better able to make her own decisions about how she would lead her life. With the fortune Lady Primrose had raised among Jacobite friends, Flora had the means to do whatever she wanted. Quickly she realized she could not settle in Skye for the present, and soon she was talking about returning to the south. The need to arrange her financial affairs in London provided a good excuse.

Before July was out she wrote to Dr Burton to say that she was about to visit some unnamed friends in the west and would call on him in York on her way to London, but that would not be before September.[14] Forbes was still feeling piqued at being excluded from the magic circle of Flora's friends and having to depend upon others for information about her. When Burton gave him the news of Flora's unexpected visit Forbes observed unhappily, 'I have never heard directly from Miss Flora MacDonald; but I have heard frequently of her.' He still had to be satisfied with acquaintance at second hand, but his hopes rose when he heard, wrongly as it turned out, that she might be in Edinburgh sometime during July.[15]

Forbes was having little luck at that particular moment with his search for Jacobite material generally. He told Burton he had heard nothing of Malcolm MacLeod, while Dr Drummond, he believed, was 'somewhat lazy' and, in spite of all his efforts, had been unable to obtain copies of a letter from the MacLeod Chief which Kingsburgh had in his possession or another from Cumberland which had been captured in transit.[16]

The Cause was not going well at this time either: the prospect of peace being made between France and Britain was exercising the minds of Jacobites who feared, rightly, that this would lose them the support of the French king. However, Burton was of the opinion that the French were still preparing for war, a thought that gave Forbes satisfaction. Towards the end of his letter he said, 'Your thoughts concerning the peace are curious, and seem to have some foundation. Pray let me know what you think of it now, whether or not it is like to come to a period, or, etc.'[17]

Unfortunately for Charles Stuart and for the Jacobite Cause it did 'come to a period' in October when the Treaty of Aix-La-Chapelle brought an end to hostilities, and the terms of the treaty banished the Pretenders to the British throne from both France and Spain.

By now Charles Stuart himself was the worst enemy of the Cause. In his frustration he was dashing from France to Spain, demanding support for a new invasion, making a thorough nuisance of himself and, in the course of it all, proving a great embarrassment to his family and friends. He felt betrayed on every side and refused even to travel to Rome to visit his father: the Bonnie Prince of 1745–6 was turning into the Wild Man of Europe of the 1750s, and this, as much as anything, destroyed hope of his family's restoration to the thrones of England and Scotland.

After a mere two months at home Flora was on her travels again. She headed south to Edinburgh in September 1748, and on to York on 5 November with a letter from Forbes for Dr Burton in her baggage. She paused only two days in York before hurrying on to London, where she remained throughout the winter.

Jacobite circles still welcomed Flora with open arms. During this visit she spent much of her time with Lady Primrose or other Jacobites, and made arrangements for the money collected for her in 1746. Sympathizers of the Cause cosseted her and fussed over her as always, and she sat for Allan Ramsay, one of the most eminent portrait painters of the day. The Scottish artist's picture portrays a very different Flora from the one Wilson painted two years earlier. Here we see a more mature, more serious woman, and one who has experienced much. The eyes are solemn and the mouth firmer. Clearly Flora had seen a lot in the two years since she was last in London to give her a more sober outlook on life. From Ramsay's portrait it is easy to believe that Flora found the return to freedom harder in many ways than her year of imprisonment.

At about this time a letter arrived from Neil MacEachain which demonstrated that he was as closely enmeshed in Prince Charlie's machinations as ever. Writing from Paris on 28 February 1749, Neil addressed her as 'Dear Florry' and said:

> I am sure it must give you a sensible joy to hear the person you once had the honour to Conduct, is in perfect good health. Soon may they enjoy any other blessings the world can give. Clanranald has his kindest compliments to you, and hopes next time you meet, you'll both be in better spirits than when he last saw you. He and I dined with somebody the very day they were took. Good God, what a fright we got!'[18]

This 'somebody' was the Prince, who had stayed on in France in defiance of the Treaty of Aix-la-Chapelle and was behaving with outrageous provocativeness to King Louis XV. The king eventually lost patience and had Charles arrested at the opera one night just before Christmas 1748 then expelled from France. On 28 February, the day Neil wrote to his 'dear Florry', the wild Prince was forced to flee from Avignon also, into a misty world of rumour and speculation. Over the following eighteen months he was 'sighted' in Sweden, Venice, Russia and Prussia, travelling under a host of aliases, including 'Thomson', the name by which he had signed his little letter of thanks to Flora and his other helpers in Skye. One unexpected place where Charles is known to have been during this time is London, where he spent a few days during the autumn of 1750. It was said that the highly efficient British secret service was well aware of his visit to England, but did nothing about it. By then arrest would have been an embarrassment to the British Government – far better to let him come and go quietly, they believed, which is exactly what he did. What a pity Flora was back in Skye by that time so that they did not meet.

In June 1749 Dr Burton, still in regular contact with her, was able to report to Bishop Forbes in Edinburgh that Flora would soon be on her way north again, and had promised to spend ten days with him at York before visiting Sir William Maxwell, a member of the prominent Borders Jacobite family, at Springkell in Dumfriesshire. Burton told Forbes that Flora was well but looked thin.[19]

Back in Edinburgh Flora delayed again, all through autumn and winter, as if unable to make up her mind to return home to Skye. She visited Forbes again on Saturday 31 March 1750, when the good Jacobite clergyman, still determined to record each last detail of every event and person related to the Rising and the Prince's escape, checked up on the names of the men who had sailed the boat to Skye.[20]

She returned home to bad news that summer: two of her half-brothers in Skye had died, apparently as a result of an accident. Forbes wrote to her at Armadale on 11 July: 'I feel somewhat of that mixture of joy and grief which would ensue upon your first meeting with your mother, – joy to see one another once more in health and safety, but grief in your mutual condolences for the affecting loss of two hopeful youths.'[21]

Back home in Skye the reason for her visit to London to arrange her finances and the delay in returning to the island became apparent. She was making up her mind about her future. She had received a proposal of marriage from Kingsburgh's elder son, Allan, a match that pleased both the Sleat factor's family, and 'One-eyed' Hugh and Marion at Armadale. Flora was a good catch for any man since she was now a woman of considerable fortune and a heroine in the eyes of many people the length and breadth of Britain.

Allan MacDonald, or Allen as he himself usually spelt his name, had much to offer too. He lived at Kingsburgh where he helped his father with his work as factor to the Chief's estates. He was a good-looking, amiable young man, convinced of his own destiny to follow his father in due course as factor to the Sleat Chief. The late Sir Alexander had planned this by sending Allan to Edinburgh to be educated under the eye of lawyer MacKenzie. Now that peace had been restored he was being groomed for the role. Allan was powerfully built, with jet black hair tied jauntily behind which made him look every inch a leader among his clansmen. This, together with his often-voiced modern opinions on farming methods, made many islanders suspicious of him: others were just plain jealous. Marriage to the heroine of the Prince's escape confirmed to these people that Kingsburgh's son had grown too full of his own importance.

When the Rising broke out in 1745, Allan badly wanted to follow his chief into the army and he became a Lieutenant in one of Sleat's militia companies under MacDonald of Kirkibost. Allan was with MacLeod of Dunvegan when the Laird was given the freedom of the town of Forres in January 1746, but he was back at Fort William by April when the Battle of Culloden was fought, and remained there during the summer of 1746, thus missing meeting Prince Charlie at Kingsburgh. Fortunately he was not stationed at Fort Augustus and so was saved the dreadful humiliation of seeing his own father brought in as a prisoner. After the Rising was over and the militia disbanded, he still longed to make a career in the Army and the chief was taking him to London with that in mind when Sleat died so tragically at Bernera. Lady Margaret wrote to Lord President Forbes in June 1747, asking for help to obtain a commission for Allan in the Dutch service,[22] but that also came to nothing. It is odd that so many others, including Flora's half-brother, James, were successful in finding their way into military careers, and we know that James came to Skye specifically to recruit for the Dutch army in the early part of 1748. Yet Allan never obtained the commission he yearned for so badly. It was like so much else in Allan MacDonald's life: he was full of ambition which, somehow, he was never able to fulfil. By the time Flora returned to the island, the factor had persuaded his son that he, Kingsburgh, was getting old and Allan was needed to help at home. This was a hard argument for the ambitious young man to refute. After all, in the natural course of events he would soon be securely ensconced in Kingsburgh as the Chief's factor. The prospect of marriage to a wealthy celebrity clinched the argument and put paid to Allan MacDonald's dreams of becoming a soldier.

Allan knew that Flora would make an excellent factor's wife. His father pushed hard for the match because he knew Flora far better than his son did, and realized that her depth of character and solid common sense would keep his son, who tended to go off in pursuit of airy-fairy schemes, on a steady path. Her fortune would also help to settle Allan.

What did Flora see in Allan MacDonald? The first thing that attracted her was the fact that he was a handsome man, intelligent and with good prospects. He belonged to the Kingsburgh family, which she knew well and respected. She was fond of old Kingsburgh and his wife, and may even have suffered pangs of conscience about being the cause of Kingsburgh's year in jail.

Even alongside the many elegant and eligible men Flora had met in the South, Allan MacDonald had much to offer. He was neither narrow nor insular, and he had ambition. His constant talk about the advanced farming methods he wanted to introduce into the island was a breath of fresh air in this stifled, narrow community. Flora saw every prospect of a comfortable, secure life with this man who one day would be factor to the Chief of Sleat, and she accepted him as her husband.

Flora and Allan were married at Armadale on 6 November 1750. MacGregor claims that the 'festivities were conducted on a large scale, and lasted for the greater part of a week', but, since he also said, wrongly, that the wedding took place at Flodigarry in the north-west corner of the island, one questions the accuracy of his account. MacGregor also tells us that Flora was married in a dress of Stuart tartan which had been given to her by a London Jacobite 'on condition that she would wear it at her marriage', yet the dress which was preserved in her family as the one she wore to marry Allan is black.[23] MacGregor describes a typical Highland wedding celebration continuing over several days, and there is no reason to expect that two people as important as young Kingsburgh and the famous Flora would have anything less.

The wedding was arranged in such haste that the marriage contract was not drawn up until a month afterwards, on 3 December. This was a five-page-long document, which showed that Flora came to Allan as a woman of considerable substance and, as was customary in those days, it assigned Flora's fortune of £700 to her husband, but bound Allan and his father to pay her £50 a year or, in the event of the couple separating, £40 a year. It took careful account of how their estate was to be shared out to their family after their deaths. The contract was signed 'Flory Macdonald' on every page, and Allan and his father also signed it. The witnesses were Donald MacDonald of Castleton, Hugh MacDonald of Armadale and Dr John MacLean, who actually wrote out the long document.[24]

The marriage of Flora and Allan MacDonald was of sufficient importance for *The Scots Magazine* to report it:

Nov. 6, 1750. At Armadale, in Sleat, Allan Macdonald, eldest son of Alexander Macdonald of Kingsburgh, married to Miss Flora Macdonald, daughter of Ronald Macdonald of Milton, deceas'd. This is the young Lady who aided the escape of the young Chevalier.[25]

The Scots Magazine brought the first news of the wedding to many Jacobite supporters in the south, including Forbes, and the clergyman's feelings were hurt. Flora had told him nothing of her marriage plans in advance and the first news he had of it from Kingsburgh came in a letter written on New Year's Eve 1750, when the old Sleat factor referred to 'the new maryed couple' and said the match had pleased everybody.[26] Forbes's disappointment showed through in his reply:

> Pray make an offer of my best wishes, in the kindest manner, to my worthy Mrs Flora MacDonald, and tell her, from me, that I looked for some few lines under her own hand to let me know her marriage day, which I and some others are quite ignorant about.[27]

He wrote to Dr Burton to give him the news and received an answer from York, saying, 'I heartily wish my worthy Flora as happy as it is possible to be on this side of the grave, and that she may live to see her children's children so too.'[28]

As the old year died and 1751 dawned, Flora hoped the eleven days of glory and four-and-a-half years of retribution now lay behind her. With Allan MacDonald at her side she looked forward to a new life in which Jacobitism would play no part. Therein may well lie the reason for her failure to tell the Stuart circle at the Citadel of Leith the good news of her changed status in life.

CHAPTER EIGHT

The Tacksman's Wife

There was a comfortable parlour with a good fire, and a dram went round. By and by supper was served, at which there appeared the lady of the house, the celebrated Miss Flora Macdonald.

James Boswell at Kingsburgh[1]

Flora and her new husband spent the first months of their married life at Kingsburgh, but from the start Allan was searching for a permanent home of their own. They could have stayed on at Kingsburgh, of course, since Allan's father, now past sixty, needed his son's support to help him manage the Sleat estates. Old Mrs MacDonald of Kingsburgh would also have been glad of the help and company of Flora, whom she liked and admired greatly, but the young couple were determined to make their own way.

This was a disappointment to old Kingsburgh, who carried the entire burden of managing the estates in the absence of the young chief, who had gone south to be educated. Lady Margaret accompanied her son: it gave her a good excuse to leave Skye, which she had grown to dislike even more intensely since her husband's death. Kingsburgh wrote to Forbes in Leith on New Year's Eve 1750, saying wistfully that, 'tho the young folk has the gaity of youth to cheer them, the old must become spiritless'. This was more than that customary mood of introspection that creeps over Scots at New Year: Kingsburgh really was beginning to feel his age.[2]

Thanks to Flora's dowry, Allan was able to apply for the lease of Flodigarry, on the north-east side of the island, when it fell due for renewal on Whitsun Day 1751. Flodigarry had been tenanted by the Martin family for generations and the sitting tenant, Martin Martin, had held it for nineteen years, but now Kingsburgh persuaded Lady Margaret to turn Flodigarry over to Allan. Flora wrote to Messrs Innes and Clark in London who were holding £800, the balance of the money raised by Lady Primrose for Flora in 1746 and additional money that Lady Primrose and other Jacobites had added to it. With this she and Allan were able to move into Flodigarry, start to make improvements to the buildings and buy stock for the farm.

The Martins were old 'enemies' of the Kingsburgh MacDonalds: factors were never popular with their tenants because they had the unpleasant task of passing on news of rent rises or reprimands from the chief, but jealousy entered into the Martins' feelings as well because they believed that the chief showed his Sleat factor too much favour. Awarding the Flodigarry tenancy to Allan added anger to their envy and ensured that the rivalry was carried on into the younger generation.

In a small community like Skye they could not avoid encountering one another and, although meetings appeared friendly enough on the surface, enmity was never far underneath. There was the case of the wrestling match between Allan and one of the Martins which went into Skye folklore. As Allan was riding past a barn where some men were threshing one day, young Kingsburgh called in to chat. Someone suggested that he and Martin, who was among them, should try a wrestling bout and, without removing his spurs, Allan squared up to his opponent. When Allan appeared to be winning, one of his spurs became entangled in a woven sack and Martin managed to pin Kingsburgh to the ground. They parted friends, or appeared to bear no ill feeling, but it was said afterwards that the crushing hold that Allan took on Martin's chest was the eventual cause of the latter's death. Later, when some youths belonging to the two families were drinking together, one of the Martins taunted the MacDonalds that their man had been beaten. A scuffle broke out in which several men were hurt, and a young cousin of Allan's composed a song about the incident, which is still sung in the islands.

Taking the Flodigarry lease away from Martin Martin turned the Martin–MacDonald rivalry into open hostility.[3] Soon after Flora and Allan moved into Flodigarry, old Kingsburgh wrote to Sleat's lawyer in Edinburgh expressing the hope that neither he nor Lady Margaret would give the lease of another MacDonald property to 'a turbulent unsafe tenant such as Martin Martin'.[4] From then on the Martins were out for revenge.

This enmity, fed by jealousy, spread to an increasing number of clansmen who resented the factor's apparent use of his office to benefit his own family, and they disliked Allan's fancy new farming ideas which flew in the face of every tradition the islanders knew. They felt they had good reason to distrust such methods, which smacked of the new order being thrust on to the clans by the powers in the south. This feeling was fuelled by resentment of the fact that Kingsburgh's son's experiments were financed by money his wife had received for her part in the Jacobite Rising, which had brought other clansmen nothing but grief, poverty and suffering.

Flodigarry suited Allan very well: it lay on the opposite side of the Trotternish Peninsula from Kingsburgh, not far as the crow flies but nearly twenty miles by the winding coastal road. A shorter track ran through the weird, wild mountain peaks known as the Quiraing.

Flodigarry lies in the shadow of the stark Quiraing cliffs, in a breathtakingly beautiful, secluded situation, hidden away in a deep cleft where a burn enters the sea. The house in which Flora and Allan lived still stands – a white cottage close to the water's edge – looking out to Flodigarry Island across a narrow sound. In an almost treeless landscape, trees grow in the sheltered valley of Flodigarry. Even today it is a remote spot. When Allan and Flora moved to Flodigarry it was a good farm, where a family might prosper, and the couple began life there full of hope.

The first few of the eight years that Flora and her husband spent at Flodigarry were the happiest and almost the only trouble-free times they were to know in their entire life together.

For Flora it was close, but not too close, to her parents-in-law, so they could lead their own lives there. Allan was able to farm by the new methods in which he had such faith, and Flora was able to raise their first child, which she was already carrying at the time they took over the tenancy.

Their son was born there on 22 October 1751, just five months after they moved. By Scottish custom a first son was usually named after his paternal grandfather and a first daughter after her maternal grandmother; the second son was given his mother's father's name and the second daughter the name of her father's mother. But Flora and Allan ignored tradition, choosing instead a name that, although familiar enough to islanders, was far from common among them: Charles. Flora chose to give her first-born the name of the Prince who had caused such upheaval in her life and Allan agreed to name his heir after the Stuart Prince whom he had never supported. The name, so unlikely in these parts at that time, serves to reveal a romantic, almost quixotic vein that ran through the character of both Flora and Allan. This detachment from reality in two otherwise prosaic people helps to explain the course of their lives later.

In 1751 there was no shadow of future misfortune for Allan MacDonald. Skye had been fortunate in the aftermath of the '45, largely because the MacLeod chief and Sir Alexander of Sleat had supported the Government and raised militia regiments during the Rising. While much of the mainland, Raasay and other islands were devastated by the Hanoverians, Skye escaped with little damage. Neither MacLeod of Dunvegan nor MacDonald of Sleat lost their estates, yet life was not easy for either chief because the Government, so anxious to persuade them to raise militia companies in 1745, now held back on payment of the costs that had come out of the chiefs' pockets. Young Sleat and Lady Margaret were chronically short of money, Lady Margaret was in debt to Kingsburgh and, when she returned to the island at about the end of 1753, she was forever complaining to lawyer MacKenzie about her lack of money and the ingratitude of the powers in Edinburgh.

With a well-stocked farm and tenants of their own, Allan and Flora were very comfortably off at this time. Allan was a skilled farmer with a good eye for an excellent cow, so that his black cattle were always in demand in the South. He also had high hopes that by introducing new methods of cultivation, as everyone in the Highlands was being encouraged to do, life would be easy for his wife and family. They made improvements to the house and farmstead at Flodigarry, and considered themselves among the better-off tacksmen on the island, living comfortably in the little house by the shore, with their own servants and gradually gathering together all the furnishings to make a home.

Although it lay little more than fifteen miles from Portree, Flodigarry was isolated and consequently saw fewer visitors than more southerly farms. Apart from an occasional neighbour passing there were rare – and welcome – calls by pedlars and packmen selling all kinds of household necessities. Strangers who arrived at any house on the island were made welcome and were entertained hospitably because they broke the loneliness and monotony of life in remote parts, and they brought news and gossip which opened windows onto the whole world. Whether there was room or not, they were always welcome.

James Boswell found this when he and Samuel Johnson stopped overnight at Corriechatachain on 6 September during their journey to the Western Isles in 1773. 'How all the people here were lodged, I know not', he wrote. 'It was partly done by separating man and wife, and putting a number of men in one room, and of women in another.'[5] Food was plentiful, the company cheerful and there was much talking and singing of Gaelic songs until even the eminent visitor, Johnson, was forgotten and Boswell, Lowlander that he was, 'joined in the choruses with as much glee as any of the company'.[6]

The clan, although the system was well into the process of disintegration by this time, was still an extended family, and Flora and Allan travelled to Kingsburgh often, or even south to Armadale, to visit their families and attend marriages and funerals, both of which usually resulted in great reunions for relatives who lived too far away to meet often. Allan's sister's husband, Ranald MacAlister, died during this time and Flora's half-sister, Annabella, married tacksman Alexander MacDonald of Cuidreach. These and other important family events were landmarks in a hard working life for Flora, and the only time the family came together.

On 18 February 1754 there was much to celebrate at Flodigarry when Flora's second child, a daughter, was born. Again they broke with tradition and did not name her Marion after Flora's mother, but Anne, the name of Allan's sister. Just a year and three days later, on 21 February 1755, a second son arrived and this time they chose to name him Alexander after Allan's father.

That same year old Kingsburgh was at last forced to tell the Chief that he no longer felt able to continue as Sleat factor. Much lobbying and contriving had already gone on over who should be appointed to succeed him, and Lady Margaret and MacLeod of Dunvegan fell out over the matter, but in the end Allan was appointed factor as the late chief, Sir Alexander, had intended. He was allowed to retain his own tack of Flodigarry.

New horizons opened up for Allan MacDonald as factor to the MacDonald estates in North Skye, an important and influential position for a young man with so many ideas. With the Chief still absent from the island, Allan had the freedom to experiment and introduce his own new schemes. The Forfeited Estates Commission, which administered the organization of all Highland lands taken from Jacobite chiefs after the '45, was encouraging new ideas which men like Allan MacDonald took up enthusiastically. They called for the introduction of longer leases of twenty-one years for tenants and enforced enclosure to turn the land over to more profitable sheep rearing. This was the start of the century of the Clearances, which was to empty the Highlands of thousands of men, women and children, who – by their emigration – gave the world the strength of Highland character to build new nations across the globe.

On the farms new methods such as crop rotation and winter herding were introduced: Allan was always in the van of these and anxious to try them. He imported sheep, he sowed rye grass and red clover, and he planted three different types of potato on his land. Then he used his influence as factor to coerce others into copying him. This ought to have transformed life for young Kingsburgh and his fellow islanders, but in the Hebrides it is not enough to try to farm by the book. Inertia among the islanders, coupled with Allan's own lack of ability as a manager, ruined some of his schemes, and bad weather and depressed prices nationally took

*Charles Edward Stuart, after J.B. Lemoyne, 1746
(Courtesy Scottish National Portrait Gallery)*

*Flora MacDonald, painted by Allan
Ramsay in 1749 (Courtesy Ashmolean
Museum, Oxford)*

The meeting of Flora and Prince Charles Edward Stuart, by A. Johnston (Courtesy Walker Art Gallery, National Museums and Galleries on Merseyside)

Cairn erected by Clan Donald to mark Flora's birthplace at Milton, South Uist

Nunton, home of the Clanranald Chief, on the island of Benbecula, is still inhabited

Detail from an advertisement offering a reward of £30,000 for the capture of the 'son of the Pretender' (Courtesy Scottish National Portrait Gallery)

The Agreable Contrast, a pro-Jacobite engraving, by W. Ebersley, compares the Prince and Flora with the Duke of Cumberland and a town trollop as a sleek greyhound might compare with an ungainly elephant (Courtesy Scottish National Portrait Gallery)

Prince Charles Edward disguised as Betty Burke, by J. Williams (Courtesy West Highland Museum, Fort William)

The inside front cover and title page of Volume 3 of The Lyon in Mourning. On the inside cover are pasted a piece of one of Betty Burke's blue velvet garters, a piece of her dress and a small part of one of her apron strings (Courtesy National Library of

The man in charge of the hunt for the Prince in the Hebrides was Lieutenant-General John Campbell, later 4th Duke of Argyll, by Thomas Gainsborough (Courtesy Scottish National Portrait Gallery)

William Augustus, Duke of Cumberland, after Sir Joshua Reynolds (Courtesy Scottish National Portrait Gallery)

Commodore Thomas Smith commanded the Royal Navy ships searching for the Prince (Courtesy National Maritime Museum, London)

Flora meeting Dr Johnson at Kingsburgh during his visit to Skye in 1773 (from Boswell's Tour of the Hebrides*)*

A bomb ketch (left), similar to HMS Furnace, *with other ships in a fresh breeze (Courtesy National Maritime Museum, London)*

Parting of Flora MacDonald and Prince Charlie (From Ascanius; or the Young Adventurer, *supposed to have been written by the Prince himself)*

John Wilkes with the cap of Liberty on a pole, the print on the wall of the bedroom in which Dr Samuel Johnson slept at Kingsburgh

Flodigarry, home of Allan and Flora. Five of their seven children were born here (Courtesy John Campbell)

Kingsburgh House, where Prince Charlie stayed (Courtesy John Campbell)

Monkstadt, home of the Chief of Sleat

The port of Leith, where Flora was held prisoner aboard HMS Eltham *and HMS* Bridgewater *during the autumn of 1746, by J Wassell (Courtesy National Maritime Museum, London)*

5

Together with all the Bonds & Securities for the Same now lying in the hands
of certain Trustees and Friends of hers in England *Surrogating*
and Substituting the said Allan Macdonald & foresaids in her full
right & place of the premises with power to him and his foresaids
to ask pursue for and receive the said princll Sum & (agents thereof
above assigned) and to grant Discharges in their own names upon
receipt thereof in whole or in part and in Generale every other thing
concerning the Premises to do use & exerce that the sd Mrs Flory Mac
:donald her self might have done before the granting of this present Assignation
And it is hereby provided & declared That albeit the present marriage
shall dissolve within year & day after Solemnizing thereof (which was on the Sixth day
of Novemr last by past) by the death of either party without a living Child procreate
thereof Yet the haill provisions & Settlements before specified conceived in favours
of either party shall stand good & effectuall, and shall not return to the granter
any Law, Statute or Practic to the contrary, notwithstanding *And lastly*
It is hereby Provided that Execution shall pass & be direct hereon at the instance
of Angus Macdonald of Milntown or his nearest male relation being past Twenty
five years of age against the said Allan Macdonald for implementing the
provisions conceived in favours of the sd Mrs Flory Macdonald & the Children of
this Marriage *Consenting to the Registration* hereof in the Books
of Councill & Session or any others Competent to have the Strength of a Decreet
of either of the Judges thereof Interpon'd hereto That Letters of horning on Six
days and other Execution necessary may be direct thereon as Effeirs & thereto they
constitute
Their Procrs *In Witness* whereof these presents are Written on this
and the four preceeding pages of Stampt paper by John Maclean Surgeon in
Isle of Skye, and Subscribed by both Parties date foresaid Before these Witnesses
Captain Donald Macdonald of Castletown Hugh Macdonald of Armadale & Mr sd
John Maclean Witnesses also to the word on the Margine of the fourth or preceeding
page Donald Macdonald Witness
Hugh Macdonald Wittness
John Maclean Witness

Flory macdonald
Allan McDonald

A page of Allan and Flora MacDonald's marriage contract, signed by Allan, Flora, and Allan's father, Alexander MacDonald of Kingsburgh, and witnessed by Donald MacDonald, Hugh MacDonald of Armadale and Dr John MacLean who wrote the document. The document can be seen at Sir Walter Scott's home at Abbotsford (Courtesy Mrs Patricia Maxwell-Scott, OBE)

Flora MacDonald, painted by Richard Wilson in London in 1747 (Courtesy Scottish National Portrait Gallery)

Allan MacDonald of Kingsburgh, Flora's husband (from MacInnes's Brave Sons of Skye)

MARRIAGES and BIRTHS.

Nov. 6. AT Armadale, in Sleat, Allan Macdonald, eldeſt ſon of Alexander Macdonald of Kingſburgh, married to Miſs Flora Macdonald, daughter of Ronald Macdonald of Milton, deceas'd. This is the young Lady who aided the eſcape of the young Chevalier. [xi. 630.]

The announcement of the marriage of Allan and Flora in The Scots Magazine

The MacDonald boys, Sir Alexander and Sir James, by Jeremiah Davison, demonstrating that by the middle of the eighteenth century chiefs had forsaken warlike pursuits for golf and hunting (Courtesy Scottish National Portrait Gallery)

Sir Alexander MacDonald, Chief of Sleat 1719–46 (Private collection)

Lady Margaret MacDonald, by Jeremiah Davison (Private collection)

Letter from Edmund MacQueen to MacKenzie of Delvine which accompanied the sample of Johnnie's handwriting (Courtesy National Library of Scotland)

Sample of young Johnnie's handwriting (Courtesy National Library of Scotland) care of most of the others. Even the mighty Forfeited Estates Commission, for all its authority and power, could not legislate for that, so Allan slowly felt himself being sucked deeper into a quicksand of debt.

Flora's and Allan's family commitment increased also: at Flodigarry two more children were added to their brood, a third son, Ranald, born on 16 August 1756, and a fourth, James, on 30 September the following year. Allan and Flora now had four sons and a daughter, all under six years of age – it was a considerable handling alongside the responsibility Allan felt they had for his ailing parents at Kingsburgh on the other side of the Quiraing. But they struggled on, as people often do under the burden of debt and misfortune until change is forced upon them.

On 18 March 1759 old Mrs MacDonald died and her passing was duly reported in *The Scots Magazine*:

> Mar 18. At Kingsburgh, in the Isle of Sky, in the 63rd year of her age, Mrs Florence Macdonald, daughter of John Macdonald of Castleton, and wife of Alexander Macdonald of Kingsburgh.[7]

She was laid to rest wrapped in the sheet on which the Prince had slept the night he stayed as her guest at Kingsburgh House. Allan and Flora now had no choice but to return to Kingsburgh to live, and Flora found herself pregnant again when they packed their belongings to retrace their path back to the house in which they had started their life together with so much hope eight years earlier. The baby, a fifth boy, was born on 30 October and they named him John.

The Flodigarry years swallowed up the whole of the fortune Flora had brought as a dowry, and the bleak possibility of failure now haunted them: what hurt most was the fact that there were some who delighted to see young Kingsburgh taken down. Allan managed to hold on to his tack of Flodigarry until Martinmas 1763, when the Martins obtained their revenge by winning it back for Martin Martin's son, Lieutenant John Martin, who purchased the stock from Allan but refused to pay for all the improvements that young Kingsburgh had made to the property.[8] On 18 November 1763, ten days before Martinmas term day, Allan wrote to lawyer MacKenzie in Edinburgh to complain about this meanness:

> Is it not a hard case that Martin Martin my successor to this tack will not buy the houses on this tack after I have been at a good deal of trouble and expence . . . to make the principal house lodgable.[9]

A disappointed Allan continued to push ahead with his modern farming ideas at Kingsburgh, but with no more success than he had experienced at Flodigarry, and by the time the young Chief, Sir James MacDonald, came of age in 1763 and returned to Skye after an absence of sixteen years, he found much that displeased him.

Sir James was worried about the deteriorating condition of his clansmen: he told MacKenzie of Delvine that the 'desolate state of the country calls loudly for some improvement,' but although he had offered to drain land at low cost, the tenants, especially those at the lower end of the social scale, rejected such help. This was not entirely due to shortsightedness (although there was an important element of that in their refusal), they just could not afford even the addition of seven per cent to their rents which the chief demanded to cover the cost of the work. All sought long leases, he complained, but did not want to pay their rent, so that by July 1763, he told Delvine, he had just succeeded in gathering in rents due the previous November.[10]

Sir James had his own ideas for improving his estates and earning higher rents by introducing 'most industrious people' from the island of Lewis. 'The islands can only be improved by Highlanders', he told MacKenzie, and, to that end, he wanted to send young men to the mainland to learn new farming methods.[11] He let out his land in very small portions so that nearly everybody who wanted some could have it, despite the fact that the Forfeited Estates Commission policy at the time was to organize larger farming units, and there was no hope of these minuscule holdings providing a family with a living. Sleat refused to give his tenants long leases, as Allan requested, giving the excuse that he did not know the people well enough. To cap it all, when the time came for a tenant to relinquish a lease, Sir James refused to give compensation for improvements made during the tenancy.

The best of Sir James's 'improvements' were no better than Allan's own, and some were a lot less practical. The basic problem was that Sir James was neither cut out to be a chief in the pre-1745 order of the clans, nor to be a landlord in the evolving new Highlands. Having been educated in the south he did not have the quality of paternalism needed for an old-style chief, neither was he sufficiently in tune with modern methods to know how to run a great estate. Sir James MacDonald was a cultured man and a scholar who had been on the Grand Tour of Europe. He was a brilliant mathematician, philosopher and linguist, excelling in 'every other branch of useful and polite learning', but he was far from strong physically.

Unfortunately he was also very much under the thumb of his doting mother, who took many of the decisions and was the real Chief of Sleat through the two decades after Prince Charlie's Rising.

Allan became the focus of much of his chief's criticism and, worse still, of the anger of Sleat's mother. Lady Margaret was besotted with James, to the complete exclusion of her other son. The sun rose and set on James and she could see no wrong in anything he did. To her son's complaints on their return to the island in 1763 Lady Margaret was quick to add her own. 'Everything in this Country in confusion', she told MacKenzie in Edinburgh, 'the falling off of Kingsburgh's resolution and activity is so very remarkable for some years . . . all gone to rack and ruin despite his annual salary.' She then turned on faithful old Kingsburgh: 'He has been blinded by his son and the indolences of old age and his own family's want of disscretion.'[12]

Surprisingly, in the light of this, the Sleat Chief awarded the old factor an annuity of £50 with a glowing testimonial to the 'long and faithful services done and performed by him to my deceased father and myself during my minority, when he was one of my tutors and curators'. The money, the chief said, was 'for making his old age placid and confortable'. It provided a welcome fillip to the meagre income now coming into Kingsburgh House, but of course it had the effect of generating even more jealousy against the favoured MacDonalds of Kingsburgh.[13]

All this carping criticism was heaped on top of the many terrible burdens that Allan and Flora had to bear already: they were in dire straits, yet were responsible for Kingsburgh who was now a weary old man, and in addition to their own half a dozen children they had to support Allan's widowed sister, Anne, and her large family until she remarried. Anne's second husband was Lachlan MacKinnon of Corriechatachain.

It is hardly surprising that the last of Flora's fortune vanished and Allan was now deeply in debt and unable to earn enough to support his extended family. The financial situation at Kingsburgh House was as topsy-turvy as it was ridiculous, with Sir James still paying interest to Kingsburgh on bonds owed to his father, although the factor now owed the Chief money. Lady Margaret accused Kingsburgh of buying up these bonds from other people with the Chief's own money, presumably rents. Poor old Kingsburgh was no longer the 'man well known for his integrity, honesty and prudence', on whose behalf she had written letters pleading for mercy in 1746: now she said 'many parts of Kingsburgh's conduct will be no rule for mine'. Her son was equally spiteful, saying to MacKenzie on 16 October 1763 that 'Kinsburgh's family are much disappointed that the whole country is not divided among themselves, and several people put to beggary on their account.'[14] Of course there were valid reasons for the Chief's complaint: Allan, always rather feckless in financial matters, had spent huge sums of the Chief's money introducing new stock and methods, which had failed, just as money expended on his own behalf had done. The failures cannot be blamed on bad or ineffectual management though: Allan's faults were compounded by the terrible Skye climate and poor cattle prices then prevailing everywhere in the Highlands. There was plenty of sense in his ideas, but not enough common sense in implementing them. Lady Margaret and young Sleat saw only that the factor's modern methods had cost them much money and decided that action had to be taken at once.

Allan was not a very careful manager of his master's money. In July 1763 he had to enclose a letter when he sent the accounts to MacKenzie in Edinburgh, saying, 'Receive inclosed the last accounts which I see is not right ballanced, but I did not observe it untill I received Kingsborough's letter as I did not look at it once I left Edinburgh.'[15] It has to be admitted that Allan was disorganized, or (to use a Scottish word) 'throughother'. On the credit side, however, he was a compassionate man who devoted much of that same letter to asking MacKenzie to intercede on behalf of the MacDonald factor in Uist who had lost his wife and fallen on hard times.

Allan fought back against the criticism of Sleat and his mother, calling on MacKenzie to plead for him from time to time. The Edinburgh lawyer must often have helped to turn away their wrath. The pleas became almost pathetic. In October 1763 Allan wrote, 'It woud be charity in you to say something for us or Such of us as have not egregriously offended Sir James MacDonald.'[16] A month later, asking Delvine to intervene to secure the transfer of the tack of Kingsburgh from his father to himself, Allan told the lawyer, 'as you are my family's patron and best friend I cannot help troubling you when I have anything to say relating to my poor family'. Young Kingsburgh never needed his mentor more badly than now because he was too frightened to approach his Chief directly. He told MacKenzie:

> This [the question of the tack] I did not sujest to my master Sir James Macdonald as I saw him so hurried at Broadford and that I was afraid he had been angry at me throw the ill will and envey that others bear to me and my father.[17]

Weighed down by worry as he was, embers of ambition still glowed somewhere deep within Allan because he told MacKenzie:

I am determined to begin immediately to inclose, plant and set quicksets and to build all my office housis with stone and lime. I mean barns, byres and miln, which I hope will be mentioned in the tack so that I may not altogether lose there value of them at the expiration of it [the tack].[18]

Allan MacDonald must have been almost the only man in Skye with hope in his heart during these barren 1760s when there was little to lighten anyone's load of worry. Even news of the death of 'Butcher' Cumberland in 1764 brought little joy to the island, where the processes of change propelled forward by the victor of Culloden ground on as surely as ever. Time was bound to have changed the clan system, but the process might have been a gradual one had it not been for the swift, painful economic revolution that followed the suppression of the Jacobites. The chiefs had already exchanged their role of 'father' of their clans for that of overbearing and often absentee landlord, and new ways from the south were swiftly rotting the fabric of a way of life that had endured for centuries.

One consequence of this was that the tacksman's role was withering away since the clan chief no longer had power to raise an army and no longer needed someone to organize his clansmen. The tacksman became a mere second landlord, renting the land and subletting it to families – a middleman who was of no use to the chiefs. The clansman no longer had the tacksman to protect him, so the chief and his factor could do exactly as they liked, and what they 'liked' was to squeeze higher rents in return for nothing, or next to nothing.

Season by season life deteriorated for the people of the island until there came that year of grief: 1766 proved disastrous for everyone – for the Jacobites, for Clan Donald and for Allan and Flora MacDonald too. But first the briefest sunburst of happiness lightened the gloom at Kingsburgh House. During the autumn of 1765 the unexpected had happened – after a gap of nearly seven years and in her forty-fourth year, Flora again found herself carrying a child. She accepted motherhood so late in life as calmly as she faced every other unlooked-for event in her life, and on 6 May 1766 her seventh and last child, a girl, was born. They named her Frances, but she was always known as Fanny within the family. Flora's family was now complete.

Fanny's arrival was also a reminder that the family was growing up. Charles, the oldest, was now fourteen, and would soon be of an age to make his own way in the world, and this gave Flora and Allan cause for sadness since they realized that there would be no living for him at Kingsburgh. Although Charles was still a boy they had already thought of trying to buy him an army commission, but this had as yet come to nothing. Anne was now twelve years of age and growing into a fine girl who could help her mother, while the four younger boys were eleven, nine, eight and six. Flora's and Allan's minds might have been sorely troubled over how they could feed, educate and set so large a brood up in the world, but they had much for which to be thankful. They could congratulate themselves that, in those times when every churchyard was filled with pathetic memorials to children who had been gathered up by famine or disease, they had managed to raise half a dozen healthy youngsters.

That year there was a reminder for Flora of the events that had made her famous twenty years earlier. On New Year's Day 1766 James Stuart, the old King over the Water, died, bringing to an end a reign that had spanned nearly sixty-five years, spent totally in exile and hope, although that hope burned as a wan flame during Jamie Stuart's bleak final years. His son, Charles, had refused to come to Rome to visit him after the disaster of Culloden because he felt that his father had betrayed him. In the two decades since Flora escorted him over the sea to Skye and to safety, Charles Stuart had had many adventures. He had roamed Europe first as the Bonnie Prince, then as the Wild Man, living for years with Clementina Walkinshaw, his mistress – or wife, as she surely was in Scots law – and their daughter, Charlotte. But after much cruel treatment, Clementina had taken her daughter and left him, so it was a lonely, middle-aged man who travelled to Rome in 1766 to claim his inheritance. There the Pope refused to recognize Charles as King of Britain. The Prince responded by huffing and puffing around Italy, powerless to assert his right to be called king but causing as much trouble as he could. His claim by now was as dead as the traditional Highland way of life that he had helped to destroy.

For Clan Donald even more devastating news came from Italy that summer, when their own Chief, young Sir James, died there. Sir James MacDonald of Sleat had never been a strong man, and his health, already poor, was further damaged as a result of a mishap while hunting in Uist in which he was accidentally shot in the leg by MacLeod of Talisker, the man who had arranged Flora's arrest in 1746. In 1766 Sir James went to Europe in search of better health, but his condition deteriorated as the journey progressed, until he was forced to stop at Rome. From there he wrote to his mother on 9 July to tell her he was glad she was not there to see how sick he was, although he said the doctor still gave him hope.[19] A second letter, written at Frascati on the 25th of the same month, told a very different story. He now informed his mother of the terrible pain he had been suffering for weeks and made it clear to her that he knew he was dying: 'I have settled my affairs, after my death, with as much distinctness as the hurry and the nature of the thing could admit of', he told her. He had appointed an executor in Rome and MacKenzie of Delvine was to look after his affairs in Scotland. The following day he died and his letter reached Lady Margaret along with the news of his death.[20] He was just twenty-four years old.

While Skye mourned, Allan and Flora MacDonald had sorrows of their own to grieve over. Shortly before Sir James died matters had come to a head and, with MacKenzie of Delvine no longer able to protect him, Allan was dismissed from his post as factor. This was a devastating blow to young Kingsburgh's pride, and when he visited Edinburgh towards the end of the year he could not face calling on his old mentor. The lawyer wrote an angry letter to which Allan replied on 22 January 1767.[21]

Young Kingsburgh's response was rambling and strange, obviously written in a state of great anguish and, like a cornered animal, he fought back. Allan admitted he had been foolish to avoid the lawyer but told MacKenzie, 'It woud be greater Charity in any man who professes friendship for me, my poor wife and seven children to recommend me to the man on whome all my dependence is.' The clear inference is that he thought the lawyer might have done more to protect him from the chief's wrath and the backbiting of his enemies.

Having made this sour gibe, Allan could not stop himself from pouring out his troubles to his old and respected friend, explaining his concern for his father and his family, all except Flora who, apart from a passing mention as 'my poor wife' at the beginning of the letter and as the children's mother later, was never referred to. It was as if he knew there was no need to worry about Flora, because she would cope calmly with the problems as usual and quietly work towards their solution. He had been criticized for trying to obtain an army commission for his son Charles. People had been jealous of his father's pension, but by the time the rents of Kingsburgh and Monkstadt had been paid his father had only £14 10s. a year left to pay for his keep and that of a servant. Not that he minded, Allan added quickly: 'Should he not pay a farthing he woud be excessive welcom with me.'

Allan then set out the facts of his dismissal as he saw them. 'I went with integrity and ane honest heart about my . . . master's business, while I managed it for Eleven years', he told Delvine, 'and tho I fell so deeply in his areers, yet I . . . had no Dishonest plan at heart.' He claimed that he had proposed to relinquish his factor's post in 1765 when he owed only £360 and he saw a particularly bad year for cattle droving ahead, but he was not allowed to. As a result his indebtedness to the chief soared:

> The factory was keept in my hands and that very year haveing Twenty Eight hundred Cattle bought; and after disposing of them and Ballanceing the Transactions of the Season, there plainly appeared £1354 13s – of a Ballance that my List of Buying inclueding the Driveing expence exceeded my list of Selling.

To us today it seems madness and utter recklessness on Allan's part to have bought 2,800 cattle, almost the equal of Skye's entire cattle export, at a time when prices were so uncertain, but young Kingsburgh always seems to have lacked the common sense that might have saved him from tumbling over the edge of the precipice of disaster. He had totally overstretched his chief's resources and paid the price by being dismissed.

When a good year appeared to lie ahead with every chance of making up much of his losses, Allan told the lawyer, he was summoned to Edinburgh. He went at his own expense to settle the accounts and draw up a plan for his successor. With the help of his father and Flora's stepfather he carried this out to the letter, only to be further humiliated. Proclamations were nailed to church doors warning clansmen not to sell Allan MacDonald cattle as the bills would not be honoured. Instead the chief ordered that the cattle should be given to Charles McSween, 'a cheating fellow who . . . that very year trip't of . . . to Antigua haveing his pockets lined with honest mens money' – including Sleat rents!

Regarding his own debts to the chief, he had by now paid back a large part of the money and promised to clear the remainder by August of the following year, but in the meantime he needed security of tenure and here he threw himself once again on to the good offices of his friend. He told MacKenzie:

> Now Dr Sir, if I have not intyrely merited your displeasure, will you not put in a favourable word for me to help throw the getting me a lace of this Tack which would encourage me to go on cheerfully with my little improvements, and help the education of my family who are now growing men and women on my hands, the oldest boy being

fifteen and the lassie thirteen and so on to the youngest – in short was there anything in the world thrown in my way which woud help their own and mothers suport I would chearfully submitt to any slavery to better them.

He was allowed to stay on at Kingsburgh, but at a greatly increased rent. Without the burden of managing the Sleat estates, Allan now settled down to look after his Kingsburgh and Monkstadt lands and his large family. He could feel easier in his mind at least that he no longer had to deal with the Chief or his mother on a daily basis. However his financial situation was not improved, for Skye remained an unhappy island of which one tacksman spoke for all when he described it as a Gehenna of misery, a place of torment from which families were being driven because they could not pay the chiefs' high rents.

PART TWO

To Carolina and War

CHAPTER NINE

A Wake for Skye

This is the best poor man's country I have ever heard in this age.

Letter from Alexander McAllister, North Carolina,
to Angus McCuaig, Islay[1]

The new chief was Sir Alexander MacDonald, younger brother of Sir James, and was different from his brother in almost every way possible. Alexander, who held a commission in the Guards, had been educated at Eton but was no scholar; he disliked Scotland and had no interest in Skye or in his clansmen, other than as a source of income. Clansmen saw little hope for their island under his chieftainship because he seldom visited his estates, and when he did he could not wait to be away again. Sandy MacDonald had a mind of his own and no one could tame him, least of all his mother who had become alienated from him because she had neglected him and poured out all her love on James. On his deathbed James MacDonald was well aware of the storm that would follow his death, and he ended his final, sad letter home by telling his mother that he had ordered lawyer MacKenzie 'to make you and my younger brother as independent of the eldest as possible'.[2]

Lady Margaret tried to give the new chief advice, much of it channelled through MacKenzie. She told Delvine she wanted her son to leave the Guards to live in Scotland, but she had little hope of his heeding her for she ended her letter with a despairing plea: 'Marry him if you can to some decent discreet woman of family.'[3]

Young Sir Alexander did marry into a good family. The new Lady MacDonald was Elizabeth Bosville from Yorkshire, a distant kinswoman of James Boswell. But marriage did nothing to calm Sandy MacDonald down. Lady Margaret was alternately ignored by him or told not to meddle. She wrote to MacKenzie in despair on 9 December 1766 on black-edged paper, for she was still mourning James: 'Sandy's behaviour to me would be a great woe if I had any sorrow to spare.'[4]

Sir Alexander's greed fed the fires of misery among all his clansmen, and these were further fuelled by cattle plague in 1769 and plummeting prices the following year. Then in 1771 Skye suffered what became known as the Black Spring: on the heels of a very severe autumn through which the island was scoured by continuous rain and wind from harvest until the beginning of the new year, winter brought snow that lay for two months. Grain ran out, leaving the starving clansmen without seed to sow. Their cows died from cattle blight, hunger or exposure, and that spring people were reduced to eating carrion. During the following summer the traveller, Thomas Pennant, saw the results of that awful spring when he visited Skye during his tour of the Hebrides. Five thousand cattle, more than the island's entire annual export trade, had perished and the suffering was heart-rending.

'The poor are left to Providence's care: they prowl like other animals along the shores to pick up limpets and other shell-fish, the casual repasts of hundreds during part of the year in these unhappy islands,' Pennant recorded.[5] Not that this was the only year or the only part of the Highlands that suffered starvation. 'The produce of the crops very rarely are in any degree proportioned to the wants of the inhabitants: golden seasons have happened, when they have superfluity; but the years of famine are as ten to one.'[6] Near Kingsburgh he saw one fine crop, a sight so unusual that he described the field as 'laughing with corn'.[7]

Over a period of twelve years the island's rents had doubled or trebled, yet its trade had decreased to a few thousand cattle. 'Cattle is at present the only trade of the island: about four thousand are annually sold, from forty shillings to three pounds a head', he said.[8]

By Pennant's time the better-off tacksmen, the only people who could afford the passage money, saw emigration to the colonies of America as their only escape. They were pushed to make the journey by economic circumstances, and pulled by the wonderful stories that came back to them in letters from family and friends who had already made the break. This good news gave hope – the only hope possible – to many islanders. As a result, throughout the second half of the 1760s, emigration fever spread like a great contagion through the south-west Highlands, across the Argyll mainland and southern Hebridean islands and northward into Skye, until no one could escape it. Everyone who had the slightest hope of raising the money (and many others who could not) wanted to leave. Large numbers were prepared to sell their freedom to any employer who would take them as indentured servants, or even to a ship's captain who would give them a free passage across the Atlantic and recoup the expense of the voyage by indenturing them to some settler in America.

The Carolinas were particularly popular with Skye people because a very large number of their own kin were already settled there, especially in North Carolina. In 1739 350 settlers, mainly from Kintyre and the islands of Islay and Gigha, had established themselves in the colony, with a number settling in the vicinity of Cross Creek, more than a hundred miles up the Cape Fear River, around the present-day city of Fayetteville. Because of their Kintyre origins they became known as the Argyll Colony and their chief trading centre was Campbellton, later renamed Fayetteville in honour of the French general La Fayette.

The Argyll colonists were mainly Gaelic-speaking Presbyterians led by men of standing: the leaders had been tacksmen in Scotland who took their tenants with them. Among these were Alexander McAlister of Balinakill, Neil MacNeill of Ardelay, Duncan Campbell of Kilduskland and James Campbell, brother of Alexander Campbell of Balole in Islay. They quickly became respected leaders in the colony, and the reports they sent back home attracted new immigrants in growing numbers as rising rents began to drive more and more Highlanders from their land. The result was a push-pull effect: higher rents and poor farming pushed while glowing reports from successful settlers pulled, until a great wave of emigration swept the Highlands during the decade from 1765–75.[9]

Allan and Flora MacDonald could not fail to hear these reports and feel envious. Might their future not lie in America too? Yet emigration was an impossible dream because they could not leave Allan's aged father, so they soldiered on, trying to eke out a living and do the best they could for their family.

The children were growing up, and by 1771 it became a matter of urgency to find a settled future for the older ones and to ensure that the younger ones received the best possible preparation for life. Flora's strong character showed through in solving this problem. She never had been a woman to sit back and wait for others to help her, but had taken charge of her fate when she was held prisoner; she had won over her enemies when they questioned her; she had shown an unwavering sense of duty which gained her many friends and brought a considerable fortune from admirers; and now she took control of the situation when it came time to seek help for her children.

MacKenzie of Delvine respected Flora for all these qualities. He had always been a good friend to the Kingsburgh family, inordinately fond of old Alexander MacDonald and attached to Allan too. He had watched Allan grow up, and was thus well aware of the young man's faults and virtues and, though often irritated and disappointed by the first, he realized that, underneath, Allan was a hard worker and had a kind heart. The lawyer's fine hand may be unseen, but it is surely present in the settling of Flora's oldest children, Charles, Anne, Ranald and John.

Lady Margaret had shown little love for the young Kingsburghs – especially Allan and Flora – in recent years, yet she was persuaded to help secure a commission for Charles in the East India Company, and Lady Primrose paid for the boy's outfitting and passage. A commission was obtained for Ranald in the Marines 'through good Capt Charles Douglas of the Ardent Ship of War', who used his influence at the Admiralty on Ranald's behalf.[10] He joined the Service in 1773.[11]

In 1771 Johnnie, a bright lad, was approaching his twelfth birthday and was in need of the kind of education he could not receive in Skye – the training for life that Allan had been given in the capital. The one man who could arrange this was MacKenzie of Delvine, but Allan was, as usual, reluctant to beg help, so it was left to Flora to write the letter asking for the lawyer's assistance. MacKenzie agreed that when the boy was ready he should come to the High School in Edinburgh where he himself would supervise his studies.

Old Kingsburgh was grateful to his friend and, now too infirm to hold a pen himself, he dictated a letter of thanks to Delvine for his kindness, 'and in Particular for Continuing the old friendship which you ever had for me and my family by thinking of taking the Boy Johnny'. He assured MacKenzie that his grandson was a sensible, well-inclined boy and promised to send a specimen of the lad's handwriting soon.[12]

A couple of months later the sample of Johnnie's handwriting was duly forwarded to Delvine, accompanied by a letter from Edmund MacQueen, Johnnie's teacher in Portree. Once again it was Flora who had arranged this. MacQueen was canny with his praise, as one might expect from a Scottish dominie, and wrote:

> Mrs McDonald of Kingsborrow has enjoined me at your desire to send you a Specimen of her son John's handwriting, which you will receive enclosed and tho it is not such as I could wish, yet it [is] as good as can be expected from one of his age considering the shortness of the time he has been at it particularly when it is but a bywork, being busy at the Latin – he reads Eutropius & gets the Grammer.

His genius is tolerably good with application suitable to his years. I am pretty well satisfied with the progress he has made, if you give any directions about him I shall follow them as far as I don't find them clash with the natural bent of his genius.

I am w^t the utmost respect, Sir.

Your very humble serv^t

Edmund McQueen[13]

Johnnie wrote twice in a large sprawling copperplate hand the words:

Art has no enemy like an

This was part of the Latin proverb 'Art has no enemy like an ignorant person'. Underneath the boy confirmed that this was his own work by signing his name, John MacDonald, in a crowded signature.[14]

The following August, by which time Flora's own future plans were settled at last, Johnnie went off to Edinburgh, a letter from his mother in his pocket for MacKenzie. In it she had written:

Dr Sir

This goes by my Son Johnie who thank God tho I am misfortunat in other respects is happy in his haveing so good a freind as you are to take him under his protection, he seemed when here to be a good natured bidable Boy, without any kind of Vices, make of him what you please and may the Blessing of the almighty attend you alongs with him which is all the retourn I am able to make for your many and repeated freindships shown to me and this family . . .[15]

Daughter Anne presented Flora with a very different problem: the girl was just sixteen years of age, but there was no money left for a dowry that would attract a husband of the right social standing. Nonetheless it was arranged in 1771 for her to become the second wife of a forty-year-old widower, Lieutenant Alexander MacLeod. Anne's husband was the natural son of the MacLeod Chief, who had acknowledged him and had given him the tack of Waternish with a good stock of cattle, and appointed him factor for the Dunvegan estates at a salary of £70 a year. In addition MacLeod inherited £500 from one of his half-brothers. From a financial standpoint the MacLeod match was an excellent one, which could only have been achieved through someone's influence, and lawyer MacKenzie was the most likely 'broker' to have arranged it. In spite of the difference in age between the bride and bridegroom, the marriage was a happy one and produced four children.

Allan's son-in-law proved no more successful as a land agent than Allan had been and he could not cope with the old chief's extravagance. As a result, when the MacLeod Chief died in 1772, it was discovered that his estates were in a muddle and he was deeply in debt. The laird's successor was his grandson, Norman, whose father had died in India several years earlier. The boy was left to sort out the confusion, which led to a lawsuit in Edinburgh over a bond for £1,000 which Alexander's father had given him to be paid for 'services' after the old laird's death. The action was a typical family dispute, with a suggestion that the old laird's heir, young Norman, persuaded him to annul the bond on his deathbed. Allan wrote to MacKenzie of Delvine in November 1772, asking him to give his son-in-law all the help he could when the matter came to court. He told Delvine 'The trustees for young MacLeod . . . gave [the old man] neither peace nor rest in time of his last sickness till he (with reluctance) signed a deed . . . dismantling the above bond.' Allan added that Alexander's antagonists were 'powerful and strong', so he would require 'all the friendship and good advice that possibly can be given him'.[16] The following year young Norman paid £100 – perhaps as much as he could afford – and Alexander resigned the factorship, sold up his tack and prepared to sail to North Carolina.

While all this was happening attitudes to emigration were beginning to change, subtly at first, but then more obviously, because the Government was coming to realize that emigration was draining Scotland of her finest people and much of her capital. A MacLeod party from Skye, who petitioned the Privy Council in London for a grant of 40,000 acres in North Carolina, was refused on the grounds that their going would impoverish the island. Yet one thing did not alter: the people themselves remained as anxious to leave as ever.

The authorities were right, of course. Skye was so short of successful tacksmen that the Chief of Sleat was being forced to bring in clansmen from the mainland to take over abandoned tacks. The incomers fared no better than those they replaced, for the Chief could not import new weather with them!

While the islanders starved, and chiefs and Government curbed emigration, the North Carolina authorities, under Governor William Tryon, were encouraging it, and islanders continued to plan their escape to the paradise of the Cape Fear Valley. Among the most enthusiastic singers of North Carolina's praises was Alexander Campbell of Balole, in Islay, whose brother had been among the original Argyll Colony immigrants of 1739. In the early 1770s Balole was very active promoting the colony. During the summer of 1771 *The Scots Magazine* quoted from a letter, written in February that year, that could well have referred to him:

We are informed from the western isles, that upwards of 500 souls from Islay, and the adjacent islands, prepare to migrate next summer to America, under the conduct of a gentleman of wealth and merit whose predecessors resided in Islay for many centuries past; and that there is a large colony of the most wealthy and substantial people in Sky, making ready to follow the example of the Argathelians in going to the fertile and cheap lands on the other side of the Atlantic ocean. [17]

In the early 1770s Balole was very active in promoting the colony. He may well have been Scotus Americanus, author of one of the most widely circulated pamphlets on emigration to North Carolina which appeared in Scotland in 1773.[18]

Campbell of Balole was in contact with Lachlan MacKinnon of Corriechatachain, second husband of Allan MacDonald's sister, Anne, about this time, painting a very flattering picture of North Carolina. Balole told MacKinnon that at Cross Creek each Highlander had a plantation of his own and they 'live as happy as princes, they have liberty & property & no Excise, no dread of their being turned out of their lands by Tyrants, each has as good a Charter as a D. of Argyle, or a Sir A. Macdonald, and only pay half a Crown a year for 100 Acres'.[19]

Among those who left Skye at this time were Flora's stepfather, 'One-eyed' Hugh of Armadale, whose wife had died sometime prior to 1771, and her half-sister, Annabella, with her husband, Alexander MacDonald of Cuidreach, and their family. Because they were refused a grant of land, they had to pool their assets and charter a ship for the party. Kingsburgh's letter of thanks to MacKenzie of Delvine for agreeing to take Johnnie was delivered by James MacDonald on his way to London to charter a ship to carry the emigrants to Carolina.

Flora and Allan desired nothing more than to go with them and, ironically, only months after their kinsmen left for Carolina, the last obstacle to prevent them from leaving fell away – old Kingsburgh 'slumbered away in death' on 18 January 1772. Allan sent the news at once to his father's old friend, MacKenzie, and *The Scots Magazine* duly recorded the event for those who still remembered all that had happened a generation before (but giving the wrong date):

> Feb 13. At Kingsburgh, in the
> island of Sky, in the 83rd year of
> his age, Alexander Macdonald, esq;
> of Kingsburgh. – Our readers will
> remember this gentleman's hospitality
> to the young pretender in 1746, his
> sufferings on that account, and his
> bold avowal of what he had done, when
> in a situation that would have
> intimidated a man of less resolution.[20]

Bishop Forbes was even more generous, writing of the 'hospitable, disinterested and worthy . . . Kingsborrow':

> Let all the world say what they can,
> He liv'd and died an honest man.[21]

The Kingsburghs lost no time in setting final preparations in motion for the journey to Carolina and it was Flora, ever practical, rather than Allan who now took command. The Kingsburgh tack had to be disposed of and provision made for the children still at home: seventeen-year-old Alexander, fourteen-year-old James and little Fanny, now six.

While all this was happening a belated, brief, brilliant star shot across the Jacobite sky – Charles Edward Stuart married Princess Louise of Stolberg, and hopes rose momentarily among those who still clung to the belief that the King over the Water would one day reign in Edinburgh. It was a forlorn hope, for the marriage proved a disaster from the outset, with Louise turning the ageing drunkard Charlie into a sorry cuckold when she eloped with an Italian poet. Even the Jacobite world now lost hope that Charles Edward Stuart would ever reign.

Visitors still came to Kingsburgh to see Flora, however. Pennant spent a night there on 22 July 1772, making the journey from Dunvegan 'over a black and pathless tract of moor and bog' to the shore of Loch Greshornish from where he sailed across Loch Snizort to Kingsburgh. Pennant was disappointed to find Flora away from home, but was welcomed by Allan and was given the honour of being allowed to sleep in

Prince Charles's bed. In the morning he left with several antiquarian relics as parting presents from his host, but he learned nothing about Flora MacDonald or her journey.[22]

By the following month Flora was back to see young Johnnie off to the High School in Edinburgh in the care of MacKenzie of Delvine. Flora had to write the letter that was sent with John because her husband was unwell 'with a pain in his side this ten days past'. She told MacKenzie she was sorry she could send no more than her thanks and her blessing with the boy, since Kingsburgh was in such desperate financial straits.

In this same letter she was able to tell him that they had made up their minds to follow their friends to America. There was a terrible sadness in every word she wrote:

> There will soon be no remembrance of my family in this miserable Island, the best of its inhabitance are already making ready to follow their freinds to America, while they have anything to bring them and among the rest we are to go . . . as we cannot promise ourselves but poverty and oppression.

They had lost 327 head of cattle and horses over the past three years, she informed him, and would have scarcely enough left to pay their creditors and start a new life in America.[23]

Things did not improve. Allan poured out the misery of the island in 1773, when he moaned that the islanders wallowed in a quagmire of lawsuits and backbiting that left no hope of improvement for anyone. He wrote:

> It is melancholy to see the state of this miserable place; the superior summoning the tennents to remove for not paying the great rents and the tennents the superior for oppression, for breaking the conditions of the tacks, and for violent profits. The factor and tenants at law . . . and forcing them out of their lands in the months of May and June without previous warning, no respect of persons as the best are mostly gone, stealing of sheep constantly, picking and thieving of corn, garden stuffs and potatos, perpetually lying, back byting and slandering, honesty intyrely fled, villainy and deceit supported by downright poverty, in its place. Most miserable is the state of this good and great family. When the next emigration is gone only old Aird and other three old men will be all that will be in Slate and Troternish of the name of McDonald.[24]

Pennant confirmed that emigration and poverty were leading to depopulation of the island and was unhappy about it:

> Migrations, and depression of spirit, the last a common cause of depopulation, having since the year 1750 reduced the number from fifteen thousand to between twelve and thirteen: one thousand having crossed the Atlantic, others sunk beneath poverty, or in despair, ceased to obey the first great command, ENCREASE and MULTIPLY [25]

The following year, 1773, Samuel Johnson and James Boswell arrived in Skye during their tour of the Highlands and Hebrides to find the subject of emigration a frequently recurring one. They saw ships preparing to sail and heard stories about why so many were leaving. Johnson disapproved of this denuding of the country of its people and said so several times.[26] Even before he reached Skye he was blaming the lairds for both the misery and the emigration. 'Were I a chief', he said, 'I would dress my servants better than myself, and knock a fellow down if he looked saucy to a Macdonald.'[27] And as he travelled on, observing emigrant ships and hearing about clansmen who were leaving, he saw nothing to change his mind.

By the time the travellers set foot on Skye on Thursday 2 September, both were fairly glowing with indignation. Their tempers had not been sweetened that day by the fact that they had spent a miserable last night on the mainland at an uncomfortable inn where they quarrelled. Both were in a state of mental turmoil when they landed at Armadale to be greeted by their host, none other than the Chief of Sleat, Sir Alexander MacDonald himself – one of the worst culprits. Sir Alexander and his wife were then staying at a house built by one of their tenants at Armadale, but were about to leave for Edinburgh. Although Johnson and Boswell had both known Sleat in London and had respected him then, they felt he was different here on his native heath among his clansmen.

'My fellow-traveller and I were now full of the old Highland spirit', Boswell confessed in his *Journal*, 'and were dissatisfied at hearing of racked rents and emigration, and finding a chief not surrounded by his clan.'

'Sir, the Highland chiefs should not be allowed to go farther south than Aberdeen', Johnson told Sleat.[28]

The Chief was not pleased. He was even less happy when Boswell foolishly bragged that the reason for coming to Skye was to visit Flora MacDonald. Boswell may well simply have been baiting the chief; if so, he certainly succeeded.

Johnson tried, without success, to find out more about the state of the island and, a couple of days after his first skirmish with his host, he was stung into telling Sleat 'Were I in your place, sir, in seven years I would make this an independent island. I would roast oxen whole, and hang out the flag as a signal to the Macdonalds to come and get beef and whisky.'

When Sir Alexander demurred his guest told him bluntly 'If you are born to object, I have done with you. Sir, I would have a magazine of arms.'

'They would rust', the chief retorted.

'Let there be men to keep them clean. Your ancestors did not use to let their arms rust.'[29]

Their four-day stay with the Chief and his wife was not happy, and Johnson complained afterwards about poor food, the absence of wheat bread and the lack of claret to wash it down, although they did have the consolation of a piper to play for them at breakfast and dinner. At tea Lady MacDonald affronted the doctor, accustomed to London manners, by having no tongs for the sugar – they had to use their fingers!

Several times during their stay on the island the travellers from the South twisted the knife in the Chief's ribs: when someone remarked that Sleat was frightened of the sea, Johnson retorted '*He* is frightened of the sea; and his tenants are frightened when he comes to land.'[30]

When Boswell published his *Journal* in 1785, the Chief was furious about the travellers' unfavourable comments about him. The whole business blew up into a great quarrel, which nearly led to a duel. Sleat was particularly incensed by a suggestion that the visit to Flora was their principal reason for coming to the island. MacDonald wrote:

> At your own behaviour everyone felt some degree of resentment when you told me your only errand into Skye was to visit the Pretender's conductress, and that you deemed every moment as lost which was not spent in her company.[31]

But in 1773 that was all in the future.

From Armadale the travellers moved on to Corriechatachain, where Allan MacDonald of Kingsburgh's sister, Anne, and Lachlan MacKinnon entertained them so generously that Boswell wrote how they enjoyed the 'joyous social manners' of the Highlands for the first time. Everyone spoke Gaelic and sang Gaelic songs until the great man from the South was quite forgotten, and Boswell found himself joining in the choruses.[32]

Although the hospitality there and on Raasay, which they visited next, was lavish, even by southern standards, Boswell and Johnson found the situation in the islands as deplorable as anywhere in the Highlands. They remained on Skye and Raasay for the whole of September, which gave them ample time to observe the poverty, the chiefs' attitudes and the exodus that was in progress. Just as it had been on the mainland, talk everywhere was of emigration, and the travellers saw ships preparing to sail to Carolina – the *Nestor*,[33] one of the largest vessels on the Clyde, lay at Portree, and Boswell watched the *Margaret*[34] sail past with emigrants on board. 'It was a melancholy sight', he remarked sadly. Even more shocking to them was the fact that, when they wanted to cash a bill for thirty pounds, the only place in Skye where sufficient cash could be found was on an emigrant ship moored in Loch Bracadale.[35] The captain could provide £30 easily – proof, if proof were needed, of how Skye was being stripped of its capital assets, and probably proof of the greed of the captains of the emigrant ships as well!

Boswell and Johnson spent the night of Sunday 12 September at Kingsburgh, where Flora and Allan made considerable fuss of them and Flora had the bed in which the Prince slept prepared for Johnson.

Kingsburgh met his visitors at the door and led them into his house, as proudly as if he had been a chief himself. He was 'completely the figure of a gallant Highlander', observed Boswell:

> He had his tartan plaid thrown abut him, a large blue bonnet with a knot of black ribband like a cockade, a brown short coat of a kind of duffil, a tartan waistcoat with gold buttons and gold button-holes, a bluish philibeg and tartan hose. He had jet black hair tied behind, and was a large stately man, with a steady sensible countenance.

The parlour at Kingsburgh was comfortable, with a good fire to warm the Skye evening and a dram going round. Dr Johnson's contentment was complete. When Flora appeared at supper Johnson took her hand and kissed it. 'I had the honour of saluting the far famed Miss Flora MacDonald', he told Mrs Thrale. Flora had recently returned from the mainland where she said she had heard Mr Boswell was on his way to Skye, 'a young English buck with him.' Johnson was delighted and warmed to her at once, as she did to him, and she talked to him freely. Flora's stay in the south had given her an excellent insight into southern manners, and she knew how to respond to this man who represented the world she had known in Edinburgh and London. As a result she was able to joke with Johnson and confide her story to him, as she had to none of the others who were curious to hear about Prince Charlie's journey over the sea to Skye. Flora was now fifty-one and unprepossessing in appearance, but Johnson admired her: he described her as a woman of middle stature with soft features, gentle manners and elegant presence. To Boswell's eye she appeared 'a little woman of a genteel appearance, and uncommonly mild and well-bred'. But her gentility soon took on a coquettishness as Johnson and she talked together.

Johnson had a cold hanging on him and went to bed early, but Boswell sat up late drinking punch with his host and, although the parlour was well furnished, with a good fire and plenty of drink, his mind strayed to Kingsburgh's financial problems and his intention to emigrate. Boswell consoled himself with the thought that 'so spirited a man would be very well every where'.[36]

Boswell shared the Prince's room with his travelling companion. The room was decorated with a great variety of maps and prints, and the beds in which they slept were draped with tartan curtains. Hogarth's print of John Wilkes with the cap of Liberty on a pole beside him hung on one wall – a comment on the views of Flora and Allan MacDonald, as well as on the sophistication of Highland homes. Boswell had to smile at the incongruous sight of the Englishman in the Prince's bed – unlike Sir Alexander, Boswell did not call Charles Edward 'the Pretender' because he considered that an insult to one who was still alive and thought differently.

In the morning Boswell found a slip of paper on a table with a few words in Latin pencilled on it in Johnson's handwriting. They said 'What is gold worth when weighed against virtue?' It was a great tribute to his hosts.

Flora had certainly made a conquest. At breakfast her guest, still a bit deaf because of his head cold, told everyone how much he appreciated having been given the honour of sleeping in the Prince's bed, and when Boswell suggested that he and Flora had arranged this between them, Flora just gave him a roguish reply: 'You know young bucks are always favourites of the ladies.'

The two were getting on so well that Johnson felt able to raise the question of the Prince's escape. 'Who was with him?' he asked, adding archly, 'We were told, madam, in England, there was one Miss Flora Macdonald with him.'

'They were very right', she replied, and recounted the entire story of the Prince's escape. Samuel Johnson listened, spellbound, to the end of her story, then said quietly, 'All this should be written down.' Boswell obediently recorded Flora's tale, together with details about the Prince which he gathered from others whom he met on the tour.[37]

When they left for Dunvegan, Kingsburgh – perfect Highland host to the last – accompanied them and, to save a long, uncomfortable ride on narrow roads, sent the horses ahead while he took his guests across Loch Snizort by boat. The gesture was greatly appreciated by Johnson, who grumbled, 'It is very disagreeable riding in Skye. The way is so narrow, one only at a time can travel, so it is quite unsocial; and you cannot indulge in meditation by yourself because you must be always attending to the steps which your horse takes.' When Johnson could neither talk nor think he was unhappy.[38]

As they crossed the loch they discussed the Highland dirk and Highlanders' table manners, and Johnson confessed that he always ate fish with his fingers because he was so short-sighted he was frightened of choking on the bones. Inevitably the conversation turned again to emigration. Allan still carried off the role of the capable, confident man whose misfortunes were only a temporary inconvenience and none of his own making, for Boswell mused again, as he had in the parlour the night before, that Kingsburgh would look just the same in America as he did seated in the boat now.

The Reverend Donald MacQueen, a Skye minister who accompanied them, gave it as his opinion that the cause of the island's trouble was that landlords listened to bad advice and consequently had golden dreams of much higher rents than could reasonably be paid, so the tacksmen left and those who had been their tenants took their place. All it needed was one bad year to ruin them. The travellers considered that the Government should intervene to induce the chiefs to change their ways. 'In France, a chief would not be permitted to force a number of the king's subjects out of the country', they remarked.[39]

Near Greshornish on the opposite side of Loch Snizort the horses waited and Johnson shambled off along the track, well satisfied that he had saved eight miles of riding on horseback. He had relished his visit to Kingsburgh House and the meeting with the heroine of Prince Charlie's escape, and wrote the words that were to become Flora's epitaph: 'Her name will be mentioned in history, and if courage and fidelity be virtues, mentioned with honour.'[40]

On 2 October, his last full day on Skye, Johnson gave a long dissertation on the manner in which chiefs ought to live, holding court like princes and behaving as chiefs had in the old days. Boswell was less passionate and commented shrewdly that emigration 'made a short settlement of the differences between a chief and his clan'.

On that last night on the island they stayed at Armadale, close to where Flora's stepfather, Hugh, had lived until his departure for North Carolina the previous year. Boswell wrote:

> In the evening the company danced as usual. We performed, with much activity, a dance which, I suppose, the emigration from Sky has occasioned. They call it *America*. Each of the couples, after the common involutions and evolutions, successively whirls round in a circle, till all are in motion; and the dance seems intended to shew how emigration catches, til a whole neighbourhood is set afloat.[41]

The dance might have been an entertainment for the visitors, but for the island it was a wake.

Emigration had reached epidemic proportions. Allan's sister, Anne MacKinnon, told Boswell that, when migrants sailed the previous year, those left behind were almost distracted and lay on the ground and tore the grass with their teeth, but this year not a tear was shed because those on shore expected to follow soon.

The brief visit brought a tantalizing breath of the outside world to Flora and served to harden her resolve to end the misery of life on the island at the first opportunity. Preparations were now begun in earnest to settle the last of their affairs and secure the future of their remaining three children – Alexander, James and Fanny – so that they would be free to leave.

Allan was tired of begging, so it was left to Flora to make a last effort to find someone to take the boys. Alexander was now in his nineteenth year and James was sixteen. Whom could they ask? Allan had once known the Duke of Atholl slightly, but refused to beg his help, so once again the unsavoury task of writing the begging letter was left to Flora. It is amazing how often Allan forced Flora to deal with matters relating to the children: Flora helped to find careers for the older ones, Allan had a pain in his side and could not write to MacKenzie about Johnnie and now he flatly refused to beg help from the Duke of Atholl.

It would be as unfair to condemn Allan for his refusal to write this letter as it would be to label him a bad farmer because of his lack of success. Allan MacDonald had faults, but he was a hard worker, he cared deeply for his family, he was generous and, as was proved later, brave.

Perhaps he refused to write the letter because he knew it would be a waste of effort. After all, The Atholls' support for the Jacobite Cause had been chequered and there was no reason why they should help Flora MacDonald now.

The letter, dated 23 April 1774, was actually written by young Alexander – perhaps Flora was still ashamed of her handwriting in spite of the efforts of Dominie Beatt in Edinburgh in 1747, but more likely she was cleverly demonstrating to the Duke that her son had some handwriting skill. The letter was frank and forthright:

> My Lord
> Necessity often forces both sexes to go through many transactions contrary to their inclinations. Such is the present one as nothing but real necessity could force me to give your Grace this trouble, & open my miserable state to your Lordship's view with the hopes of getting some comfort through your wonted goodness of heart to many who have been in less tribulation of mind than I am at present.
>
> The case is as follows – my husband by various losses & the education of our chidren (haveing no other legacy to leave them) fell through the little means we had, so as not to be able to keep this possession, especially as the rents are so prodigiously augumented; therefore of course must contrary to our inclination follow the rest of our freinds who have gone thir three years passed to America; but before I go would wish to have one or two boys I have still unprovided for in some shape or other off my hands. The oldest of the two called Alexander is bordering on 19 years of age, hath a pretty good hand writeing, as this letter may attest, went through the most of the classicks & the common rules of Arithmetick, so that he is fitt for whatever providence and the recommendation of well wishers may throw in his way; your Grace's doing something for him would be the giving of real relief to my perplexed mind before I leave (with reluctance) my native land & a real piece of charity.[42]

She told the Duke how Charles, Ranald and John were settled, then turned to Alexander:

> Had I this boy off my hands before I leave the Kingdom I could almost leave it with pleasure, even tho' I have a Boy and a lassie still depending on the protection of kind providence.

136

This freedom I am hope full your Grace will forgive as nothing but the care of my family could prevail with me to use such.[43]

She finished with a reference to her own fame, the only time she ever used this to try to benefit her family.

Mr Macdonald, though he once had the honour of a little of your Grace's acquaintance . . . could not be prevailed upon to put pen to paper therefore I with the assistance of what remained of the old resolution went through this bold task. And with prayers of a poor distressed woman (once known to the world) for the prosperity of your family.

I am, with the greatest esttem & respect

Yr Grace's most obedient Servant

Flora mcdonald[44]

She received no reply so far as we know and certainly no offer of help came from the Duke.

The Chief of Raasay, who already had such a large family of his own that another scarcely mattered, generously agreed to take care of little Fanny, but there was no one left who might look after her sons: there was nothing for it but to take them to America.

The last thing to be done was to relinquish the tack of Kingsburgh, and this was negotiated and handed over to the new tacksman, William MacLeod of Ose.[45] With that completed, Flora and Allan were free to leave, and in the late summer or early autumn of 1774 they sailed for North Carolina.

Tradition says they spent some time at the home of Flora's Argyll relations at Largie before they sailed, but they could not have stayed there for more than a week or two since Flora's letter asking the Duke of Atholl to take the boys was only written from Kingsburgh at the end of April.

Flora's daughter, Anne, her husband, Alexander MacLeod, and their children accompanied the Kingsburghs, and some of the Kingsburgh servants were probably taken too, since we know that in North Carolina Allan had eight servants indentured to him for five years. But, of course, these could have been acquired in America.

In his *Dictionary of Scottish Emigrants to the USA*, Donald Whyte records two other Skye men who sailed at the same time as Flora. One, James MacDonald, settled in Anson County, where he married the widow

McQueen, and the second, John MacDonald, was the son of the Reverend Hugh MacDonald of Portree. He is also believed to have settled in the same county in North Carolina as the Kingsburghs.[46] James Banks of Fayetteville in North Carolina recorded in a biography of Flora, published there in 1857, that one of Flora's fellow passengers, named Bethune had died only about five years earlier.[47]

Tradition is quite firm that Flora sailed from Campbeltown in Argyll in August 1774, although her husband states twice in subsequent claims for compensation from the Government that they emigrated in 1773, and in a third that they embarked for North Carolina 'in the Autumn of 1774'.[48]

August was a popular month for emigrating because the voyage took about two months, which meant that settlers arrived at the end of the harvest when barns were full and there was plenty of food to last through the winter. This also allowed time to find and clear land for the next spring's sowing.

Tradition and nineteenth-century writers such as James Banks name the ship in which Flora sailed as the *Baliol*, but there is no surviving evidence that a vessel of that name existed. *Baliol* was more likely a clerical error in transcribing the name *Balole*. Campbell of Balole in Islay was involved in the shipping of emigrants from the Hebrides to North Carolina, and we know he had been in contact with Flora's family, so it is likely that he helped arrange their voyage. In a letter written on 31 May 1774, Hector McAlester in Scotland told his brother, Alexander McAlester, in North Carolina, that Campbell of Balole 'setts off . . . by the first of August'.[49] This fits in with Flora's August 1774 departure in a ship belonging to *Balole* or chartered by him to take Hebridean islanders to North Carolina.

Parts of the record book of William Dry, Collector of Customs at Brunswick on the Cape Fear River, have survived and it contains the name of the *Cato*, which arrived on 1 December 1774. She was bonded by Customs at Greenock in August, called at Skye and arrived with 312 Highland passengers on board. This may have carried Balole's party. Other ships claimed to be Flora's are the brigantine *Jessy*, which sailed from Greenock at the end of July, the *Ulysses*, which left Greenock on 18 August and arrived at Wilmington on 18 October, carrying '111 Scotch passengers', and the *Carolina Packet*, advertised to sail from Scotland between 1 and 8 September.[50] However, the records are by no means complete.

The fact that no ship is recorded in the Campbeltown customs books proves nothing, since the authorities in those days were much more interested in cargo (and duty payable on it) than passengers, and records seldom referred to emigrants. Many ships were plying between Scotland and Cape Fear at this time, and surviving North Carolina records show that during the last quarter of 1774 at least ten ships arrived in the colony from the Clyde, north-west England and the north of Ireland. Any one of these could have picked up Flora's little party at Campbeltown on its way round the Mull of Kintyre without anyone bothering to record the fact.

Flora may have left Scotland with relief and looked forward to a new and more secure life in North Carolina as she embarked at Campbeltown, but the two months ahead were to give her no pleasure. She had no love for ships: an uncomfortable boat journey to Skye had cost her a year's freedom, much of it spent cooped up in ships, and she had experienced at least one narrow escape from drowning while travelling between the mainland and Skye. But having spent most of her days on islands, she accepted boats as a disagreeable but essential part of daily life. Sailing from Uist to Skye was one thing: crossing the Atlantic was another. We have the word of one of her countrywomen for that. Janet Schaw, an Edinburgh 'Lady of Quality' and sister of a wealthy planter in North Carolina, sailed to the colony from Burntisland in Fife in October of the same year as Flora.[51] Her journal of the voyage makes horrifying reading, and it was no worse than that of many other emigrants. Miss Schaw had to share a room five feet wide by six feet long with another member of her party, while her maid slept on the floor between the two beds. That was luxury compared with the squalor of the hold into which poor emigrants were packed. The owner and captain cheated rich and poor alike out of food and money to such a degree that Miss Schaw complained, 'It is hardly possible to believe that human nature could be so depraved as to treat fellow creatures in such a manner for a little sordid gain.'[52]

A terrible storm battered Miss Schaw's ship until the cabin was flooded and much of their food washed overboard, including live poultry which they carried to provide fresh meat. For the rest of the journey their diet consisted of neck beef, New England pork 'on a third voyage across the Atlantick', which had to be suspended over the side of the vessel on a string in order that the seawater might render it 'tolerably fresh'. They cooked this and ate it, provided a shark had not managed to steal it while it hung in the water.[53]

Mortality rates in emigrant ships were high. On the *Nancy*, which sailed from Dornoch the year before Flora's journey, half of the 200 emigrants on board died and only one child out of fifty under the age of four who left Scotland saw America. Of the seven babies born during the voyage, only one survived and all the mothers died.[54]

Flora, travelling with her daughter, who may have been pregnant at this time, and two grandchildren, still babies, must have lived in fear through every hour of the voyage, not just for herself but for all of her family.

There is no evidence that Flora's journey was as eventful as that of the Lady of Quality, or that many of her fellow emigrants died on the way – certainly all of Flora's family arrived safely. Yet landfall at the mouth of the Cape Fear River must have filled her with a sense of joy, deliverance and thanksgiving as heartfelt as that of the Pilgrim Fathers themselves. This was North Carolina, a place about which she had heard many wondrous reports, and she looked forward to a new start among her kinsmen who were already there. North Carolina held all Flora MacDonald's hopes for the future.

CHAPTER TEN

Lairds of America

In America now are we,
In the shade of the forest for ever unfailing,
When the winter departs and the warmth returns
Nuts and apples and sugar will grow.

Gaelic lullaby composed for his daughter
by John Macrae, who emigrated from Scotland
to North Carolina in 1774[1]

North Carolina lived up to the expectations of Flora and her clansmen. The colony was filled with forests which were the source of its wealth – wood, pitch, turpentine and tar, which kept the Navy supplied and gave the inhabitants the nickname 'tarheels'. Land was plentiful and cheap, the climate was warm and it was reputed to be a haven for debtors from other colonies so, all in all, this was an attractive place for ambitious or impecunious Scots to settle.

Her first sight did not impress the Lady of Quality, who described the mouth of the Cape Fear River as nothing more than a 'dreary Waste of white barren sand, and melancholy, nodding pines'.[2] But then she had not come from the bare, treeless Hebrides. The pines, however wearily they nodded, were exhilarating to Skye people and the first habitation in the colony was a welcome sight.

Fort Johnston, where the ship had to stop to present her papers and pay a fee, was a small, defence-work standing on the west bank of the Cape Fear River. It was crudely built of large blocks of a kind of cement made by mixing lime, oyster shells and sand, and bonding the mixture with water. It looked drab, a lonely God-forsaken place that could not have withstood a determined attack from pirates or enemy warships. Indeed, it could hardly have intercepted any ship that chose to ignore it. With an ancient sloop, HMS *Cruizer*, lying at anchor in the river, rotting and gathering barnacles, Fort Johnston provided a far from intimidating first defence for the colony.

Another stop was made at Brunswick, a small settlement of no more than 'a few scattered houses on the edge of the woods',[3] standing on a low bluff some twelve miles upstream, because this was the official port of entry for Cape Fear, with the customs house located in it. There was no reason for the Kingsburghs to land at Brunswick because the rival port of Wilmington, another twenty miles up the Cape Fear River, was a newer town but already far more prosperous. Wilmington was also a more convenient point of disembarkation for anyone bound for the interior of the colony because its excellent harbour, situated near the confluence of the North-east and North-west Cape Fear Rivers, attracted merchants who traded with the communities of settlers for a hundred miles inland along each of the two rivers.

Allan greeted America as he had welcomed Samuel Johnson at his front door in Skye, rigged out in Highland splendour down to the last detail of tartan plaid and bonnet with the cockade.[4] Perhaps he wanted to show that a man of importance and a Highland tacksman had arrived among them; perhaps it was simply that these were the only 'good' clothes he possessed. The Scottish merchants in the town were just as impressed with this fine Highland figure as Johnson and Boswell had been when they first met the tacksman of Kingsburgh. They accepted Allan at once as a man of rank and a leader in their community.

Duane Meyer, author of *The Highland Scots of North Carolina*, commented 'The arrival of Flora MacDonald in the Cape Fear settlement was an event of great importance. She was a symbol of Highland bravery and independence.'[5] If Allan was received with respect, Flora was welcomed as a celebrity in America for her name was as well known there as the woman who had saved Prince Charlie in 1746 as it was in Scotland. Her daughter, Anne, who was actually with her mother at the time, told Alexander MacGregor that 'various demonstrations on a large scale, were made to welcome her to American territory',[6] and tradition relates that a ball was held in her honour. J.P. MacLean, in his book, *Flora MacDonald in America*, suggests that Anne turned heads in the town. 'She was greatly gratified by the special attention bestowed on her daughter, Anne, then entering into womanhood, and of surpassing beauty', MacLean wrote.[7] Anne was at this time still only twenty years of age, but had already been married for three years. She was the mother of two children and was probably already pregnant with her third. She was an attractive young woman, there can be no doubt about that, but if anyone was the centre of interest in Wilmington that autumn it was Flora herself.

Wilmington was a pleasant and prosperous town, containing a large number of successful Scots and Scotch-Irish merchants. It must soon have shocked the Kingsburgh MacDonalds, however, to find how mixed Wilmington's population was – ranging from their well-heeled countrymen to itinerant sailors (many of them Scots too) and river raftsmen, who ferried goods and people up and down the Cape Fear Rivers and who had a wild reputation in Wilmington. If Flora and Allan expected to find themselves in a busy, peaceful place they were in for a surprise. Wilmington in the autumn of 1774 was bubbling with discontent, its people sharply divided among themselves and North Carolina had just had its own Boston Tea Party at Edenton. The Lady of Quality heard of it as soon as she arrived. 'The Ladies have burned their tea in solemn procession, but they had delayed however until the sacrifice was not very considerable as I do not think anyone offered above a quarter of a pound.'[8]

The Kingsburghs would have known almost nothing of America's troubles before they arrived, or at least they thought them no more than a bit of discontent confined to Massachusetts and the northern colonies. The King's troops would quell the whole distasteful incident as effectively as they had suppressed the Highlands and Islands in 1746. There was little hint of the widespread dissatisfaction that was soon to lead to open rebellion and the War of Independence, engulfing every one of the thirteen American colonies.

The Kingsburgh MacDonalds could not have appreciated how different the colonists were from people back home either. Settlers in America came from a wide range of countries and cultures: they were remote from London and had built a way of life for themselves that made them very different in character from the British – freer, more enterprising, adaptable and without England's (or Scotland's) stultifying, strict social structure. Britain could contribute nothing to the Carolinians' day-to-day lives, and certainly it could not dictate or advise what they should do in response to an Indian attack, a raid by pirates or even a dispute over rights to a piece of land. By the time the authorities in London had spoken events had moved on, so the colonists were accustomed to making up their own minds.

In one important respect, however, London did rule America: trade. A series of laws, strongly biased in Britain's favour, ensured that America was a captive market for British manufactures. Virtually every item traded beyond the thirteen colonies generated profit for Britain. Exports and imports, even those to and from many other European countries, had to be shipped by way of Britain, adding hugely to costs. Many products were listed as 'enumerated goods', which meant they had to be sold to Britain only to be resold by merchants there at a great profit. Trade in the reverse direction led to duty and handling charges, which increased the prices the colonists had to pay for the goods they needed, sometimes far beyond their real or reasonable cost. Colonists were forbidden to trade all kinds of basic commodities, even with one another. This legislation controlled such necessities as wool and iron. As one complained, 'A colonist cannot make a button, horseshoe nor hobnail but some sooty ironmonger or respectable buttonmaker of Britain shall bawl and squall that his honour's worship is maltreated, injured, cheated and robbed by the rascally American republican.'[9]

Discontent grew when Britain introduced new taxes to help finance the maintenance of sea and land forces to defend the colonies and help reduce the debt resulting from the Seven Years War. The final straw for many, especially the Scottish and Scotch-Irish Presbyterians, was the Quebec Act of 1774, which recognized the Catholic Church in Canada. That was more than the Presbyterians could stomach.

North Carolina had her own long-standing quarrel with the London Government over justice, which had led to open revolt a few years earlier and was put down without mercy by the Governor of the time, William Tryon. Tryon's successor, Josiah Martin, inherited growing discontent in the colony so that, by the time Flora and Allan sailed in August 1774, anger had reached such heat that leaders of the malcontents in North Carolina's Colonial Assembly had already summoned a revolutionary congress. This gathering in turn voted to send representatives to the first Continental Congress called by the rebels at Philadelphia for the following month, all of which was the talk of Wilmington when the Kingsburghs arrived, although its full implications were probably lost on the newcomers.

The heroine's arrival at Wilmington provided a diversion in the dull world of a small colonial town, and those who were defying the King's laws in the colony no doubt found that her presence added a delicious *frisson* of rebellion. The women gave a ball in Flora's honour, tradition claims, but if so this must have been one of the last to be held there before war broke out. Already supporters of the growing Patriot faction were openly disapproving of such wasteful frivolity as parties and dancing, and by the following spring they had banned 'expensive diversions and entertainments'.[10]

There was nothing to detain the newcomers for long in Wilmington. Allan and Flora were anxious to be on their way inland, for it was now late autumn and they would have to find somewhere to live soon if they were to be settled on a plantation in good time to prepare for the spring sowing. They were also anxious to be reunited with Flora's half-sister, Annabella, and her husband, Alexander MacDonald of Cuidreach, who were waiting for them at their plantation of Mount Pleasant in Cumberland County, a hundred miles up the North-west Cape Fear River from Wilmington. Cuidreach and his family had settled there in July 1772 among the more recent arrivals from Scotland, the 'new Scotch' as they were dubbed by other people in the area.

Mount Pleasant, now known as Cameron's Hill and in Harnett County, lay about eighteen miles from the twin settlements of Campbellton and Cross Creek, which stood only a mile apart at the head of navigation on the North-west Cape Fear River, just beyond the point where North Carolina's hundred-mile wide coastal plain of unending low sandhills turned into the hilly uplands known as Piedmont. As at Wilmington and Brunswick, there was no room for two settlements so close together, so one had flourished at the expense of the other: Cross Creek had become a busy trading centre and left Campbellton behind. Just a few years after Flora's arrival the two settlements united, and in 1783 the name was changed to its present name of Fayetteville.

To reach Cross Creek, Flora and her family had to travel across the sandhills on horseback, or in wagons along the road through thick forests of giant trees hung with moss and mistletoe. But they were much more likely to have taken one of the many boats that plied up and down the Cape Fear Rivers, crewed by Wilmington raftsmen, and carrying passengers and goods to and from the coast – cattle, horses, hogs, grain and wood from the plantations, which were traded for stores of every kind, imported from Britain. As well as flat-bottomed cargo boats there were numerous passenger craft, even fine barges like that belonging to the wealthy planter, John Rutherford, which had an awning to fend off the sun and was rowed by 'six stout Negroes in neat uniforms'. But Flora was unlikely to have travelled in such style or comfort.[11]

The journey from Wilmington to Cross Creek took six days of hard rowing against the current, an astounding experience for people accustomed to the starkness of Skye's barren terrain. The Lady of Quality found the north-west branch of the river exceedingly beautiful after the drabness of the Cape Fear estuary: 'Nothing can be finer than the banks of this river; a thousand beauties both of the flowery and sylvan tribe hang over it and are reflected from it with additional lustre'.[12]

It was hard to take in the full glory of the North Carolina landscape because great forests enfolded the spacious country to the point of claustrophobia. In the Sandhills country between Wilmington and Cross Creek there were no high peaks, just mile after mile of low, rolling hills clad in woodland, with here and there a settler's plantation. Even in late autumn when the deciduous trees had all shed their leaves and only the long-leaf pines remained green, this gilded country presented few grand vistas. Oaks, elms, sycamores, magnolias and other exotic trees such as Scotsmen had never seen at home, reached down to the water's edge, and the walnuts, hazels and hickory shed their fruit. All were there to be gathered so easily that the Lady of Quality one day made passable wine from wild grapes which clung to the river banks: she was appalled that nobody in the colony made use of this bounty. Dense moss overhung the river banks and Candle Bay Myrtle grew in profusion everywhere, supplying wax which settlers used to make candles. Hummingbirds foraged among giant honeysuckle, while heron and crane flew low over the river. At the edge of the woods one could see deer, fox, wild turkey, quail and partridge. To new arrivals from the Scottish islands this must have been the Garden of Eden – the entrance to paradise.

To Flora and Allan Mount Pleasant lived up to its name, and there they found a warm welcome awaiting them from Flora's half-sister, Annabella, and her family. Again, tradition speaks of welcoming parties for the Kingsburghs before Flora and Anne settled down with their kinfolk, while Allan and Anne's husband prospected to find suitable places of their own.

Cuidreach owned two hundred acres, delightfully situated on a hillside at Mount Pleasant which he had bought on his arrival in the Colony in 1772. He was highly successful and already owned a second plantation farther west in the neighbouring Anson County. During the two years Cuidreach had spent at Mount Pleasant he had cleared additional land, extended his house, added to his stock of animals and planted orchards. He now had a good stock of cattle, horses and hogs. With his wife, Annabella, and four daughters he led a very contented life, surrounded by family treasures brought all the way from Skye: silver, fine furniture, linen and no fewer than sixty books.[14]

Cuidreach's son, Donald, arrived from Scotland about this time, and his other sons, James and Kenneth, also settled in Cumberland County. Annabella's father, 'One-eyed' Hugh of Armadale, owned two plantations in Anson County, fifty miles further inland, near Cuidreach's second plantation, so from the first Flora could feel that this was her kinsmen's country.

North Carolina brought the Kingsburgh family peace of mind for the present and hope for the future. They were among family and friends but, equally important, still surrounded by those familiar and beautiful furnishings, ornaments and books that they had known at home. Flora was remembered as spending much time sitting out of doors at her half-sister's house, beside a natural well, which is still known as Flora MacDonald's Spring. There, it is said, she smoked a pipe and dreamed about the past in Skye or the future in America. On Sundays she walked a mile to church at Barbecue Creek, and she was remembered long after by someone who saw her there as 'a dignified and handsome woman to whom all paid respect'.[15] The log church that Flora attended has now been replaced by a modern building of red brick, but the graveyard is full of headstones that commemorate the Highlanders who worshipped there in Flora's time. The only exception to this general admiration came from a Mrs Black who, it was said, 'did not have an exalted opinion of Flora MacDonald and never spoke of her pleasantly'.[16] Everyone else, from her family to her enemies, held her in high regard.

Although this part of North Carolina had not been settled exclusively by Highlanders, the Gaelic-speaking people from the Scottish Highlands and Islands constituted the biggest single national group in the area and impressed their stamp on the community – a capacity to retain their identity, close kinship and the lingering moral code of the clans. They did not transplant the clan system to their new home, but it did survive in a small way since so many tacksmen from the Highlands who become land-holders in North Carolina brought indentured servants dependent on them. Alexander Schaw, brother of the Lady of Quality, wrote home in 1775: 'Many Highland gentlemen are now in that country, several of whom have been officers, and still retain their influence among the people.'[17] The description fitted Allan to a T because, from the day he arrived, he was treated as a kind of chief among his kinsmen and other clansmen, not only because of his own superior position but because his wife was a heroine. His vanity was well satisfied.

The Highlanders suffered from one disadvantage: they were cut off from the rest of the colony by differences of language, custom, dress and attitude to work. Lowlanders and the Scotch-Irish of Ulster contributed more to the community at this time, providing North Carolina and other colonies with clergy, teachers, doctors and merchants.

Idyllic as the new country appeared at first sight, it brought many problems, not least the burning, humid summers that felt unbearable to those accustomed to the chilly, rain-drenched Highlands. Often the hot, clammy days ended in dramatic thunderstorms whose lightning flashed blue among the tree tops. Fevers often raged through communities, especially in the low-lying swamps of the wide coastal plain, but even in the healthier Piedmont illness was ever present. Wolves, wildcats, snakes, and even cattle and hogs (which were allowed to wander freely over the countryside) could be more dangerous than any wildlife one might encounter in Scotland. Bears were a mixed blessing: they seized a settler's hogs, but on the other hand they made excellent eating and provided useful fur and fat. There were other hazards too: mosquitoes and those accursed 'chiggers' which still make life miserable in the North Carolina forests today. No bigger than the point of a needle and unseen, they penetrate clothing and burrow under the skin to create a torture of itching and raise little red lumps. They affected man and beast in Flora's Carolina. The Lady of Quality complained about them and the Reverend Charles Woodmason, who settled in the Carolinas in 1776, wrote:

> Myself greatly tormented with Seed Ticks, by my lying in the Woods. Seed Ticks are a small insect no bigger than the Point of a Needle with which ev'ry Leaf and Blade of Grass is covered . . . they bite very sharp . . . get into the Skin cause Inflammations, Itchings and much torment.[18]

The inflictions of North Carolina chiggers equalled any Hebridean midge torture.

Because of the number of huge tree-roots everywhere, land was hard to clear and almost impossible to plough; consequently many people simply used hoes to prepare small areas for planting. Yet they grew crops successfully – Indian corn, wheat, oats, peas, beans, flax and sweet potatoes – but the soil quickly became exhausted, and when that happened it was easier to abandon it and open up new fields than to try to fertilize and revitalize it. The settlers raised cattle and hogs, and almost all had excellent orchards that produced superb crops. In the forests there was plenty of game to be shot or trapped – from wild turkeys to pheasant – all excellent supplements to the family diet.[19]

Work was hard, but the new world was generous to the Highlanders, even to those who arrived with nothing. Alongside the successful settlers, many others were very poor and, according to the refined senses of the Episcopalian, Woodmason, these lived like savages, touched by neither religion nor education, and unwilling to work. Woodmason was prejudiced against Presbyterians. He was thwarted in his efforts to 'civilize' these settlers by the intransigence of the Ulster Scot Presbyterians who, he said, would rather their children ran wild than allow them to be instructed by a minister of the Church of England. Woodmason said he encountered people living in destitution, too lazy even to cut wood to make a fire and swapping wives like cattle. In his view they were worse than the Indians.[20]

The Lady of Quality confirmed much of this, recording that the cattle were left to forage for themselves or starve, and that many inhabitants produced only enough for their own needs, and the rest of the time wandered through the woods with a gun or sat at home drinking New England rum, which she was convinced weakened the blood.[21]

Allan MacDonald and his kinsmen were above all that. While Flora waited at Mount Pleasant, he and his sons travelled around Cumberland and neighbouring Anson Counties in search of somewhere to settle. Although poverty had driven the Kingsburgh family from Skye, Allan had arrived with sufficient funds to buy a property and to stock it. It was said that he settled in the colony with £700 of capital.

It has always been assumed that Allan eventually bought a plantation in Anson County (now Richmond County), from one Caleb Touchstone, and named it Killegray. However the late Rassie Wicker, who spent much of his life working in North Carolina as a surveyor during the first half of the twentieth century, devoted considerable time and energy to locating exactly where Flora and Allan did settle. When Allan came to make his claim for compensation from the British Government at the end of the War of Independence, he listed a tract of 475 acres and a separate 50 acres. He also claimed the loss of 'Caleb Tulishstone's riffle'.[22]

Wicker proved that Caleb Touchstone obtained a grant of 200 acres of land at Mountain Creek in 1754, which passed to Stephen Touchstone in 1756. Caleb also had 475 acres plus a detached 50 acre tract on Cheek's Creek, about 1½ miles north-east of the small settlement of Pekin, and 5 miles or so north of Killegray. This plantation is known locally as Old

Baldwin's Place. Wicker's exhaustive searches failed to discover any deed or court record of this plantation, or any mention of Allan or Flora. This is not altogether surprising since many of the records have been lost or destroyed and circumstances may even have prevented Allan from registering the land properly.

Allan MacDonald, fiercely proud of his Kingsburgh kinship, would never have given his plantation the name Killegray – that was the name of a Clan MacLeod island, lying between Harris and North Uist in the Long Island of Scotland and with no MacDonald connection. Killegray, on the border of Richmond and Montgomery Counties, belonged to a settler by the name of Alexander MacLeod, the same name as Allan's son-in-law, which might have given rise to the confusion.

One tiny piece of evidence puts the truth of Wicker's theory beyond doubt. In the Public Record Office in London, the late Dr Donald MacKinnon, an authority on MacDonald history, discovered a letter written by Governor Martin to his secretary in May or June 1775. It stated that he was going to place some important papers 'with my friend Mr MacDonald of Kingsburgh, living upon Cheek's Creek, in Anson County'.[23]

Flora herself told us that 'her husband purchased a plantation with the stock of different cattle thereon, on which they lived for near a year'.[24] As they lived happily at Cheek's Creek only until February 1776, this suggests that the spring of 1775 was well advanced before they took possession of their land, and the outbreak of the American Revolution soon after probably prevented them from registering the deed.

Wicker described Allan and Flora's property as he found it:

> Back of, and at the foot of the dyke is the old spring, walled in with rock. Beyond the spring, the land rises for a distance of about a half mile, terminating in an abrupt bluff facing the creek. At this point the hill, or mountain, is precipitous – it is utterly impossible to climb it, and its peak stands perhaps one hundred and fifty feet above the river. There is barely room to walk between its foot and the river bank. On the opposite side of the river, another mountain of equal height and slope, leads away to the north. Between these two hills are the remains of two old mill dams, both built of rock.

An elderly resident told him that the Baldwins, who gave their name to the property, operated a mill at the lower of these two dams. The upper one was there before the Baldwins' mill was built, and was presumably

Allan's grist mill, which Allan himself described as located beside a good run of water and able to produce enough flour in a year to keep the whole family in bread.[25]

Allan MacDonald settled in the Touchstone property at Cheek's Creek, Anson (later Montgomery) County, in a part of North Carolina that was somewhat isolated from the majority of their Highland kinsfolk, and among longer-settled Ulster Scots and Germans. To this plantation, set among low hills and winding creeks, he brought Flora, his two sons, Alexander and James, and their eight indentured servants, three women and five men. Around seventy acres of land had already been cleared for cultivation, giving them a good start for their farming, and they had excellent orchards of peaches, apples and other fruit, as well as a house with a separate kitchen building, a barn, stable, keeping house and crib for holding Indian corn. Flora filled her new home with the furniture, linen, silver and books that she had brought all the way from Kingsburgh, and she felt that this truly was a new world that would offer them a way of life that would be the envy of those they had left behind in Skye.[26]

Her daughter, Anne, and her husband, Sandy MacLeod, settled in Cumberland County, about 25 miles from Cheek's Creek, virtually halfway between the Kingsburghs and the Cuidreachs at Mount Pleasant. They named their property Glendale after the birthplace of Sandy's mother in the shadow of the twin mountains in Skye, known as MacLeod's Table.

Wicker also unravelled the mystery of the whereabouts of Glendale:

When Alexander McLeod and Anne, his wife and the daughter of Flora McDonald, looked about for their American home, they chose the three hundred acres on Wad's (then called McDeed's) Creek which Kenneth Black had bought from Thomas Wadsworth. They probably bargained with Kenneth for its purchase, but it appears that this deal was never consummated, as Alexander made no claim for it, but only for personal property. They nevertheless gave it the name of Glendale.[27]

Kenneth Black's wife was the woman who disliked Flora, but her feelings had no effect on her husband's subsequent kindness to the Kingsburghs. For confirmation of Sandy MacLeod's estate, Wicker quotes from a taxation list of 1777, an old land plan and pieces of local lore gathered over many years. One old man, when asked how Glendale came to be named, answered: 'It got its name from old Glendale himself, who got into trouble and had to go back to Scotland' – a description that fits Major Alexander MacLeod. The property lies in what is now part of Moore County, just a few miles south of the present-day town of Carthage, but MacLeod also had land beside Cuidreach's in Anson.

Flora MacDonald, her family and kinsmen were once again a small, closely linked community, all settled within a radius of 50 miles of one another: the Kingsburghs at Cheek's Creek, Flora's stepfather just five miles away, her daughter and son-in-law twenty-five miles distant at Glendale and her half-sister and brother-in-law twenty-five miles farther off at Mount Pleasant. Because of their close kinship to the chiefs of the MacDonalds of Sleat and Clanranald, and the Dunvegan MacLeods, they were by far the most important members of the community socially – natural leaders of the Highlanders in the inland settlements of North Carolina. They were all far too busy that summer to have much time to spend together, yet they had to meet, talk and make decisions that were to have momentous consequences for them. Many of the longer-established American colonists decided that the time for grumbling and petitioning London was over, and Allan and Flora found that their new homeland was in a state of war before the seeds of their first harvest were properly showing through the ground.

CHAPTER ELEVEN

Loyal to Whom?

There are three or four Gentlemen of consideration here, of the name of McDonald . . . whom I should be happy to appoint Captains . . . being persuaded they would heartily promote and do credit to His Majesty's Service.

Letter from Governor Martin to Lord Dartmouth[1]

With seventy acres of land ready for the plough the MacDonalds had plenty to keep them occupied throughout the spring of 1775. The fact that the land had been 'cleared' did not mean it had been turned into rich arable fields: the Carolina forests were so dense and the trees so immense that the only way to 'clear' ground was to burn the undergrowth and young trees, remove a ring of bark from the larger ones and leave them to die. Even when these trees dried out and could be burned they left roots too large to be dug out, so they had to be left to rot. In the case of the long-leaf pine this took longer than the settler was likely to live! The process had to be repeated each year to prevent the forest from taking over again.

Often planters simply grubbed holes in the ground and dropped their seed in, rather than attempting to plough it because the crude wooden ploughs they used constantly struck unseen roots and either stopped or broke. As Rassie Wicker said, 'These were veritably tasks which separated the men from the boys'.[2]

Allan must have felt glad he had been forced to take his two sons to America with him, for it required all their energy in addition to that of his five indentured male servants to plant out the cleared land in time to harvest a crop that first year.

Flora had to toil hard, too: even with three female servants to help, her life must have been one of drudgery. She might have been a tacksman's wife and a lady close in kinship to the clan chief back in Scotland, but in North Carolina only the richest settlers' wives were ladies of leisure. On a Carolina plantation a woman had to work from before dawn until after dark. She was responsible for the cleaning of the house, cooking, growing vegetables, tending the geese, ducks and hens, and making a home for her family. In addition she had to help with the outside work. Unless she was lucky enough to live near a trading centre, such as Cross Creek, and had sufficient money to purchase all her needs from traders there, she also had to make everything from candles and feather bolsters to clothes for her children. For a well-connected but impecunious woman like Flora MacDonald, every day was one of unending work.

In Skye, life had been dominated by the sea: at Cheek's Creek the all-pervading woods ruled. Much as Flora disliked the sea, there must have been times when she looked on North Carolina's forests with similar intense distaste – anyone from Skye would have. Like the seas around the Hebrides, the forests were both a provider and a predator: they supplied timber to build homes, logs for fuel, as well as oil, wax and rich crops of nuts and fruit, but they were also an unrelenting enemy determined to recover every acre that was taken from them.

On a remote plantation life could be lonely, with days on end when no outsider visited, but Flora MacDonald was accustomed to that: those early years of her married life at Flodigarry in Skye had prepared her well. She and Allan did not need company, but they got plenty of it. Before the first green wisps of growth were showing through on their fields, strangers were beating a path to their door to such an extent that Flora must have wondered how she would feed them and when her husband would find time to push ahead with his own essential work.

The reason was that the discontent they had first heard talk of on their arrival at Cape Fear was growing, and growing fast. Communities were already divided within themselves, even here where the Highlanders were in the majority and considered themselves superior to the money-grubbing merchants of the tidewater or coastal plain. It has to be admitted that merchants in Wilmington and Brunswick in turn considered the backwoods of the interior an unsavoury place populated by swindlers and layabouts.

As 'new Scotch' arrivals, Flora and Allan could not feel involved in this rivalry or talk of rebellion, the reasons for which they could barely understand. However everyone was forced to take sides sooner or later, and when that time came the Kingsburgh MacDonalds, like a large number of their kinsmen, found powerful reasons for casting their lot with the King. The recently arrived Highlanders had seen enough of war and its aftermath: after all, many were now in Carolina as a result of Prince Charlie's Rising and in that affair they had suffered and seen kinsmen and friends lose homes, family, livelihood and even lives. Flora had a whole year of her life snatched from her for aiding the Prince, and, while stationed with the militia at Fort William, Allan had seen how traitors were treated. They blamed the social upheaval in the generation that followed the '45 on Hanoverian vengeance and believed that it was an important cause of the poverty from which the only escape was emigration. What the Redcoats had done in Scotland in 1745–6 they could repeat in America in 1775.

Allan MacDonald's position was further affected by the fact that he had sworn loyalty to King George in order to obtain his commission in the militia, and even now, thirty years later, his profound Highland sense of honour bound him by that oath. But another powerful inducement persuaded him to cast his lot with the Crown: from the moment he arrived Governor Josiah Martin accepted him not just as a leader, but as the principal Highlander in the community – a chief of the clansmen. Like all Highland leaders, Allan was a highly political person who found the lure of power irresistible. He was hugely flattered by all this attention and threw in his lot with the Loyalists immediately. This created jealousy among other Highland settlers, particularly Farquhard Campbell, a merchant who ran a trading vessel between Cross Creek and Wilmington and, until Allan came on the scene, had been undisputed 'chief' of the Highland community. Allan probably did not become aware of Campbell's annoyance until it was too late.[3]

Alexander McAlester, one of the original Argyll colonists of 1739, was another Highlander who threw in his lot with the Patriots and joined the Revolutionary Committees of Safety then beginning to spring up everywhere in the colony (although there never was one at Cross Creek). To the alarm of Loyalist settlers these committees were soon flexing themselves to assume power, so Governor Martin, unable to curb them, made secret approaches to Allan MacDonald and other Highlanders, and was heartened by their favourable, even eager, response.[4]

Martin was not the best man to be in charge of the colony at this delicate time: he was honest but stubborn and tactless, obsequious to those above and overbearing to those below. He was no diplomat, but more than made up for his lack of statesmanship by his tenacity to the King's cause.[5]

As early as 16 March 1775, Martin wrote to General Thomas Gage, the British army commander in America, asking for weapons and ammunition to arm the Highlanders and the Regulators, a group who had rebelled against illegal taxes and corruption a decade earlier but had now come round to supporting the Crown.[6] He called a meeting of the Colonial Assembly at New Bern for 4 April, only to have the Patriots insolently summon their own Provincial Congress in the same town on the preceding day. In the face of such provocation Governor Martin prorogued the Assembly, the last British Colonial Assembly ever in North Carolina.[7]

The governor continued to negotiate with Allan, sending messengers to Cheek's Creek to persuade him and the Highlanders to remain loyal. Allan was treated like a clan chief and responded like one, assuring Martin that he would assist when the time was ripe. Flora wrote later that while her husband was being exhorted to remain loyal he was under extreme pressure to join the rebels, but he realized that he had to come out on one side or the other and naturally chose the Loyalists.[8]

The volcano of revolution erupted during the first week of May, when news of skirmishes – and alleged British cruelties – at Lexington and Concord spread through Carolina. The Battle of Bunker Hill followed – this was war, with communities now openly taking sides. Supporters of the rebels were dubbed Patriots or Whigs because most had Whig political sympathies, and King George's followers were labelled Loyalists or Tories. Even at this early stage the War of Independence affected Flora directly. Ranald, her third son, now a second lieutenant in the Marines, was drafted to America, where the Marines played a significant part in the American Revolution. He served with the 6th Company of the 2nd Battalion, stationed at Boston, and fought in the first engagements of the war. His father (without actually naming him) claimed he was wounded at Bunker Hill, but the *Leicester and Nottingham Journal* of 17 June 1775, by coincidence the day of the Battle of Bunker Hill, listed MacDonald among the wounded at Lexington and Concord. Two days after Bunker Hill Ranald was promoted to lieutenant in lieu of John Haddon, who had himself been promoted to take the place of a dead officer.[9]

Governor Martin was not the only man in America to realize the potential value of the Highlanders to the King: Allan had a cousin, Captain Alexander MacDonald, an army veteran living on Staten Island, New York, who saw the possibility of raising a regiment of Highland emigrants for the King. Captain Alexander claimed that the idea was his and was put to General Gage as early as October 1774, probably the exact month in which Allan and Flora set foot in America, but it was only taken up the following April when credit for the idea was given to Colonel Allan MacLean![10]

On 12 June Gage issued an order empowering MacLean to raise a corps of two battalions each of ten companies, named the Royal Highland Emigrants. The first of these battalions largely comprised men from New York and Canada, and the second was to be recruited from Highlanders in

Nova Scotia (then separate from Canada) and North Carolina. This battalion, with headquarters at Halifax, Nova Scotia, came under the command of Major John Small, with Captain Alexander as senior captain. Within four days of being appointed, Alexander had commissioned his cousin, Allan, into the Highland Emigrants as a captain and made young Alexander a lieutenant. After the Marines serving in America were returned to the Home Fleet in 1778 and Ranald had recovered from his wounds, he too went to Nova Scotia where he served with the new regiment, thanks, no doubt, to the influence of his father's cousin, Captain Alexander MacDonald.[11]

Unaware of the honour being accorded him in the North, Allan was giving ample confirmation of his loyalty in North Carolina and Governor Martin came to depend on him. Messages shuttled between Cheek's Creek and Government House at New Bern, bringing Allan and the Governor even closer together. Martin even asked Allan to guard secret documents for him, writing to his secretary:

> Finding that Lord Granville's papers may be deposited to the greatest security with my friend Mr MacDonald of Kingsborough, living upon Cheek's Creek, in Anson County, I am resolved to place them under his guardianship, provided they may be removed in safety.[12]

Allan had become the Governor's 'friend' and was accepted as totally loyal. Martin even undertook the long and hazardous journey to Cheek's Creek himself and stayed there as the Kingsburghs' guest, giving Flora more work to act as hostess to the King's representative in the colony, in addition to running the plantation while her husband was busy playing politics. Governor Martin had to travel in the utmost secrecy and ordered his secretary to tell anyone who asked that he had gone to the town of Salisbury. The visit confirmed his faith in Kingsburgh and, as a result of the correspondence and this secret stay, the Highland leaders were brought together again to reaffirm their support for the King. Following this meeting Allan was delegated to travel to the coast to advise the governor that the Piedmont Highlanders were 'ready and willing to obey his orders and command'.

It was now high summer in the colony, with broiling hot days – not an easy time for a Scottish islander, who had never experienced a Carolina summer, to travel. Mosquitoes and chiggers were a plague, but there was worse: rebel groups might be concealed anywhere in the dense forest, so

Allan had to travel in disguise and with great care. Riding through this hostile country was unnerving: 'empty' forests are far from silent places at any time and, on this journey, every snapping branch or bird call must have brought a shiver of fear, for it might be a group of Patriots stalking him.

Allan MacDonald's loyalty took him 150 miles through comfortless and unsafe country to reach the Governor, who by now had been forced to take refuge in Fort Johnston, that drab little fortification which had been the Kingsburghs' first sight of habitation on their arrival at the mouth of the Cape Fear River. In spite of all Allan's secrecy, the Patriots soon had wind of his mission and sent out two parties to intercept him.

About this time the Lady of Quality told of a secret meeting in Wilmington, which was attended by 'some ambassadors from the back settlements on their way to the Governor to offer their service, provided he could let them have arms and ammunition as might empower them to raise men by proper authority'. Flora's son-in-law, Alexander MacLeod, was reputed to have been among this particular group, but Allan could well have been there too.[13]

The visit was common gossip in the town and, if Miss Schaw knew so much, it is little wonder that the Patriots were also well informed of the Loyalists' movements. The only surprise is that MacLeod and Allan succeeded in evading capture and reached the oystershell and lime fortress safely. Kingsburgh was away from home for two weeks on this mission and stayed with Governor Martin for several days. It cost him £28, which he paid out of his own pocket. He returned home with authorization to negotiate with the Regulators with a view to uniting them with the Highlanders to form a fighting force to defend the colony. These journeyings of Allan MacDonald and others called for great courage, since they might well have been killed if captured. They must have frightened Flora too.[14] While carrying a message to Cheek's Creek during July, one of Martin's messengers, Samuel Williams, had his house broken into and ransacked, and he only evaded capture because his wife managed to get a warning to him in time. On another occasion Williams watched from a hideout in the forest while two hundred Patriots scoured the country for him.[15]

The response of Kingsburgh's kinsmen prompted the Governor to send a letter to the Earl of Dartmouth, Colonial Secretary in London, at the beginning of July. It was a pathetic message which began by recounting in pitiful detail his impotence to govern, and how he had sent his pregnant wife and their children to safety before he was forced to spike the cannon at the Governor's palace and flee New Bern for refuge in Fort Johnston. He told Dartmouth he still believed that if General Gage would send support he could save the colony, for he could muster a sizeable army, which would include '3000 effective men' from among the Highland settlers. He asked Dartmouth to restore his own former army commission, which he had sold because of ill health some years earlier, and to grant commissions appropriate to their rank to the leading gentlemen in the colony in the event of war breaking out. Allan MacDonald and his son-in-law, Sandy MacLeod, were numbered among these:

> I would most humbly beg leave to recommend M^r. Allen McDonald of Kingsborough to be Major, and Captain Alex^d Mcleod of the Marines now on half pay to be first Captain, who besides being men of great worth, and good character, have most extensive influence over the Highlanders here, great part of which are of their own name and familys, and I should flatter myself that His Majesty would be graciously pleased to permit me to nominate some of the Subalterns of such a Battalion, not for pecuniary consideration but for encouragement to some active and deserving young Highland Gentlemen who might be usefully employed in the speedy raising of the proposed Battalion. Indeed I cannot help observing My Lord, that there are three or four Gentlemen of consideration here, of the name of McDonald, and a Lieutenant Alex^d McLean late of the Regiment now on half pay, whom I should be happy to see appointed Captains in such a Battalion, being persuaded they would heartily promote and do credit to His Majesty's Service.[16]

This letter, although expressly sent in the care of the Lady of Quality's brother, Alexander Schaw, did not reach the Colonial Secretary until the end of October. Like every other letter or order, it became caught up in that terrible time warp of slow communication between Carolina and London, London and Boston, and Boston and Carolina. Every letter, every order and every piece of advice or information took weeks to be relayed on each leg of the journey, so that, by the time it arrived, events had moved on. This was no way to put down a rebellion and it contributed greatly to the ineffectiveness of Governor Martin's rule in North Carolina.

Within days Martin was forced to abandon Fort Johnston and live aboard the dilapidated old ship, HMS *Cruizer*, moored in the Cape Fear River. He escaped in the very nick of time: the following day he watched helplessly from the ship as Fort Johnston was burned to the ground by Patriots.[17]

Soon after he received a bitterly disappointing reply from General Gage in Boston – intercepted and read by the rebels first, of course – to his request of 16 March for arms and ammunition. Gage had nothing to spare apart from a small amount of gunpowder which he said he had no means of transporting to North Carolina.

The Patriot Committees of Safety in the colony turned their attention to the Highlanders during July, and especially to Allan MacDonald for it was an open secret that Cheek's Creek was the centre of Loyalist support. On the 3rd they decided to enquire into Kingsburgh, instructing the chairman of their committee, Cornelius Harnett, to write to Allan:

> to know from himself respecting the reports that circulate of his having an intention to raise Troops to support the arbitrary measures of the ministry against the Americans in this colony and whether he had not made an offer of his services to Governor Martin for that purpose.[18]

News of the raising of the Royal Highland Emigrants must have reached Martin soon after he despatched his letter to Lord Dartmouth asking for authorization to raise his Highlanders in the colony, but he ignored it and went ahead with his plans involving Allan. Martin must have felt bitterly disappointed, believing at times that his own side was working against him just as surely as the Patriots. He refused to be browbeaten by his superiors or the enemy. At the beginning of August, when the Patriots called another Provincial Congress at Hillsboro, Martin issued a fiercely worded proclamation from his refuge aboard HMS *Cruizer*, denouncing the rebels.[19] But the Patriot response to this 'fiery proclamation' was simply to laugh at him and dismiss it as 'false, scandalous, scurrilous, malicious and seditious'.[20] In spite of all their bravado, however, the Patriot delegates meeting at Hillsboro were much less assured than they sounded. They set up a committee to visit immigrants who had recently arrived from Scotland to explain to them 'the Nature of our Unhappy Controversy with Great Britain'. Farquhard Campbell and Alexander McAlester served on this committee.[21]

Both sides continued to woo the Highland Scots vigorously as summer turned to autumn, often at great personal risk because North Carolina, virtually without a government, was now a place full of fear. Burning, looting and even killing became commonplace. The Patriots' committee and two Presbyterian ministers moved among the settlers to persuade them of the right of the Patriot cause, and in this they had some success, especially among those Highlanders who had been long established in North Carolina. As in Scotland in 1745, when being a Highlander did not guarantee loyalty to Prince Charlie, the settlers of the western part of the colony remained sharply divided.

Allan and Flora MacDonald's loyalty remained steadfast and, with Martin's encouragement, Allan did not wait for authorization from London to set about recruiting a loyal army. He worked selflessly through summer and autumn to persuade the clansmen to join a company of volunteers, which he had begun to raise. At Glendale, Sandy MacLeod was similarly occupied so that, between them, Kingsburgh and Glendale drilled and trained two companies of clansmen into soldiers. At Cheek's Creek Flora was left to run the plantation through the unbearable hot, humid harvesting days while her husband and their sons were playing soldiers instead of threshing and filling the barns with their first Carolina harvest. What should have been a serene, happy time for Flora became one of restlessness, secret assignations, political intrigue, uncertainty and even fear.

When the Colonial Secretary replied at last to the Governor's letter of 30 June he promised little help: some arms and light field guns were to be despatched to Gage so that the general might forward them, if needed, to Carolina, along with a battalion of men. He ordered the Governor to sound out the Highlanders in order to establish precisely how many men could be mustered, and told Martin that, if the response did not add up to a worthwhile fighting force, then the volunteers should be absorbed into the Royal Highland Emigrants. He flatly refused to restore Martin's old army rank.

The Patriots continued to work among the Highland settlers that autumn to win more of them over, or at the very least to neutralize them. The Reverend James Campbell, minister of Cross Creek, was very pro-Patriot, which influenced some Scots, and on 16 October the Governor wrote ruefully to Lord Dartmouth in London of waning support among the Highlanders and the Indians:

I have heard . . . with infinitely greater surprise and concern, that the Scotch Highlanders on whom I had such firm reliance have declared themselves for neutrality, which I am informed is to be attributed to the influence of a certain Mr Farquhard Campbell an ignorant man who has been settled from his childhood in this Country . . . and has imbibed all the American popular principles and prejudices.[22]

Campbell was clearly still taking his revenge for being displaced as leader of the Highland community in the back country.

At long last London agreed that Sir Henry Clinton should be ordered from Boston with two thousand men, and on 27 October a letter went to Martin telling him that seven regiments would sail from Cork about 1 December for Cape Fear. Unfortunately at this critical moment General Gage was replaced by Major-General William Howe as commander of the British forces in North America, and Lord Dartmouth was succeeded as Colonial Secretary by Lord George Germain, neither of whom had much interest in Carolina – as far as they were concerned this war had to be won in the north.

At this point two Highland officers turned up in North Carolina claiming that the Highlanders in the colony must abandon their plan and join three new companies of the Royal Highland Regiment which they were going to raise in the colony. These two, Lieutenant-Colonel Donald MacDonald and Captain Donald MacLeod, carried authorization to select and appoint officers for the three companies. For their dangerous journey the two Donalds had been given the cover story, in case of capture, that they had been wounded at Bunker Hill and were on their way to live with friends in Carolina. Far from welcoming them, Martin simply ignored the pair and pressed on with his own plan.

Allan and his son-in-law, Glendale, wanted nothing to do with the emigrants' regiment either. Viewed in a charitable light, Allan did not wish to abandon his family among enemies at such a dangerous time. Less kindly it might be said that it suited Allan MacDonald's vanity better to remain in the colony as leader of his own militia company than to join an unknown and unestablished regiment in which he would be no more than a captain. Perhaps the truth lay somewhere in the middle. The most Donald MacDonald managed to wring from Kingsburgh was a promise that he would go to Nova Scotia if unable to raise a large enough force among his own clansmen.

Although outranked by the officers from the north, Allan MacDonald remained the key figure in the fight to save North Carolina for the King. Because of Flora's fame and his own enthusiasm for the Loyalist cause, it was natural that the Highlanders should look to the Kingsburghs for leadership, so when the governor sent an emissary, Alexander MacLean, to the back country to establish how many Highlanders could be raised, he was ordered to talk to Allan. Following secret meetings, MacLean reported that 3000 Highlanders could be relied on, with 1000 stand of arms, but privately he believed that twice as many could be mustered.²³ This encouraged Martin in his belief that the Highlanders were crucial to the defence of the colony, so, when word arrived from Howe that Clinton's force was on its way from Boston to join the seven regiments due from Ireland, the Governor decided the moment had come to rally the Highlanders.

His plan was that the Highlanders should march to the coast near the mouth of the Cape Fear River and link up there with the invading troops, who would arm them, and together they would defeat the rebels. This force was to be put under the command of the officers from the north, Donald MacDonald and Donald MacLeod, with 'two others who have been employed on the regiments duty, and whose complement of men appears, also, to be raised'. These 'two others' were Allan and his son-in-law, MacLeod of Glendale.²⁴

On 10 January 1776, Governor Martin sent out the 'fiery cross' to rally the Highlanders to the King's flag. The words of his proclamation had the familiar ring of all those declarations, orders and proclamations that had run through the Highlands in 1745 – awesome words to chill the heart of every man and woman who had lived through that momentous time:

> I do hereby exhort, require and command in the King's name, all His Majesty's faithful subjects, on their duty and allegiance forthwith to repair to the Royal standard . . . at the same time pronouncing all such Rebels as will not join the Royal banner, Rebels and Traitors; their lives and properties to be forfeited.²⁵

Hard on the heels of this proclamation he despatched his loyal lieutenant, Alexander MacLean, to Cumberland and Anson Counties with a special message for Allan MacDonald and other Highland leaders. The time had come to rise.

CHAPTER TWELVE

A Second Culloden

We will never submit till the bayonet is removed and your tyrannical Acts of Parliament are repealed. These are the sentiments of all degrees of men in British America, a few tattered Scotch Highlanders excepted.

Letter from a Gentleman in Philadelphia[1]

At Cheek's Creek the Governor's emissary was warmly welcomed when he presented the order naming twenty men in whom Martin was putting his trust. The first name on the list was Allan MacDonald, even before that of Lieutenant-Colonel Donald MacDonald the commander of the force. Kingsburgh's son-in-law, Sandy MacLeod, came third. It was a singular honour for Allan MacDonald to be regarded as so important in the community, and Flora could certainly have claimed credit for this, although she never did.[2]

Flora seldom talked of her involvement in political matters, either in 1746 or in 1776, and when she described her Carolina experience she summed up the events leading up to the rising in a sentence:

When the American Rebellion brock out, and Congress forcing her husband to joyne them, being a leading man among the highlanders, and seeing he would be obliged to joyne either party, he went in disguise to Fort Johnston on the mouth of the River Capefear, and there settled the plan for riseing the Highlanders in arms, with Governor Martin.[3]

As the wife of Allan MacDonald, Flora saw it as her duty to be loyal first to him (and she remained so throughout their life together), to be a dutiful clanswoman to her chief and to be a faithful subject of her king. She never doubted where her duty lay and, when the time came in January 1776, she kept faith.

Governor Martin's proclamation called on the Highlanders to be at the mouth of the Cape Fear River by 15 February to meet the force he expected from Ireland, which gave the leaders less than a month to muster their men. Old Lieutenant-Colonel MacDonald, now generally referred to as General MacDonald, called for the leaders from the various districts to rendezvous with their men at Cross Creek on 5 February, ready to march to the coast.[4]

Colonels were appointed from various districts, including Flora's stepfather, Hugh MacDonald in Anson, now in his late seventies or early eighties, but still burning with all the ardour of an old soldier. Like so many of his kinsmen who had supported Prince Charlie secretly in 1746, he too rallied to the House of Hanover in the American War. Allan was appointed lieutenant-colonel, the highest rank the governor had it in his power to grant, and his son-in-law became first captain. Allan and Flora's son Alexander was made a captain, and young James was given a junior commission.

Although Allan and many other clan leaders responded enthusiastically, the Patriots' work of hectoring, threatening and wooing the Scots throughout the preceding six months proved effective and many stayed at home. Things were not going wholly in the rebels' favour, however, for several leaders of the community who had previously supported them now came over to the Loyalists. Even Farquhard Campbell changed sides, although it would be an exaggeration to say that Campbell became a Loyalist, since what he did was court both sides and give information about one to the other.

With so many Whigs among their neighbours the 'Carolina clans' had to be rallied in secret. North Carolina tradition maintains that balls and parties were held to bring the Highlanders together to enlist them and that Flora helped to organize these. Since Cheek's Creek was one of the principal rallying centres it is likely that such gatherings were held there.

General MacDonald called a muster at Cross Hill just outside Carthage, on the lands of Dr Alexander Morrison, another Skye man who had arrived in 1774. The Regulators and the Highlanders were each to bring their promised three thousand men. First the Regulators proved an enormous disappointment. Few set out to join the general, and fewer arrived at the rallying point. One group of five hundred men turned tail and scattered when they heard a rumour that a company of Patriots was approaching on the road to Cross Hill, leaving Colonel Donald MacLeod, who had gone out to meet them, without so much as a guide to lead him back to Cross Creek.[5] Of the three thousand promised, no more than a few hundred men had rallied by 12 February, in spite of promises of generous financial and land grants.[6] There would have been even fewer had they known that the promised army from Britain was still lying in its transports in Cork harbour. The fleet due to sail at the beginning of December was only now ready to depart and left the following day, 13 February.

Unaware of all this, Colonel MacLeod hurried back to Cross Hill to discover that Allan and his friends were faring badly too. He met Kingsburgh, Glendale, Colonel James Cotton and other leaders with about five hundred Highlanders. Even old Hugh of Armadale was believed to be present, although he was far too old to have taken an active part and his name never appears in any of the Loyalist documents. Thomas Rutherford, who had turned coat, reported that, because of the idle and false reports being spread by wicked and ignorant men, 'great numbers of his Majesty's liege subjects have failed to attend'.[7]

Some clansmen were persuaded to join because they believed that Governor Martin himself was on his way to Cross Creek with a large army to unite with them there. When this did not happen many blamed Allan MacDonald for deliberately misleading them and simply drifted off home, angry with Kingsburgh at being deceived. Undaunted, Kingsburgh and his friends marched their five hundred men to Cross Creek while others scoured the countryside in search of more recruits – forty here, ninety there, so that when muster day arrived on 15 February they had around 1,400 men, including Regulators and Highlanders, but only 520 weapons. Two more days spent rounding up additional weapons yielded another 130 firearms, and on 18 February they marched out of Cross Creek and off to war, a force of 1,500 men with only 650 guns and 80 broadswords among them.[8]

There can be no doubt that it was only because of the enormous influence of Flora MacDonald's name and Allan's enthusiasm that General MacDonald was able to muster even that number. No wonder the affair became known to Americans as the Insurrection of the MacDonalds. Those old enough to remember the Rising of 1745 must have recalled Prince Charlie's struggle to raise an army in the Highlands then. Kingsburgh dug deeply into his own pocket to buy equipment for himself, his sons, servants and for many of the volunteers as well. The schedule of his claim after the war covered everything from horses to rum to warm the Highlanders on their march. He paid the expenses of meetings with Regulators and Highlanders and even supplied blankets, shoes and shirts, all of which amounted to just under £300:

To my travelling expenses from
the Highland settlement in Anson
County in North Carolina to Fort
Johnston on the River Cape fear
being fourteen days from home to
settle the plan of riseing the
Highlanders with Governor Martin
who was at that time at the Fort.   28   0.   0.

To the value of 9 Stands of Arms
purchased from Messrs Marshall and
George Milln, both Merchants, of
Cross Creek @ 3 10 0 each   31   10. 0.

To Silver mounted Riffle bought of
Mr George Milln   9   9.   0.

To Caleb Tulishstone's Riffle   7   0.   0.

To Cask of Rum bo't of Mr Gillis at
Cross Creek for the use of the
Highlanders on the Expedition   7   10. 0.

To the value of five Horses taken from
me and two sons, when made Prisoners
after the Engagement the Highlanders
had with Genl Caswell at Moore's Creek,
with two Batt Horses included   85   10. 0.

To my own Family Arms, including my
three indentured Servants' Arms   42   9.   6.

To Blankets, Shoes and Shirts
purchased and given to the Common
Highlanders   18   9.   4.

To my own and two Sons' Baggage,
with Saddles &c., being robbed of
everything but barely as we stood   58   0.   0.

To expenses at different Meetings
with the Regulators and Highlanders
&c. and money given to different Expresses   11   15.   1.

                                                         _____

                                                          299   12. 11.[9]

The story preserved in North Carolina maintains that Flora waved Allan
and their two sons off from their home at Cheek's Creek, but legend is
unreliable. A strange letter purporting to have been written by Flora just
before the Highlanders marched turned up in a Clan Donald publication a
century ago. It said:

> Dear Maggie,
> Allan leaves tomorrow to join Donald's standard at Cross Creek, and I
> shall be alone with my three bairns. Canna ye come and stay with me
> a while? There are troublesome times ahead, I ween. God will keep
> the right. I hope a' oor ain are in the right prays your good friend –
> Flory McDonald.[10]

Although the letter has an uncomfortable sanctimonious nineteenth-
century ring to it and its language is pure theatrical Lowland Scots –
unreal even to southern Scottish ears – an old lady, living in Fayetteville
in 1849, claimed that Flora had sent it to the woman's older sister at the
time of the Revolution. It is interesting to compare it with *The
Autobiography of Flora MacDonald*, a strange book described as edited by
her granddaughter, Flora F. Wylde, and published in Edinburgh in 1870.
In this Flora recounts her story to a girl named Maggie, a name that is
purely a literary device, and the language she uses is as arch as the
Fayetteville lady's letter. The letter, which has vanished, is patently an
invention: so too must surely be the same woman's claim to have
watched Flora review the Highland troops as they left Cross Creek: 'I
remember seeing her riding the line on a large, white horse, and
encouraging her countrymen to be faithful to the King,' she said,[11] but
such an act would have been totally out of character with Flora's likely
response to the situation in which she found herself in February 1776.
Perhaps she did travel to Cross Creek to say farewell to her husband and
sons; perhaps she did ride there on a white horse; but she certainly never
played Joan of Arc or Queen Elizabeth of England in front of the
mustered army.

In 1776 Flora MacDonald was much more likely to have been sitting at home with her own thoughts and fears than parading on a white charger to encourage the Highland army as it marched out of Cross Creek to win North Carolina for King George.

One could almost wish that the story of Flora on the white charger might be true and that she really did review the Highland army as it left, because she could not fail to have been moved to see her husband, two sons, their kinsmen and indentured servants all following the British flag. Kingsburgh had made this possible through his courage, determination, loyalty and generosity in paying out of his own pocket for arms and clothing for many of the men. Of course there was his vanity too, that counted: at that moment he came as near to being a chief as he ever would in the whole of his life. Without Allan MacDonald there would have been no army and no defence of North Carolina. That day, Sunday 18 February, as he rode out of Cross Creek, he had his reward: he was third in command of the only army the British had in the colony, and bore the rank of lieutenant-colonel, the highest rank possible for him to hold.

Yet Allan's little army did not bear close examination. It was a force with little crusading ardour, largely without weapons and composed of men who were bewildered to find themselves caught up in a quarrel they did not understand. Some were even frightened, or resentful of the fact that Kingsburgh and his friends had lured them into this situation. This was what they had left Scotland to escape and they had no heart for a fight now.

The Highlanders marched no more than four miles from Cross Creek before they learned that the Patriots, under Colonel James Moore, had arrived at Rockfish Creek, a mere four miles farther downstream. The following morning the Highland general made up his mind to surprise the enemy after dark and, in preparation for the attack, he paraded all his men who had weapons. Some made it clear they were unwilling to fight; others just melted away into the forest. 'Some of the soldiers, suspecting that such a project was in view one Capt. Sneed with two Companys of Colo. Cotton's Corps ran off with their arms very early that night', it was reported.[12] Then the bobbing Farquhard Campbell arrived with news that Colonel Richard Caswell, who had been ordered by the New Bern Committee of Safety to march against the Highlanders with the district's militia and minute men, was about to join Moore with six hundred men. The Patriots were closing in and the Highlanders would soon be outnumbered. Campbell's view was that they should avoid battle for the present, so General MacDonald decided to cross the Cape Fear River and march on towards Wilmington. On the morning of 20 February the men were again assembled and given a rousing harangue to put fire into them. The general inveighed against those who had deserted the previous evening and told his army that, if any man was 'so fainthearted as not to serve with the resolution of conquering or dying', he should say so now. At this 'there was a general huza for the King except from about 20 men of Colo. Cottons Corps who laid down their arms and declared their courage was not warproof'.[13]

Allan MacDonald's son-in-law, Glendale, was sent ahead with a detachment of a hundred Highlanders to secure the Black River bridge fifteen miles further on. This would enable the Highlanders to push on downstream through thick forest and rough country, which at this time of year was far from the hospitable Carolina that Kingsburgh had known when he travelled up from Wilmington less than eighteen months earlier. All the way they were stalked by Patriot spies.

The Patriots had quickly mustered their men when they learned that the Highlanders were assembling at Cross Hill, and by now they were on the march. Messages shuttled back and forth between the two sides, but by Friday 23 February General MacDonald, realizing that the enemy had closed in, drew his men up in battle order and asked for volunteers to lead them into battle. Eighty 'able bodied Highlanders' stepped forward: they were armed with every broadsword the army possessed and put under the command of Captain John Campbell. MacDonald would still have preferred to avoid battle and march straight to the coast to meet the invading force expected there at any moment, but he had no choice now – he had to fight.

Two Patriot colonels, Alexander Lillington and John Ashe, each with a small force, were the first to reach the bridge over the Black River at Widow Moore's Creek on Sunday 25th, where their men began to dig themselves in to defend the crossing. The following day Caswell joined them to bring the Patriot numbers up to a thousand men, well positioned to intercept the Loyalists.

The Highland army's march from Cross Creek had been long and hard for poorly trained men, and when they arrived within six miles of the bridge late on the evening of Monday 26th they were glad to pitch camp for the night beside the swampland which lay along that part of the river. During the night the Highland general became ill, leaving Colonel MacLeod to take charge. Allan MacDonald now stood second in command. A council of war was called at which the leaders argued over whether to attack Caswell's force or not – the older, more mature men believed the

Patriots were too well positioned, but the younger officers were all for pressing on across the bridge with a surprise onslaught on the enemy emplacements on the opposite bank. These younger leaders, totally lacking in military experience, were determined to have their way and in the end the older faction had to give way and agree to attack. So before one o'clock in the chill February night the men were roused and ordered to form up in battle order.

In the darkness the army edged round the swampland as best it could, forever stumbling and slithering in mud and water. Although the river lay only six miles from their camp, dawn was less than an hour away by the time the clansmen reached the bridge at Moore's Creek. The Americans had withdrawn hurriedly from an encampment on the Patriots' side of the river, but embers of their fires were still smouldering when the Loyalists arrived. Heartened by this, MacLeod decided to storm the bridge immediately, using his hand-picked Highlanders armed with broadswords to lead the charge.

Claymores and Gaelic war cries had frightened bigger armies into defeat than this Whig band, and he believed that they would triumph again in the Carolina dawn. With Captain Campbell he brought his eighty Highlanders forward to the bridge, and gave the battlecry: 'King George and broadswords'. The clansmen raised their swords and rushed the bridge. Too late they realized that the Americans had removed many of the planks at the middle of the bridge and greased the wooden beams. As the Highlanders poured towards the black chasm at the centre of the bridge they were raked by deadly gunfire from Caswell's soldiers. MacLeod himself struggled across the bridge by dint of slithering along one of the beams, but no sooner had he reached the other side than he too was cut down by enemy fire. Behind him the Highlanders fell wounded or dead, and many simply vanished into the deep swirling water of the Black River and were drowned. The main part of the army, on seeing what was happening, turned and fled.

The Battle of Moore's Creek Bridge was over in minutes, a defeat almost as violent and swift as Culloden, and just as complete. Once again Highland bravery and the broadsword had counted for nothing in the face of devastating musket fire. But the most humiliating aspect of the defeat was that the Highland charge had been foiled by a trick.[14]

Caswell did not follow up his victory as quickly as he might have done – he could not easily cross the broken bridge to pursue the fleeing Highlanders, and when he did he wasted time gathering in the spoils of battle. Moore's Creek had cost him only a couple of soldiers, while fifty Highlanders lay dead in the creek or on its banks. Day by day the mountain of booty grew, until by 10 March the conquerors claimed (with exaggeration) to have collected 350 guns and shot-bags, 150 swords and dirks, 1,500 excellent rifles, 2 medicine-chests fresh from England (one of them valued at £300 sterling), 13 wagons and horses and an enormous amount of money.

MacLeod's death left Allan MacDonald in command of the defeated army, a fact that he pointed out with pride when he came to make his claim for compensation from the British Government after the war. There was no longer any army to command, but Allan and his remaining fellow officers rallied the remnant of their force as best they could, holding a hasty council of war at which they decided to return to Cross Creek, with around ninety of their men who still remained. From there they intended to disperse to their homes.

Colonel Moore arrived soon after the battle was over and, while he set out to seize Cross Creek, Caswell and his men began to gather in soldiers and others suspected of being Loyalists. Moore quickly caught up with Kingsburgh and his men at Smith's Ferry on the Cape Fear River, surrounded them and took every one of them prisoner. Within two days the Americans held nine hundred men – more than half the Loyalist army – including almost all the officers of importance. The general was easily captured where he was hiding in a hole near the place where he had lain ill; his surgeon, aide-de-camp, secretary, adjutant and chaplain were also taken. Then the other brave MacDonalds were brought in one by one, including Allan of Kingsburgh, his sons, Alexander and James, and Alexander MacDonald of Cuidreach. Rassie Wicker believed that old Hugh MacDonald was among the prisoners, too, and certainly a 'Hugh MacDonald' appeared on the list compiled by the committee appointed by Congress to report on the insurgents and other suspected persons held in April 1776. The Hugh MacDonald who was taken into custody was described as a freeholder living in Anson County, which certainly describes 'One-eyed' Hugh. Wicker stated: 'Evidently the old war horse could not resist when the drums rolled, and the pipes played . . . There is no record of the disposition of his case, but he was evidently paroled, and returned to Anson, where he died about 1780.' More likely old Hugh was merely brought in after the battle as a 'suspected person' and was soon freed. Three of Kingsburgh's indentured servants and numerous other MacDonalds were also taken.[15]

The prisoners were sent to gaols in various parts of the country where the rank and file were quickly paroled, but the officers were held until parole or exchange could be arranged. Allan's younger son, James, was freed or escaped and made his way back home. Allan MacDonald was marched with his fellow officers to Halifax, 150 miles north of Moore's Creek Bridge, close to the Virginia border, a place as remote as it was possible to find in North Carolina from the influence of the Highland settlements. Halifax was a trading centre of some importance in those days, a place similar to Cross Creek or Wilmington. It had a small gaol – a bleak two storey brick building – into which between two and three dozen Highlanders were crowded, cold, wretched and uncomfortable, and all the more miserable because they had no blankets, no bedding, no fire, no candles and no comfort. A bleak depression came over Allan and his health began to suffer.[16]

While the Highland officers were marching to Halifax, Moore occupied Cross Creek with two thousand jubilant Patriots who rounded up every suspect and helped themselves to whatever they fancied. They divided all the salt in the town among themselves, leaving the townspeople none, and they seized a box of gold coins, claimed to be worth £15,000, which was found hidden in a stable. Many merchants and people of importance were arrested and sent to join the prisoners in Halifax gaol, but most were freed a month later.

Precisely how and when Flora first learned the shattering news of the Moore's Creek defeat we do not know, but what she heard was the worst that could have happened. Word spread quickly through Cumberland and Anson Counties to Cheek's Creek, telling her of the defeat and that her husband and friends had all been killed or taken. She clearly never knew precisely what happened in the battle, so what she wrote of it in 1789 was probably gleaned from her husband later. She told Sir John MacPherson then that:

> after marching 200 miles and driveing the enemy from two different posts they had taken, [the Highland army] made a night attack on General Caswell at the head of 3000 Congrass troops, who were intrenched on the other side of Moors Creek, the bridge being cutt down excepting the two side beams on which a noumber of highlanders got over, but were bet back with considerable lose, the enemy haveing 3 piece of cannon planted in front close to the bridg, which forced the highlanders to retire back 12 miles, to the place from whence they marched the night before.[17]

At the time Flora knew nothing for certain of her family's fate, but sat alone at Cheek's Creek, sick with sorrow, only her three female servants for comfort, waiting for news of her husband, her two sons, her son-in-law and their servants, who had marched away so proudly less than a fortnight before. If her stepfather was arrested that added to her worries. These days were the longest in Flora MacDonald's life, longer even than those she spent as a prisoner in a British warship in 1746. Flora MacDonald's North Carolina dream was over before it had properly begun – its end the more shattering by its unexpectedness. Flora waited at Cheek's Creek utterly devastated.

CHAPTER THIRTEEN

The Years of Fear

Now, sir, permit me to say; when you'll know, the dispersed and distress't state of my family, you will at least sympathize with me, and pity my oppress'd mind.

Letter from Allan MacDonald to
Continental Congress[1]

Flora's son, James, a lad of only eighteen, was the only member of her family to come home, the only glimmer of good fortune in two years of unrelenting wretchedness for the heroine. James was able to reassure her that his father and brother, Sandy, were safe, although both were held by the Patriots. That gave her hope, but it was by no means a reason for rejoicing because there was ample evidence of the bitterness that now lay all around her in North Carolina. No one was safe – in enemy hands or out of them.

Flora described her husband's capture and imprisonment, and gave us the only version we have of her own harrowing experiences in the two years following Moore's Creek. Of Allan she said:

> The common highlanders then parting with my husband, Mr McDonald of Kingsborrow, and their other leaders, excepting about ninty faithfull followers, who with their leaders made their way back to Smiths Ferrie on the Higher part of the Capefear, where Col. Martin with 3000 Congress men mett them, surrounded them & made them prisoners, Mr McDonald and about 30 other gentlemen were draged from goal to goal for 700 miles, till lodged in Philadelphia Goal, remaining in their hands for 18 months befor exchanged.[2]

Her account of her own difficulties and the brutality she faced at once highlights not only her suffering, but that of all the other families left alone in North Carolina. She remembered it vividly when asked to describe it thirteen years later:

Mrs Flora McDonald, being all this time in misery and sickness at home, being informed that her husband and friends were all killed or taken, contracted a severe fever, and was deeply oppressed with stragling partys of plunderers from their army and night robbers, who more than once threatened her life wanting a confession where her husbands money was. Her servants deserting her, and such as stayed grew so very insolent that they were of no service or help to her.[3]

Flora stayed on at Cheek's Creek with James for as long as she could, suffering great indignities now that the Revolution had become a bloody war in which neighbour fought neighbour and even members of the same families were enemies. No one was safe from Patriot soldiers, civilian committees or even marauding bands of robbers from either side taking advantage of the turmoil of war. Settlers on neighbouring plantations who had lived in harmony for years became bitter enemies.

Visitors, once so warmly welcomed at Cheek's Creek, were now dreaded because they might be robbers or officious Patriot zealots threatening and asking questions, and there was nobody within miles to bring help should it be needed. No one was to be trusted except the closest and most trustworthy of friends. It was a life of constant fear.

Men like Ebenezer Folsom abused their authority. In May 1776 Folsom was put in command of a Patriot force at Cross Creek, with orders to keep the Tories in order in Cumberland and the adjacent counties. He behaved so arrogantly that both Loyalists and Patriots grew to hate him and petitioned for his removal. In 1777 he was tried for usurpation and abuse of power.

Carolina became a place of hatred and feud where neither person nor property was safe. Both sides were guilty of cruelty, but the families of those who had mustered to the King's call to arms suffered worst of all. The terror continued for many of them beyond the end of the war when the civil courts took over with the same degree of cruelty, all of which has been glossed over by American historians. As Robert DeMond put it, 'Historians of the revolutionary war have entirely ignored the hardship which was willingly endured by this large group.'[4]

Flora was brought before one of the committees of safety. She behaved with the same composure and dignity as had won over her enemies in 1746, but it failed to help her now. Allan's cousin with the Royal Highland Emigrant Regiment in Nova Scotia heard about this incident and wrote to Kingsburgh:

I am also happy to hear of Mrs Macdonald's Wellfare & her Spirited behaviour when bro^t. before the Committee of Rascals in North Carolina. I don't doubt but She & the Other Gentlewomen there will be sorely oppressed by the Savage Cruelty of those Wretches who at present has the Upper hand of them.[5]

Fear and anxiety brought on severe attacks of fever, during which she had only James to nurse her. Yet even in those unbearably burdensome times Flora MacDonald's uncompromising sense of duty drove her on. Ignoring the fact that it was extremely dangerous to travel in North Carolina, as soon as she began to recover from her fever Flora felt compelled 'to visit & comfort the other poor gentlewomen whose husbands were prisoners with Mr McDonald, as they blamed him as being the author of their misery in riseing the highlanders.'[6] Flora was doubly brave: well aware of the criticism of her husband which was now circulating among the Highland community, she felt she had to face these people and offer them what explanations and comfort she could. In order to do what she saw as her duty she ignored all the dangers and rode around the countryside to visit the Highland families who were surely no worse off than she herself was. Unfortunately on one of these journeys she fell from her horse and broke her right arm. This, she said, 'confined her for months, the only phishitian in the collony being prisoner with her husband'.[7]

Left with no comforter but young James she remained in this desperate condition for two years, constantly subjected to insults and robbery. She lost the books and other treasures she had brought from Skye, including her exquisite silver, which is still in Carolina in private hands. It comprises four pieces – a tray bearing the monogram F McD, a jug, sauceboat and ladle – and ownership can be traced back only as far as the 1780s since when it has been in the possession of the same family. The silver has been described as 'prized because of its beauty of Old English craftsmanship, more prized because it was the gift of admiring friends in London when, as the Prince's Preserver, she was the centre of popular interest'.[8]

North Carolina legend claims that Flora sold the silver in Wilmington to pay her fare back to Scotland from Charleston, but Flora MacDonald did not return directly to Scotland from Carolina, so she certainly did not sell her silver to pay her passage. How Flora MacDonald came to part with the silver plate will probably never be known, but whether she sold it voluntarily or had it taken from her by one of the roving bands, Allan considered it to have been 'plundered by the enemy' and included it in his claim for compensation. If not actually stolen from her home the silver may have been taken from Flora and sold off to pay alleged debts, as happened to so many of the Loyalists' possessions at this time.

For her own safety Flora moved several times during those eighteen unhappy months. Precise information as to her whereabouts is scarce, but tradition is strong enough to allow us to know broadly where and how she lived.

Rassie Wicker believed that Flora was with Anne for part of the period in question. Certainly she would want to be with her daughter during Anne's confinement with her fourth child which took place during 1776. Wicker examined local fact and tradition and came to the conclusion that she lived with Anne, either at Glendale or on another one-hundred-acre plantation belonging to Kenneth Black, the man from whom MacLeod had rented his Glendale land. This second settlement was on Nick's Creek near Pinehurst. Wicker wrote:

> It is unlikely that the houses at either Glendale or the Nick's Creek place were commodious buildings; certainly not roomy enough for Flora and her eight servants in addition to Mrs McLeod, her four children and her twelve servants. It is the writer's opinion that a large part of these were assigned to the plantation on Nick's Creek, while Flora and her daughter, with perhaps three or four women servants, occupied Glendale.[9]

In the light of the fact that some of the menservants were taken prisoner at Moore's Creek and Flora's own statement that others deserted, it is unlikely that she and Anne had anything like twenty servants between them. At most they probably had no more than half a dozen, mostly women, some unreliable, but a few as faithful to the Kingsburgh family as the Kingsburghs were to their king. Fanciful claims have been made that Flora's servant girl, Kate, who accompanied her to her prison ship in 1746, was with her in North Carolina, but this must be nonsense. Kate vanished from the story when Flora sailed from Leith to London in HMS *Bridgewater* and the most likely explanation is that she was sent home to Skye at that time.

At Glendale there was no more security for Flora than at Cheek's Creek. Her son-in-law, Alexander MacLeod, in his claim said:

> his property [was] plundered and destroyed to a considerable amount, his wife [far advanced in her pregnancy] driven for refuge to

a near relative's house twenty four miles distant, and the children who could not make a sufficiently expeditious escape [were] with their nurses, separated in the woods.[10]

The Patriots caught the children, but fortunately some loyal servants managed to convince them that the youngsters were their own. The robbers then turned on one of the menservants, demanding to know where Glendale's money and valuables were hidden, but he refused to tell. Glendale's losses were considerable: his claim for more than £1,500 included his fine furniture and books – no fewer than 360 volumes – which he had brought from Skye.

Another strong North Carolina tradition maintains that Flora and Anne spent much of this time at the Cuidreach plantation, which was twenty-four miles from Glendale, and possibly she did seek refuge there for a while. However, according to Alexander MacDonald of Cuidreach's claim after the war, life at Mount Pleasant was just as unsafe. Cuidreach told the Claims Commissioners:

> Your memorialist's family consisting of a wife and five children . . . suffered cruelties which exceed description, being frequently plundered of the common necessaries of life, and at last stripped from even their body cloathes and turned out of their house into the woods, where they must have perished for want of food and cloathing had not their miserable plight wrought on the feelings of one of their captains who had the humanity to conduct them within the British Lines and was rewarded with all the money your memorialist had at command.[11]

Apart from suggesting that Annabella was not in a position to help her half-sister and Anne, Cuidreach's claim demonstrates that pity could sometimes be shown by Patriots towards Loyalist families. The Cuidreachs reached Charleston and sailed home to Britain from there, arriving in London in February 1783.

Anne MacLeod was much more likely to have stayed on Kenneth Black's plantation with her mother than at Mount Pleasant. Black was a staunch Loyalist to the point that he was eventually murdered because of his adherence to the King's cause, and he would willingly help his friend Glendale. Anne's husband escaped after Moore's Creek and hid in the forests for six weeks (one wonders if Black helped here also?) until he was able to make his way to the coast and join the governor. In spite of Patriot offers of a reward for his capture, Glendale managed eventually to reach New York.

Many tales were handed down from generation to generation, telling of destruction of property, burning of houses, robbing, terrorizing and humiliating. Some of these concerning Flora are so preposterous that one suspects they may have originated as propaganda stories. One recounts how two of Flora's daughters fell into the hands of Whigs while on a visit to friends, and had the rings pulled from their fingers and silk handkerchiefs snatched from their necks. Then the soldiers put their swords into the girls' bosoms and split their dresses down the front. All this is not hard to disprove – Flora had only one daughter with her in America. Yet the story resolutely refuses to go away. A similar incident may well have happened to someone else, or it may be pure fiction put about by anti-Patriots to discredit the enemy. Whatever its source the tale persisted.

Another, carrying the hallmarks of revolutionary propaganda, concerns Flora's departure from the one-hundred-acre plantation. It relates that one of the servants became ill with smallpox and lay at death's door when Flora had to flee suddenly. She could not take him, but hesitated to leave him behind, so in desperation she smothered him with a blanket and had him buried. There cannot be a shred of truth in such a story: a servant probably did die and was buried hurriedly before Flora fled from one of the gangs of robbers, and her enemies built a story round it to discredit Flora and her fellow Highlanders.[12]

In prison Allan learned a little about his wife's suffering and complained to the Committee of Safety in Philadelphia that General Philip Schuyler, the Patriot general in the north, had led him and his fellow prisoners to believe that their families would be provided for, yet his wife was living in great need. He could do nothing more than complain: he was powerless to help Flora and, indeed, he had plenty of troubles of his own.

At Halifax he pined in the cramped, comfortless gaol, far from his family and unsure of what was happening to them. He was allowed to keep one of his servants with him, which made life easier, but he missed his family and fretted over the humiliation of the defeat at Moore's Creek Bridge. Soon he was joined by old General MacDonald, who had still not recovered fully from the illness that had kept him from the battle.

The Americans were jubilant about their victory: so elated in fact that, when their Provincial Congress met at Halifax in April 1776, it passed a resolution calling for complete independence from Britain. Moore's Creek

Bridge had been a catalyst which put North Carolina in the van of the movement towards the United States' Declaration of Independence the following July.

They may have sounded confident at that moment, but the Americans still feared invasion from the force under Sir Henry Clinton and the still-awaited British fleet. The soldiers from the north arrived but could not land, so they hovered at the mouth of the Cape Fear River. At long last the fleet of warships and transports from Britain reached Cape Fear at the beginning of May. The Americans were determined that the Highlanders would not remuster to join these invaders, so they proposed to send the prisoners out of North Carolina altogether, to Virginia and Maryland. Key prisoners were to be banished to the Patriot heartland of Philadelphia – those 'such as appear to us from their rank and influence over an Ignorant and restless part of our Inhabitants to be capable of doing us the most mischief'. There were twenty-six in all in this category and, of course, they included Allan and his son. In spite of the almost universal bitterness on both sides, the American leaders could still show compassion – about this time the Patriots commented:

> We are sorry to be compelled to an act of such severity as this sending of these men at such a distance from their unfortunate families; but the security of our country makes it indispensably necessary for should they have an opportunity of exerting their pernicious influence at a time when we may be invaded by a powerful army, the consequences might, and probably, would prove fatal.[13]

In Kingsburgh's case they wavered for just long enough to send a message to General Schuyler, asking if he would allow Allan to be sent home on parole. Without waiting for an answer, the Provincial Congress, which met in Halifax during April, decided 'that in consideration of the candor of Allen MacDonald, and his being in a low state of health, recommend him to be admitted to his parole of honour'.[14] He was not allowed to go home, but the conditions were similar to parole granted to General MacDonald the previous week – Allan was to remain confined to the town, he had to report daily to the authorities and he was not to be allowed to correspond with anyone who opposed the Patriots.

Humanity did not extend to all involved in the cause of Independence, and the parole was not properly implemented. Allan and the general were still held under guard in the room they shared in Halifax Gaol, and before

April they were on their way to Philadelphia. Regardless of his poor health, Allan was forced to set out on this four-hundred-mile journey on foot. It was like walking from Skye to Manchester in unbearable heat, along dusty roads that passed through unfriendly settlements and hostile towns. He complained bitterly when he reached Petersburg, Virginia, telling a friend, 'To walk on foot is what I can never do the length of Philadelphia.' [15] But he did. There was no choice – he and his fellow Highland officers had to trudge on through the growing heat of the southern spring to Fredericksburg, Alexandria and Baltimore. By 19 May they were in the new gaol in Walnut Street, Philadelphia. Allan still had his son, Alexander, with him, which brought him a little comfort and companionship.

Philadelphia Gaol, though brand new, was far from pleasant, and the prisoners were held closely under guard by the Pennsylvania Committee of Safety. Philadelphia's melting hot, humid summer days were oppressively heavy, while the nights were cold, and prisoners in the town gaol had insufficient blankets and few comforts. A week after Allan's arrival the Committee of Safety asked the Continental Congress what subsistence allowance should be given to the Highland officers, and Congress granted them $2 a week for their board and lodging, to be repaid on their release.

The Highland officers in Philadelphia Gaol were not the only Scots to suffer. From now on life for all of their countrymen – Highlanders and Lowlanders alike – in every part of America became progressively more difficult: in the south because of the Highlanders' dogged loyalty, and in the north because of the important contribution that Scottish regiments were making to Britain's war campaign. To be a Scot was enough to bring down the wrath of the authorities and of the mob who mindlessly drove out many moderate men and women who might have contributed much to the emerging American nation after the war. In 1776 the Scots were the only people to be singled out by name when the Declaration of Independence came to be drafted. Thomas Jefferson's draft included the line: 'At this very time too they [the British authorities] are permitting their chief magistrate to send over not only soldiers of our common blood, but Scotch and foreign mercenaries to invade and destroy us.' Congress removed this offensive sentence from the version that was approved at Philadelphia on 4 July 1776.

These were days of tremendous excitement in Philadelphia, with constant comings and goings of delegates to Congress and, on 8 July, the Declaration of Independence was read publicly in the town. From his cell in the gaol, which stood directly opposite the State House where Congress met, Allan could hear the rejoicing. On the following day he was sent to Reading, fifty-five miles up the Schuylkill River, where many Loyalist prisoners were being held. A week later his son was allowed to join him at Reading but, although the town was so full of British prisoners, Allan and Alexander were the only two Carolina Highlanders held in it. The move cost Congress £7 10s., a sum to be charged back to the prisoners in due course.

Life at Reading was more tolerable since the two were allowed to have a servant with them and all three were given $5 a week allowance – if the money arrived on time, which could never be depended on.[16] Inflation depressed the value of even that modest amount month by month, until Allan was forced to petition Congress for more the following year. 'Drink, Lodging and Cloathing and in short everything is so extravagantly high priced that Prisoners must be in a very miserable State', he wrote on 5 April 1777. 'Two dollars, the common allowance per week being of greater service ten months before now, than Six these days.'[17]

Yet Allan was able to replenish his wardrobe and still cut a dash as a Highland gentleman: on 10 May he wrote to Alexander Bartram, a merchant in Philadelphia, to order material for two summer waistcoats as well as scarlet cloth and 'furniture' to make a third. As an afterthought he asked also for material to make 'two pair of Breeches of wheat coarded or plaine stuff'.[18]

But the one thing that eluded him was that which he longed for most – freedom. Others taken at Moore's Creek Bridge had been exchanged long before: at the end of 1776 Allan complained to Congress that he and his son were the only North Carolina prisoners for whom no exchanges were being arranged. It did no good. He petitioned several times again to be exchanged for an American prisoner and Congress offered to hand him over in return for a Colonel Lute, then on parole in the town. The British, however, would only rank Allan as a captain and refused to match him with an officer of higher rank. Governor Martin's generosity in conferring the highest rank it was in his power to give now proved a terrible handicap to Kingsburgh, who was forced to waste away a second sweltering, humid Pennsylvania summer in confinement.

News of Flora and other members of his family was still filtering through from time to time, as can be seen from a petition he submitted on 18 July 1777. In this he told Congress:

I am here with one of my Sons – seventeen months a Prisoner. My wife in North Carolina 700 miles from me in a very sickly tender state of health, with a younger son, a daughter, & four Grand Children. Two sons in our Service of whom I heard little or nothing, since one of them had been wounded in the Battle of Bunker hill – and two in Britain, of whom, I heard no account since I left it. Them in Carolina I can be of no service to in my present state, but were I Exchanged I would be of service to the rest if in life.[19]

The two sons 'in our Service' were Kingsburgh's oldest son, Charles, and third son, Ranald, who was now acting as cousin Alexander's adjutant in Nova Scotia. America at war was a magnet for young men with a spark of adventure, particularly those with poor prospects, or younger sons whose opportunities at home were limited. It offered excitement, a chance to make their mark, and opportunities to climb the social and financial ladder fast. Charles had abandoned the East India Company at the start of the war and sailed for America with the idea of buying himself an army commission. This had the irresistible advantage that it also brought him nearer to his parents and his brothers. On 18 May 1776, through the influence of cousin Alexander, he too was commissioned as a lieutenant in the Royal Highland Emigrants.

From mid-1776 on, Allan MacDonald and his sons, Charles and Alexander, all held commissions in the new regiment, and it was this commission that eventually gave Kingsburgh hope of freedom. After nearly eighteen months, during which he had seen every other Carolina Highlander officer released, he realized that he stood little chance of being exchanged as a lieutenant-colonel in the Carolina Militia, but he might be successful as a captain of the Royal Highland Emigrants because there were more prisoner officers of lower rank available for exchange. He petitioned Congress again during the Summer of 1777, telling them that, although he was a lieutenant-colonel in the militia, he held a captain's commission in the regular army, and he was sure the British commander-in-chief, Sir William Howe, would exchange him in either rank. He now suggested that he should be released on parole in order that he might negotiate an exchange for himself and his son. Congress agreed and on 21 August 1777, after all but one week of a miserable eighteen months as a prisoner, Allan MacDonald set out for New York accompanied by Alexander to seek some way of winning complete freedom for both of them.[20]

PART THREE

To Nova Scotia and Skye Again

CHAPTER FOURTEEN

Freedom at Last

I am also happy to hear of Mrs Macdonald's Wellfare & her Spirited behaviour when brot. before the Committee of Rascals in North Carolina.

Letter from Captain Alexander MacDonald to
his cousin, Allan MacDonald of Kingsburgh[1]

The British occupied New York in September 1776 and held it until after the war ended in November 1783. It became the headquarters for the British army commanders and an important link with Britain. By the time Allan MacDonald arrived there, a year after its capture, the harbour was crammed with hundreds of ships and the town was bursting at the seams with soldiers and refugees. A fire at the time of the British occupation and another just before Allan reached it resulted in a terrible housing shortage so, while the rich lived well, the poor spent icy winters and broiling hot summers in a makeshift canvas shanty town. The enemy was never far away so the place was permanently on a war footing, yet army officers and wealthier civilians enjoyed a hectic social life of dinners, parties, balls, the theatre and concerts. New York offered the brittle pleasure of a frontline garrison town that knows war can bring all the gaiety to an end at any moment, but, in 1777, it was the place to be for anyone who wanted to be at the heart of things, and that suited Kingsburgh. He settled there to enjoy its social life while he pleaded with General Howe to offer an American prisoner for exchange with him.

But Howe was not interested in Kingsburgh or his plight: he was busy outmanoeuvring George Washington at the Battle of Brandywine and attempting to strike at the Patriot heart in Philadelphia. Wagging Patriot and Loyalist tongues said that the rest of his time and attention was taken up with his mistress, Mrs Elizabeth Loring, to the neglect of his military duties. Whether due to General Howe's occupation with matters of war or of the heart, Allan MacDonald was left to his own devices to arrange an exchange for himself and his son after their arrival in New York in late August or early September 1777.

He succeeded with remarkable speed: he stated in his claim to the British Government at the end of the war that he was exchanged in August that year, but surely he meant only that he was freed to arrange his exchange during that month. According to the record of pay issued to North Carolina officers by Governor Martin, Allan MacDonald served 626 days, from 10 January 1776 to 27 September 1777, which suggests that this was the official date of his exchange.

The Royal Highland Regiment now existed officially: it was put on establishment on 25 December 1776, with the second battalion still stationed at Halifax, Nova Scotia. Allan's cousin, Captain Alexander MacDonald, wrote to Allan on the last day of the year 1777 to say, 'Nothing can give me greater pleasure than to hear of you & Your Son being Safe out of the hands of the Rebels.'[2] This was in response to a letter written by Allan on St Andrew's Day, 30 November, which must have told cousin Alexander about the exchange. Captain MacDonald urged Allan to head north to Nova Scotia at once to join the Royal Highland Emigrants for which he was desperately recruiting at the time. 'For Gods sake dont Stay long Come to us before the Winter sets in & bring all the fine fellows you possibly can get along with you', Alexander pleaded.[3]

As an additional incentive the captain gave Kingsburgh news that his son, Ranald, was with him in Nova Scotia and was looking forward to seeing his father. Perhaps the best news he sent Allan, however, was details of the accumulated back pay that Kingsburgh could draw in New York. Allan was perpetually short of money, but at no time more acutely than now when he was in New York where living costs were high and ways of spending money endless. Allan did not dash off to Nova Scotia at his cousin's request for two reasons: he was waiting for word of Flora and he was busy in New York raising a company of eighty-four Gentlemen Volunteers from Virginia and North Carolina.

Life became progressively harder for Flora and other Highlanders' wives in North Carolina while their menfolk were held in prison. Marauding bands of robbers were just part of their torment – officialdom added its own dimension to their suffering. As early as 1776 local committees of safety compelled some Highland settlers to leave, and the Provincial Congress passed its first law to confiscate the property of those who would not take an oath of loyalty, and to banish them from the state. There is no evidence that the Kingsburgh plantations were taken from Flora, and it was decreed that women and children should not be molested, but Flora certainly did not live there in peace after Moore's Creek Bridge. By April 1777 even more stringent laws were passed and Loyalists began to stream out of North Carolina, bound for Canada, the West Indies, the Bahamas, East Florida and back to Britain. In July a large vessel sailed with many Tories, their wives and children, the majority of them Scots. The following October the *North Carolina Gazette* reported that Flora MacDonald, with a great number of overloyal people, had sailed from Charleston for Scotland, but Flora MacDonald of Kingsburgh was certainly not among these fugitives.

Kingsburgh kept himself busy while he waited for news of his wife. He proudly boasted to his cousin that he had raised a company of '100 gentlemen volunteers from Carolina then in New York' and equipped them with splendid uniforms at his own expense,[4] but the response he received was cool. Captain MacDonald replied tartly, 'I Darr say you and your Vollunteers make a formidable figure in the Dress you have Describ'd to Me'. The Captain would far rather his cousin had brought his volunteers to Nova Scotia where they were needed for his regiment. 'I had rather you was here at the head of your own Company in our Regiment than Commanding a Com^y. of Provincials wch as we have a great many Enemys may be made a handle of to hinder our Establishment', he told Allan.[5]

Kingsburgh used up a lot of his money fitting out his company of volunteers. In Nova Scotia his sons were going through every penny of their own as well as whatever they could squeeze from their father's allowance until Allan once again found himself deeply in debt. His cousin helped him to obtain every penny of arrears of pay that he could for himself and for Alexander, who had been in prison with him, but he could do no more than give advice about how Allan should spend his money. There was more sorrow than anger in Captain MacDonald's letter in reply to Allan's financial problems:

You tell me you have contracted a Great Deall of Debt. I Darr Saie you must have lieved Expensive but it is high time now my Dear Allan to Study Oeconomy your 3 oldest Sons are provided for Espetialy if this Reg^t will be Establish^d therefore has no right to Expect any more assistance from you, if you was worth ten thousand a year.[6]

The three 'oldest sons' referred to were, of course, Charles, Ranald and Sandy who was still in New York and hoping for a captaincy.[7]

Ranald was to deliver this letter to his father in New York and tell him all about Nova Scotia, in the hope that this might tempt Allan away from playing clan chiefs and army commanders. Not a bit of it: a fortnight later cousin Alexander was writing again to warn that Ranald would be asking for money to buy higher commissions for himself and his brother, Charles. It was one of those 'I feel it is my duty to tell you' letters, informing the recipient of something he will not want to hear. 'These Circumstances are as galling to me to relate as they can possibly be to you to hear them but I think it my Duty from the Sincerest Friendship to acquaint you with them', he told his cousin.

The boys had inherited their father's inability to manage money, especially Charles, whom cousin Alexander described as 'a fine young fellow for whom I have the Sincerest regard . . . very Sensible & very Clever when Sober but rather unhappy when he is in any ways disguised in Liquor'. Charles was living it up in Nova Scotia and needed to be kept on a tight rein. Alexander advised Allan to question Ranald closely about all this as soon as he arrived – 'with the power & authority of a parent Command Ronald at his peril to tell you the truth of all he knows Concerning Charles & his behaviour' – but not to reveal where his information had come from.

'I beg you to keep tight hand & learn them to live upon their pay Especially as you have other things to do with Yr money & other people to provide for', the captain advised, adding that the real solution was for Allan to come to Nova Scotia where he could keep an eye on the young men.[8]

On 19 February 1778, the captain wrote to Allan again, but with growing impatience. The Kingsburgh boys were still spending money with all their father's abandon. Cousin Alexander had already been forced to give both Ranald and Charles advances against their father's account and he was becoming tired of it. Charles was again the main offender, having borrowed £10 from his father's cousin, despite the fact that he had an income of more than £37 a year. 'If all this is not Sufft to Support Chars what will other poor Subalterns do who has not a farthing but their bare subsistance?' cousin Alexander asked sharply.[9]

For very good reasons the boys had been discouraging their father from leaving New York. Nova Scotia in winter was a remote, bleak, deadly boring place with none of the compensations of New York's lively social life, but, of course, even more important was the freedom they had when their father was not present to curb their enjoyment. Captain MacDonald was angry with the MacDonald boys and tired of playing the heavy father to them. He told Allan:

I understand that Charles & Ronald are entirely ag^st your Joining the Regiment I dont know w^t good reason they can have for it but One thing I am sure of it is absolutely necessary that you should be as near them as possible to overawe their Conduct & assist them with your good Advice & without you clearly see that you can do better for yourself by staying where you are I w^d earnestly recommend it to you to Join the Reg^t as soon as possible with all the Offrs & Recruits you can possibly bring along with you As well for the above Reasons as for the Character of the Regim^t.[10]

As if it would make any difference he proffered an additional carrot to tempt Kingsburgh: 'Bad as this place was always reckoned This is certainly the Most peaceable Corner now in America.'[11]

Allan ignored his cousin's plea. He now had a compelling reason for remaining in New York: here he was at the heart of things, and something was being done at last to get Flora out of North Carolina. Flora herself told later what happened, writing in a mixture of the third and first person: 'Her husband and son-in-law Major Alex^r McLeod obtained a flag of truce from Sir Henry Clinton and Admirall How, which brought me, my daughter and her children from Wilmingtown in N. Carolina to New York.'[12]

That makes Flora's escape from North Carolina sound simple – it wasn't. Having obtained the flag of truce, her son-in-law, Alexander MacLeod, sailed to the mouth of the Cape Fear River in the sloop *Sukey and Peggy* and anchored off Brunswick on 21 February 1778. Foolishly believing that the papers he carried would guarantee his safety he went ashore to buy meat, only to be seized by Colonel Ward of the North Carolina Militia and put under guard. He was not allowed to contact his friends on board the ship. Ward and General John Ashe each sent reports to Colonel Caswell, the hero of Moore's Creek Bridge, who had now become Governor of North Carolina. Their reports were backed by another from local Patriots in the town who told Caswell, 'We must beg to acquaint you that Major MacLeod, who brings the Flag, was one of the principal acting officers in the Insurrection in this State by the Highlanders and was himself in the engagement at Widow Moore's Creek.'[13]

Against all that advice the Governor accepted MacLeod's flag of truce and ordered that he should be allowed to leave North Carolina 'with his wife and son and Mrs MacDonald and her four children with their indentured female servants'. Here the Governor confused the two families: it was Alexander's wife who had four children and his mother-in-law, Flora, who had only her son with her. MacLeod was told to lose no time because 'the more expeditious he is in getting away, the greater satisfaction he will give the State'.[14]

The *Sukey and Peggy* sailed up river to Wilmington, where she remained under constant guard while Glendale sent urgent messages to the back country to order Flora and Anne to come as fast as they could and join him on board the ship. Flora's son, James, was included in the arrangement for the families to leave, but there is no record that he accompanied them, and both he and his half-cousin, Donald, turned up in North Carolina later fighting on the British side.

Flora's half-sister and Donald appear to have stayed on to look after old Hugh, who was now near to the end of his life. Donald had another good reason for remaining: his grandfather had made over his plantation to him so he would have wanted to protect it. Allan signed an affidavit to the effect that Hugh of Armadale had handed his property over to his grandson when he backed Donald's claim for compensation from the British Government and said he had witnessed the signing of the deed of transfer.[15] Hugh died in about 1780, and the site of the grave where he is reputed to be buried is still pointed out by his descendants beside Old Mount Carmel Presbyterian Church in the foothills of North Carolina's Uwharrie Mountains.

We have only tradition on which to rely for the details of Flora's departure from Carolina, but this suggests that the order to leave came as a surprise to her and she abandoned the house at which she was staying in great haste and confusion. With Anne and her family she hurried to Wilmington and boarded the *Sukey and Peggy*, which still lay under guard, and sailed north. Once again Flora found herself making a voyage under the most disagreeable conditions – 'in the dead of winter, being in danger of our lives for the most of the voyge by a constant storme'.[16] She sailed to New York.

Flora escaped in the nick of time, for during the spring of 1778 the British turned their attention to winning the war in the south and began a campaign that lasted three years, and in which Flora's sons were involved. By the time this started she was reunited with Allan at last: it had been two years and two months since they parted as the Highlanders marched to war.

Although New York was far from being a peaceful or happy place when Flora reached it in April 1778, it must have held something of the happiness of 1774 in it for the Kingsburghs. Allan and Flora were there with their daughter, Anne, her husband, Alexander MacLeod, and their four children. This was a time of contentment in spite of all the comings and goings of ships and soldiers, and the ceaseless flow of news of war. Anne's husband was on half pay, so he returned to London with his family in October 1778 to try to obtain an army commission again and to apply for recompense for the money he had laid out to raise the Highlanders in Carolina. After months of wrangling and pleading he succeeded, and he returned to America a couple of years later where he fought in the Carolina campaign.

In New York after Flora arrived, Allan continued to devote himself to his eighty-four volunteers who paraded in the splendid scarlet and blue uniforms he had bought for them. Through these brief, baking summer months he was able to put thoughts of joining his regiment aside and even to ignore his financial worries. It proved to be a short-lived spell of happiness, however. Allan might push his financial problems to the back of his mind, but cousin Alexander in Halifax could not. Writing to William MacAdam in New York at the beginning of June, to enclose a letter for Allan, Alexander wrote, 'Should he [Allan] be Straightened for Cash you may venture to endorse his bill on me for any sum within or about 100 G^S'. The captain had already cleared an account for £160 'advanced to the Same Gentleman before'.[17]

Captain MacDonald had other Kingsburgh worries, apart from Allan's finances, to cope with at this time – the young Kingsburghs were still a sore trial. Sandy, who was now with the regiment in Halifax, was taken seriously ill as a result of a wound he had received earlier, probably at Moore's Creek, and had to undergo an operation, and Captain Alexander needed another officer to stand in for him. He asked Charles to take over his brother's duties, but was refused on the grounds that Charles expected his parents, whom he had not seen for many years, to arrive shortly. There seemed to be no end to the selfishness of the young Kingsburghs and the trouble they were prepared to give their father's cousin.[18]

This was not a happy time for Captain MacDonald. France and Spain had joined in the war on the side of the Americans and MacDonald blamed the London Government for the mess in which the British found themselves. He was full of bitterness over the leaders' mismanagement:

The honor and Grandeur of Great Britain were never in a more despisable situation than the present owing entirely to the Misconduct of the Villainous Minority and I hope in God if the Army is obliged to leave America that the first thing they will do when they land in Britain is to Scalp every son of a Bitch of them.[19]

He was losing patience with Allan MacDonald, too, and in August issued an ultimatum. Writing again to William McAdam, he instructed:

If Capt Murd. McLean or Capt Allan Macdonald Should be there tell them as I have said before its very Surprizing w^t keeps them there that I will Certainly Stop their Credit from receiving any more money if they dont Join the Reg^t or Assign Sufficient Reasons to the Contrary.[20]

That forced Allan to capitulate at last and to travel to Nova Scotia to join his regiment in October. On arrival he was posted to command the garrison at Fort Edward, a strongly fortified defence at Windsor, just where the Avon and St Croix Rivers converge and flow into the Minas Basin. The fort consisted of a square earthwork with ramparts and a wooden palisade enclosing barracks, officers' quarters, brewhouse, bakery, kitchens, stores, magazine and a fortified blockhouse. Only the blockhouse remains today, one of the oldest buildings in Nova Scotia, a squat, square, two-storey wooden building with an overhanging upper storey which has slits in the floor of the overhang to repel attackers. Fort Edward was well placed to protect the forty-mile overland route from the Bay of Fundy to Halifax, and during the American War it served its function in protecting the province from at least two planned American invasions.

Cousin Alexander had agreed that Flora might be with her husband at Windsor, so it was arranged that she should follow him to Nova Scotia almost immediately, although she still had not recovered fully from her ordeal in North Carolina. It was now late autumn and not a good time for a voyage from New York to Halifax, but Flora probably had no choice because Allan could not afford for her to stay on in New York. The sea journey was sheer hell: recalling it later, she said that, by the time the ship reached Halifax 'I . . . was very nigh deaths door, by a violent disorder, the rough sea and long passage had brought on.'[21]

There was clearly some hurry to get her to Windsor before winter closed in to block the forty-mile long track across the isthmus to Windsor. '[We] were alowed to stay there [Halifax] for eight days on account of my tender state', she wrote. 'The ninth day sett off for Windsor, on the Bey of Minas, throw woods and snow and arived the fifth day.'[22]

The route across Nova Scotia, beautiful in summer, climbed through pine forest and crossed a rocky ridge of magnificent beeches, elms and maples, before dropping down on to farmland and orchards on land drained by the French for the last few miles' drive to Windsor. With no proper road at this time it was a hard, exhausting winter journey, and next to impossible for a sick woman.

Worse was to follow. At Fort Edward the quarters in which she stayed with Allan, most likely part of the cramped and spartan officers' quarters, were miserable and bitterly cold. Nova Scotia's climate could hardly have been more different from what she had left behind in North Carolina and it was certainly colder by far than anything she ever knew in Skye. She recalled it vividly years after: 'There we continued all winter and spring, covered with frost & snow, and almost starved with cold to death, it being one of the wors[t] winters ever seen there.'[23]

Flora felt miserable and low all through that dreadful winter of 1778–9, in spite of the fact that she had Allan and two of her beloved boys, Charles and Alexander, with her at Fort Edward – Ranald who must have missed being reunited with his mother since the Marines serving in America were returned to the Home Fleet in 1778. Cuidreach's son, Kenneth, who had been General MacDonald's aide-de-camp at Moore's Creek, was also in Nova Scotia. The Kingsburgh boys were no longer the boys she and Allan had watched grow up in Skye: they were smart young army officers who had inherited some of their father's sense of self-importance, and they also had an appetite for drinking and living which shocked their mother. Their financial affairs reminded her of her husband's fecklessness with money too. Reunion was therefore joy mixed with disappointment.

Above all Flora missed Anne and Annabella, but some compensation came in October when Allan's cousin, Captain Alexander MacDonald, joined them with his wife, Suzie. The captain was devoted to Suzie and referred to her affectionately as 'my fat frow' because she was pregnant at the time. He would do anything for Suzie, sending off for everything she asked for: best green tea, sugar and 'a piece of black satin for a neglishee and petticoat for my wife who is a pretty lusty woman'. When Suzie craved oysters he ordered several casks to be sent. They already had five children. Two sons had been sent home to Scotland to be educated, but their other three children were with them in Nova Scotia.[24] Another friend at the fort that winter was the Reverend John Bethune, who had travelled out from Skye in 1773 and had been chaplain to the Carolina Militia. He was now Chaplain to the Regiment.

Fort Edward was not only cold: life there was empty and dreary in the extreme, in spite of the fact that cousin Alexander did all he could to make it more pleasant and to involve the women in what little entertainment could be provided. Just after St Andrew's Day he wrote in a letter:

We Spent a very sober decent St Andrew here Chusing rather to entertain the Ladies with a dance than sitting long after Dinner and getting ourselves drunk. After all our Oconomy it will rather come heavy upon our Young Gentlemen there being so few of us. The Ladies desire to be remembered to you in the Kindest Manner & w^d be happy to see you at our Room (where we meet once a fortnight) to see you dance Guillicallum over two broad Swords lain across.'[25]

No wonder he said 'You must not expect any news from here' in another of his letters.

The young MacDonalds, Alexander and Charles, hated the dull existence in this remote fortress and longed to get away to Halifax where life was much more exciting. In December Captain MacDonald sent a letter to General Francis McLean in which he said:

Our Young fellows are so fond of dancing and seeing the Ladies at Halifax they are constantly plaguing me for leave to go down there and they'll think it hard when I'll refuse them I have given leave to Lieut Alex^r Macdonald to convey his Brother Lieu^t Charles as far as Halifax and ordered him immediately upon his Arrival to wait upon you for Approbation to stay a few days.[26]

Otherwise life consisted of coping with deserters and backbiting among the officers and men, and smoothing over the riots and brawls that boredom brought on when the men went to Halifax, a naval base where rivalry among sailors and soldiers proved as heady as the brew they drank in the bars.

Christmas came and went, and on 18 or 19 January Suzie gave birth to her sixth child. Both mother and child died and the captain was devastated. He wrote to MacAdam in New York:

I have nothing now to trouble you with but the Melancholy Acco^t of Mr^s Macdonald's Death and left me behind a Miserable wretch with five children much at a loss wch way to turn myself to provide for them Shou'd God Spare my life to see them able to do for themselves.[27]

Sensible, stable Flora was a godsend to Suzie's grieving widower during this very trying time. Suzie's death took away all the pleasure the captain might have derived from the fact that, at long last, his regiment, the 84th

Regiment of Foot, the Royal Highland Emigrants, was playing its part in the war. For Flora the loss of Suzie was a bitter blow: the girl had been her only congenial female company in this desolate place and now she felt utterly alone. Her misery was made worse during the summer when she had another fall in which she dislocated the wrist of her good arm and damaged some tendons, as a result of which she was confined to the house for two months. In spite of the fact that the regimental surgeon attended her, she never really recovered from the accident and both of her arms gave her trouble for the rest of her life.

Lonely and miserable, Flora began to dread the thought of another winter in this bleak place, but where could she go? She was fifty-seven now and every year hung heavy on her. She discussed these feelings with Allan for hours on end – Carolina had not proved the paradise they had been led to expect and now it contained more enemies than friends, Nova Scotia was cold and lonely, and she felt homesick for the Long Island and Skye, and for her youngest children, Fanny and Johnnie, whom she had not seen for five years. Her heart called her back to Skye and the Hebrides, although she and Allan both knew that in the Islands they had no tack to which they could return, no money, no prospects – nothing. But they did have relations and clan kinsmen there, and at that moment kinship felt more important by far to Flora MacDonald than wealth or comfort.

Allan agreed that she should return to Scotland and managed to secure a berth for her on the twenty-four-gun ship *Lord Dunmore*. Accompanied by three other ladies and two gentlemen, she sailed for home in October just in time to escape winter. A late autumn Atlantic voyage was preferable to a second Nova Scotian winter. Biographies of Flora are filled with ridiculous tales of her voyage home. Alexander MacGregor's account is typical:

> The vessel in which she sailed was met by a French privateer, and a smart action took place. During the engagement Flora refused to take shelter below, but prominently appeared on deck, where, with her wonted magnanimity, she inspired the sailors with courage, and assured them of success. Unfortunately her left arm was broken in the conflict, and she was afterwards accustomed to say that she had fought both for the House of Stuart and for the House of Hanover, but had been worsted in the service of each.[28]

The account in her granddaughter's 'autobiography' is even more fanciful:

All went well until the vessel encountered a French ship of war, and we were alarmed on finding that an action was likely to take place. The Captain gave orders for the ladies to remain below, safe from the skirmish; but I could not rest quiet, knowing my husband's spirit and energy would carry him into the thick of the fighting, therefore I rushed up the companion-ladder . . . and insisted on remaining on deck to share my husband's fate, whatever that might be . . . Thinking the sailors were not so active as they ought to have been . . . I took courage, and urged them on by asserting their rights and the certainty of victory. Alas! for my weak endeavours to be of service I was badly rewarded, being thrown down in the noise and confusion on deck, I was fain to go below, suffering excruciating agony in my arm, which the doctor pronounced broken.[29]

Both tales obviously have the same origin and illustrate the way in which successive biographers have accepted and repeated myths and half-truths without question. Flora did say something approximating to MacGregor's remark about the Houses of Stuart and Hanover, but her version of the alleged encounter was very different:

In our passage, spying a sail, made ready for action, and in hurreying the ladys below to a place of safety, my foot sliping a step in the trap, fell and brock the dislockated arm in two. It was set with bandages over slips of wood, and keep my bed until we arrived in the Thames.[30]

The incident does demonstrate one thing: in moments of crisis Flora always took the initiative. It was she who took command and helped the other women to safety.

Flora reached London towards the end of the year 1779, thirty-three years after she had first arrived in the city as a prisoner. This time there were no enthusiastic Jacobite ladies to fawn over her, no men begging her to tell them her story and no Princes to spoil her. It was a quiet homecoming and, although London was not her beloved Hebrides, it was welcome after the ordeal of the past five years.

If she looked forward to peace or contentment she was going to be disappointed. Soon after she landed she received news that her son, Alexander, who had been sent home because of his poor health, was missing. The ship on which he had sailed from America failed to arrive in Britain and it was feared that it had foundered. Fate had not finished with Flora MacDonald yet.

CHAPTER FIFTEEN

Home to the Islands

I may fairly say we both have suffered in our person, family, and interest, as much if not more than any two going under the name of refugees or loyalists, without the smallest recompence.

Letter from Flora MacDonald to
Sir John MacPherson[1]

News of Sandy's disappearance was the final straw: Flora, hitherto indomitable, collapsed completely. Already worn out by the long sea voyage and suffering great pain from her injuries, her health broke down on learning that her son's ship was missing. Flora suffered what she described as 'a violent fitt of sickness, which confined me to my bed in London for half a year, and would have brought me to my grave, if under Gods hand Doctor Munrow had not given his friendly assistance'.[2]

Dr Donald Munro was the son of the second of the three Alexander Munros – father, son and grandson – who held the Chair of Anatomy at Edinburgh University successively throughout the eighteenth century. Donald Munro's mother was a MacDonald of Sleat, so the clan kinship grapevine was clearly functioning well in the English capital. Flora did not say whether she stayed with the doctor during this time or, indeed, indicate where she resided in London. Allan's cousin, Alexander, in Nova Scotia, had a sister living there and Flora could have stayed with her. Lady Margaret MacDonald of Sleat, now an old woman, was also in London then, but it is unlikely that Flora would have been invited to stay with her since the chief's widow had virtually ignored the island heroine since the day the Prince passed through Monkstadt, and Flora and old Kingsburgh took all the blame for helping him.

In *The Truth about Flora MacDonald* Allan Reginald MacDonald suggests that she was probably in the care of Jacobite friends, and this may well have been the case.[3] Lady Primrose, who had befriended her in 1746 and raised a subscription for her, was now dead, and most of her other Jacobite admirers of 1746 had also gone – dead or scattered all over the country. But there were still Jacobites around. Thirty-three years had passed since she first sailed into the Thames to be treated as the most admired prisoner in the capital, but now no one took much notice of her, in spite of the fact that, during the past five years, she had proved herself more of a heroine than in that brief sunburst of glory when she accompanied Bonnie Prince Charlie over the sea to Skye in 1746.

Slowly Flora recovered her strength and by the spring of 1780 she was able to begin the long journey home to Scotland. By the middle of May she was in Edinburgh, where she stayed with Mrs John MacKenzie of Delvine and was reunited with her son, John, now a young man of twenty. Lawyer MacKenzie, her very dear friend of long ago, had died two years earlier, but he had made a good job of raising Johnnie while the Kingsburghs were in America and Flora was grateful.

She continued to consult doctors in Edinburgh and must have been a regular visitor to the apothecaries in the city, for she arranged for her mail to be directed to her 'at Mrs MacDonald's laboratory Lawnmercat'. At that time Mrs Charles MacDonald, a clanswoman, had a chemist's shop in the Lawnmarket at the top of the capital's Royal Mile. Physicians in the city recommended Flora 'to make all possible speed to the highlands for the benefets of goat Whey', so she wrote at once to Donald MacDonald, a merchant in Glasgow and a friend of Cuidreach's son, Kenneth, to tell him she intended to travel first to Skye and then to settle in the Long Island. She asked MacDonald to arrange for her belongings to be sent to her care of Boisdale in South Uist. She was in a great hurry, for she told the merchant, 'I mean to remove from this place as soon I receive your Answer'.[4]

June was well advanced by the time Flora managed to make all the arrangements for her journey. This time she chose the longer overland route by Inverness rather than risk the sea journey by Kintyre. Her injured arms made riding so difficult that it took three painful days to reach the Highland capital. She referred to her travelling companion on the ride North as 'my young Squire,' which suggests that it was Johnnie who escorted her home. After resting a further three days to ease her aching arms, Flora took the road to Skye. 'I had the good luck to meet with a female companion from that to Skye', she told Mrs MacKenzie in a letter dated 12 July. 'I was the fourth day, with great difficulty, at Raasay, for my hands being so pained with the riding. I have arrived here a few days ago with my young daughter.'[5]

Fanny, no longer the child left behind in 1774, was now a blossoming fourteen-year-old girl. Joy and pride shine through Flora's description of Fanny as she found her: a girl 'who promises to be a stout Highland "Caileag," quite overgrown of her age'.[6]

Flora did not travel on to Uist immediately as she had originally intended. Her daughter, Anne, was staying at Dunvegan Castle on Skye, as the guest of her husband's nephew, the MacLeod Clan chief, so Flora joined her there with the intention of remaining only for a short time. But Anne, horrified to see her mother's ill health, had other ideas. Flora stayed on at Dunvegan, which became her home for most of the ensuing three years. Here, Flora and Anne were joined by Anne's husband in 1781 and Flora enjoyed the comforts of a home, with occasional visits to the Outer Isles, while she waited expectantly for news of her husband and boys.

Two letters from Allan were waiting for her at Dunvegan, bringing news of himself and of Charles. The second was dated as recently as 10 May – less than two months before. It seems that her husband was able to communicate with her more quickly than the British Government could send despatches to its generals in America!

She reported Allan's news back to Mrs MacKenzie: 'He was then in very good health and informs me that my son Charles has got the command of a troop of horse in Lord Cathcart's regiment.' This merely served to make her more melancholy about her missing son: 'Alas! I have heard nothing . . . about my son Sandy, which, you may be sure gives me great uneasiness.'[7] 'I still hope for the best', she added sadly.

The MacDonald menfolk in America were as deeply committed to the Loyalist cause as ever, and Flora hung on every report that reached Dunvegan. 'I hope', she said, 'we will soon have peace re-established . . . as it's a thing long expected and wished for . . . especially by poor me, that has my all engaged. Fond to hear news, and yet afraid to get it.'[8]

Allan was now at least fifty-seven years of age and not in the best of health, so he saw no active service with the 84th Regiment other than to guard Nova Scotia from invasion. To begin with he had command of the 8th Company, with his son, Sandy, as his lieutenant, but after Sandy left on his ill-fated journey home Allan was assigned to the 6th Company where he remained right up to the end of the war. Although he was never sent any further away than Sydney in Cape Breton, where his company guarded the harbour entrance, commanding a company of the 84th Regiment in Nova Scotia was no easy posting, for Windsor lay just across the Bay of Fundy from Maine and was always under threat of invasion from there, or sea attack by the French Navy. In November 1781 he wrote to his cousin, Balranald, in Uist, that the harbour was being fortified 'as we expect very early in the spring to be besieged here'.[9] In the event Nova Scotia was never seriously attacked by the Americans, but that did not make Allan's task any the less vital.

Those of the younger generation did not remain in Nova Scotia during this time because they were desperate to see more action, just as Allan himself had been in 1745. With Ranald back at sea the others' chance came when the campaign in the south began to go better for the British: Charleston fell to them and the British Legion began to wreak havoc in the southern colonies. The nominal commanding officer was Lord Cathcart, but the notorious British Legion was effectively under twenty-three-year-old Colonel Banastre Tarleton, an officer whose campaigns were as fiery as his bright red hair and matching personality. Tarleton boasted of having butchered more men and lain with more women than any man in the army, and he was probably not far wrong in his claim. The green uniforms of Tarleton's highly mobile force were feared wherever they appeared in the south to help win South Carolina back and to break Patriot power in North Carolina temporarily. Charles, James and Annabella's son, Donald, all served under Tarleton during this time: Charles, a captain, fought at Charleston, Waxhaw, Camden, Catawba and Cowpens, and James, a lieutenant, was severely wounded at the Battle of Camden in 1780 and had to be retired on half pay. According to Allan, Alexander's health became 'much impaired by constant Light Infantry service in New York, etc.', and he had to be sent home to recuperate. It was on the voyage back to Britain that his ship went missing.[10]

Ranald served on HMS *Alcide* and HMS *Shrewsbury*. Aboard HMS *Alcide* he found the excitement he missed in Nova Scotia: he took part in the biggest naval battle of the war, the Battle of the Saints on 12 April 1782, when Admirals Rodney and Hood cornered the French Navy among the Caribbean Islands and won back control of the Atlantic for Britain. When the French flagship, the 112-gun *Ville de Paris*, was battered into surrender, Ranald went aboard her and served in her afterwards.[11]

Wherever he sailed with the Navy, Ranald kept asking about his missing brother. On 16 October 1780 he wrote to his mother from New York with news that Flora could not wait to share. As soon as she read Ranald's letter she passed the news on to her cousin, Donald MacDonald of Balranald, on 10 December:

Dr Sir

I cannot but attempt writing you the unexpected, joyful news I
received this day from Ranald, dated October the 16, from New York
about my Dr. Sandy. I shall give it you in his own words, you will be no
doubt much surprised to hear that Sandy is still in the land of the
living, they were taken up at sea by a vessel from lisbone, and carey'd
to the Coast of Brasil, this news put me in such confusion that I can
scarce hold the pen. I have great reason to be thankfull for all their
preservation. He writs me that he got a letter from his father in June
from Halifax and that he was then in very good health and that
Charles and James was well, he regrets that his Brave Captain lost his
Leg, his ship suffered greatly. This is two Letters I receiv'd from him
within this ten days, he writs me that General Clinton with 6 thousand
men was going to embark to assist Lord Cornwales, who was blocked
up by the French fleet, they had 28 sail, the Enemy 34 Sail of the line
of Battle-Ships. God send us good account of them. God bless him
poor man he never refuses an oppertunity in writing to his Mother I
am very glad to hear that the Children are upon the mending hand,
the major desires to be kindly remembered to you and Mrs McDonald,
youl except of the same from your affectionate Cousin F mcD.[12]

At home, the time had come for young John to be launched into a career
with a cadetship in the Bombay Infantry in India, and from the moment his
ship sailed until a letter reached her with news of his safe arrival, Flora worried
herself sick about him. Sandy's fate was in her mind whenever she thought of
John's voyage, and the relief in her letter thanking Mrs MacKenzie for
sending her news of Johnny's safe arrival could not be hidden:

I return you my most sincere thanks for your being so mindful of me
as to send me the agreeable news about Johny's arival, which relieved
me of a great deal of distress, as that was the first accounts I had of
him since he sailed.[13]

Almost as soon as he landed, John managed to secure a commission in
the Bengal Engineers, the start of a career that made him by far the most
successful of all Flora's children.

While she waited and worried, Flora spent her time between Dunvegan
and the Long Island. She lived the life of a nomad with no home of her
own, and could not have afforded one even if she had wanted to settle.

Instead she moved from relative to relative and friend to friend. During the latter part of 1781 she was with Allan's sister-in-law Peggy MacLeod of Knockcowe in Skye; then she visited Peggy's son. That same year she spent time in North Uist with her cousin, Donald MacDonald of Balranald, who had succeeded MacDonald of Kirkibost as the Sleat Chief's factor on the island. She also lived at Kirkibost with Mrs MacDonald, the widow of the old factor, and the woman who had travelled from the Long Island to Skye the day before Flora and Betty Burke made the journey and had been at Monkstadt when Flora arrived. It was she who was searched so closely by the militia.

From North Uist Flora moved to Milton in South Uist, her old family home, and stayed with her brother Angus for a time. She was still at Milton in the early part of 1782, but wrote to Mrs MacKenzie, 'I am now in my brother's house on my way to Skye, to attend my daughter, who is to ly-in in August.'[14]

It was not an ideal life, but infinitely preferable to what she had left behind in America. She described her own health at this time as tolerable 'considering my anxious mind and distress of times'.[15]

Months passed, but her 'dear Sandy' did not return and hope faded slowly. Ranald's report became 'hearsay' and then it was accepted as totally without foundation. Flora realized that Sandy would never return, and painfully slowly she came to terms with her loss. 'I have no reason to complain', she told Mrs MacKenzie with resignation, 'as God has been pleased to spare his father and the rest.'[16] But God had not spared all the rest. Soon she received another blow – Ranald, too, was reported missing.

On 9 September 1782 the *Ville de Paris* foundered off Newfoundland with Ranald on board. In fact it has been claimed that Sandy was lost with the ship too, but that is manifestly untrue. Sandy was lost much earlier: Flora herself told Sir John MacPherson that she heard her son was missing on her arrival back in Britain from Nova Scotia in late 1779.[17] Allan believed Ranald went down with the *Ville de Paris*, writing in his claim, 'What added to the utter misery of your Memorialist was the loss of his third son, Captain Ronald McDonald of Marines, in the *La Veill de paris*.'[18] Some writers have suggested that Ranald was not lost with this ship and in fact that the *Ville de Paris* did not sink at all, a confusion that arises from the fact that a new *Ville de Paris* was launched at Chatham in 1795 and given the name to perpetuate the memory of 'such a notable prize in the history of the Royal Navy, the pride of De Grasse's fleet and quite the finest ship at that time'. Ranald was still on the Marines' officers' list published in January 1783, but news took so long to travel in those days that this means nothing. His will is more important. Dated 31 August 1780 and naming Allan and Flora, it was proved in London on 29 October 1783 and said that he died in September 1782 – the month of the loss of the *Ville de Paris*. Although we cannot say for sure that Ranald was lost with the prize ship, all the evidence points to that probability.[19]

Poor Flora never felt more alone than throughout that long year when she was without a home of her own, in constant pain from her injured arms and, in spite of having her two daughters near her, far from her husband and her boys. She was weighed down by grief for Sandy and Ranald, of whom both she and Allan seem to have been particularly fond. All she had left to hope for was that at long last the war in America might end. It was reaching its climax, but its outcome was obviously not what she would have wanted.

At last the government in London realized the war was lost and hostilities ended before 1782 was out. Peace was confirmed by the Treaty of Paris the following year. America was independent: Flora had suffered for another lost cause and the future for her and her family was less secure than ever.

The Peace of Paris brought the Americans a great victory, but that did not satisfy the Patriots who showed little mercy or magnanimity towards the beaten Loyalists. They frequently flouted the articles of the peace treaty, and persecuted and prosecuted Loyalist settlers, denied them their rights and confiscated their property. While this was happening the British Government left those who had sacrificed so much to fight for them largely to their own devices.

In North Carolina loyal settlers faced many injustices, although it must be said that there were also some individual acts of clemency and generosity. It was only in 1786 that an act was finally passed pardoning all Loyalists. Many Highlanders returned home, among them both Charles and James who were back in Skye by 1784. Other families fled to Canada and Nova Scotia, where soldiers who had served in the war swelled their numbers. Those who had suffered and fought together now settled together to start a new life in the north.

The London Government lost no time in cutting its losses in America. On 7 October 1783 it announced that the 84th Regiment would be disbanded: three days later Allan MacDonald mustered with his men of the 6th Company at Windsor to be dismissed into retirement on half pay. As a reward for their service 105,000 acres of unsettled Crown land to the east of

Windsor in the present-day Hants County was allocated to the Royal Highland Emigrants Regiment 2nd Battalion veterans. This lay in an area bounded by the Shubenacadie and Nine Mile Rivers, and west from Grand Lake to the Kennetcook River. The township where the families of men of the 2nd Battalion of the 84th settled was named Douglas, probably in honour of Sir Charles Douglas, Commander of Halifax naval station and the man who helped Ranald MacDonald to obtain his first commission. Colonel John Small, who commanded the battalion, had Douglas ancestors, so he may have chosen the name partly for that reason. Although no papers have been discovered to pinpoint the exact location, it is known that Allan accepted and took up seven hundred acres in the Kennetcook area.[20]

Generous as these land grants sound they offered no life of ease, particularly for men who had been officers until recently and now wanted to continue to live like well-heeled gentlemen. For Kingsburgh it was particularly hard since he was now over sixty years old and was without means to pay for help to clear and prepare his land. Yet he persevered and cleared a few acres on which he built a little house of which he was proud during the spring and summer of 1784. As he worked he saw a new dream, a new life with Flora on their own farm in Nova Scotia.

Half pay did not go far, but Allan always had high hopes: the British Government had set up a commission to examine Loyalist claims for compensation for losses of property in the former British colonies, with awards to be made on the basis of loyalty, service and the extent of the claimant's losses with evidence of these checked or corroborated. Allan MacDonald considered himself well qualified for generous consideration on all three counts, but unfortunately no one could be sure how these would be interpreted by the commissioners, or even whether any particular claim would be entertained at all. The tendency was to ask for too much rather than too little, and the commission, well aware of this, was inclined to look with suspicion on every application. And it certainly helped to have someone of influence to support one's claim, or to intercede with the Commissioners. Many of Allan's friends and kinsmen also lodged claims, among them his son, James, his daughter, Anne, her husband, Alexander MacLeod, cousin Alexander of Staten Island, MacDonald of Cuidreach and Cuidreach's son, Donald.

When he decided to settle in Nova Scotia Allan filed his claim through an agent. This was drawn up in Halifax on 3 January 1784 and forwarded to the commissioners in London, where it was marked 'Received on 12th March, 1784'.[21] This asked for £1,086 compensation for his losses, a sum that buoyed his hopes as he worked on his land during the summer. By autumn cash was running short and there was no word of settlement of his claim: in fact stories were filtering through to Nova Scotia that claimants who appeared in London in person were dealt with much more expeditiously, so Allan decided to leave his land, on which he could not work during the bitter Nova Scotian winter anyway, and sailed to Britain to press his claim harder. He had every intention of returning when he received his money.

Off to London Allan went, and on 8 February 1785 he submitted a new claim, this time for £1,341 for the loss of his plantation, servants and belongings in Carolina, and just under £300 for costs incurred in raising his militia company and taking part in the campaign which ended at Moore's Creek Bridge. Returning claimants had told him of the commissioners' meanness, so Allan resolved to make as certain as he could that his losses would be covered. He was also determined to win as much sympathy as he could so, having told the whole tale of his misfortunes in America, he ended with a heart-rending plea:

> Your Memorialist hopes that the Right Honorable Board will order the contents of the annexed Schedule, being money expended and value lost by an old, worn out officer in the service of his King and Country, lost the comfort and strength of his old age, his Estate, his all, and an old Wife, a daughter and himself to support, with only a very small income, this money would contribute to make his living easy in his old days, and now in reduced and infirm state he is in, having neither Dwelling or Place of Abode but his Regimental Grant of Lands on the River Kennetcok, in Nova Scotia, where he has a little neat Hutt, and cleared a few acres last Summer, means soon to return, had he but the Money to carry out his improvements which he was obliged to give up last October for want of cash.

Allan had every intention of making a new start even at an age when others would have given up. He put the spectre of failure in Skye and North Carolina behind him and was still game to start again to build a new life for himself and Flora in Nova Scotia. That must have taken great courage.

He detailed his losses to the Commissioners:

To the value of my Large Plantation, containing
75 acres of which 70 were cleared and in
cultivation, which three good Orchards of Peach
and Apple and other Fruits, the Grounds extant   300.   0.   0

To the value of Dwelling House, with Barn,
Keeping House, Kitchen, Stable and Crib for
holding Indian Corn   60.   0.   0

To a Grist Mill in a good Run of Water, by
permission of Assembly, the yearly income of
which keeped the whole family in Bread   120.   0.   0

To the value of my Little Plantation of
50 acres, of which 30 were cleared land
and in cultivation, with a good orchard of
Peaches, Apples and other fruits, including a
Farm House, Barn and Crib   110.   0.   0

To the value of Horses robbed and taken of
both Plantations   96.   0.   0

To the service of five indentured Men Servants,
hree years of their time being unexpired   150.   0.   0

To the services of three Women Servants Ditto   45.   0.   0

To the amount of the value of Books,
Plate and Furniture plundered by the
enemy   500.   0.   0.

By amount of Sundrie articles saved
by Mrs McDonald of above Effects   40.   0.   0.
     460.   0.   0

     1341.   0.   0[22]

Costs and losses incurred through his military activities in support of King
George totalled a further £299 12s. 11d.

The commission had been due to sit until 25 March 1784, but the work of examining claims dragged on for a further five years, so that the final report to the government was made only on 15 May 1789. During the five years through which the commission sat, it received more than five thousand claims totalling over £10,350,000, and refused to consider another 950. In all the British Government awarded just over £3,000,000 to Loyalists for their losses.

Allan MacDonald's submission was duly heard, but his award was small – £440, with £276 for loss of income. Others were treated with equal meanness. Anne asked for £960 and received £160, while her husband submitted petitions for more than £2,000 and was awarded less than £500.

The award was not enough to enable Allan to return to Nova Scotia with his wife and start to build a new life: in any case, sensible Flora, conscious they were both well over sixty and in poor health, was unlikely to have encouraged him in such a venture. So the land grant on the Kennetcook River was allowed to lapse and, in the report of the commission administering the Nova Scotia grants for 1800, Allan's property was listed as reserved for the use of one of the commissioners, John McMonagle, presumably in payment for his services as a commissioner.

With his small recompense from the Government and an income amounting to half his army pay, Allan returned to Skye in 1785. Of the eleven years during which he had been away from the island, he had spent fewer than three with Flora and he hadn't seen his daughter, Fanny, since he handed her over to Raasay as a child of eight. She was now nineteen.

Much imagination has gone into reports of Allan's homecoming. Some simply recorded that he and Flora came back to the island together; others that Flora was at Portree to meet him and that they returned to Kingsburgh, the tack of which had been held open for him all the years he was absent. Allan did not have any rights to Kingsburgh – he had given these up when he left for America in 1774, and the house and land were still let to William MacLeod who had taken them at that time.

It was a subdued reunion, but touching – two elderly people, racked with the aches and pains of old age, coming together again after a long separation and much suffering. The only joy offered to them was to be together and to be reunited with most of their family. They had nowhere to stay, so Anne offered her parents and her young sister, Fanny, a home with her at Dunvegan, where they were welcome to stay until they found somewhere permanent. Fortunately the MacLeod chief, now an army general, was still away in India, so the two families were able to live in the castle as if it were their own.

Allan and Flora visited Uist – tradition relates that, for a time, they made their home at Daliburgh, not far from Flora's birthplace on South Uist – and when their son John wrote to his mother on 5 May 1787, he addressed the letter to Mrs MacDonald, late of Kingsborrow, South Uist, by Dunvegan.

John was doing remarkably well in the east. He was posted to Sumatra as a surveyor and quickly rose to the rank of colonel. He made a good marriage to a widow, Mrs Boyle, a general's daughter. Unfortunately she died when their second child was born and Johnnie mourned deeply for her. 'I lost the best of women', he told his mother. Both of his children also died young.[23]

John married again, another good marriage to Frances Chambers, daughter of the head of the Bengal Justiciary, and they had nine children, one of whom they named Charles Edward and another William Pitt. John was able to retire at the early age of forty-one to live at Exeter in Devon and write. He was a prolific writer on engineering subjects and a renowned map maker. His maps of St Helena and Sumatra are to be found in the British Library.

As early as May 1787, when he was only twenty-seven, John had amassed a large enough fortune to be able to relieve his parents of their financial worries. He sent his mother a letter, written in haste on board the Indiaman *Ravensworth* in the Straits of Sunda:

> I have ordered £100 to be given to you immediately for your and Fanny's use, and £40 to Anny. I have also ordered two thirds of the Interest of £1400 to be given to you annually and the other third to Anny. If Fanny marries with her parents' consent she is to have £100.[24]

It is interesting, although perhaps not surprising, that John made over the allowance to his mother and not to his father. As a young man with a good grasp of financial affairs, he realized how hopeless his father was at managing money.

Johnnie's settlement of an annuity on his parents was timely: soon afterwards a tack fell vacant, which would enable his parents to settle close to their old home at Kingsburgh. The Reverend William MacQueen of Snizort died in September 1787,[25] leaving Penduin vacant, and Allan was able to take over the lease. He and Flora moved there towards the end of the year.

In the same year Flora saw two of her sons settled: Charles, who had given them so much worry in Nova Scotia, married Isabella, the daughter of James MacDonald of Aird, and James took the lease of Flodigarry. James, always known as 'Captain MacDonald of Flodigarry', married Emily MacDonald of Heisker and Skeabost in Skye and they had six children.

Allan and Flora were now living in comfort with four of their five surviving children settled close to them. At long last they knew financial stability – the first peace of mind they had enjoyed since the far-off days after they took up residence in their first home at Flodigarry nearly forty years earlier. Unfortunately neither was able to enjoy it: Flora was now sixty-five and racked incessantly by arthritic pains in both arms as a result of her falls in America and on board ship, and Allan became virtually unable to walk.

The world beyond Skye moved on and in January 1788 Prince Charlie died, a fat, drunken, pathetic old man of sixty-seven. He had been King over the Water since 1766, but no one – not even the Pope or the King of France – recognized him, so he was left to grow old in loneliness. His only comfort during his final years was his daughter by Clementina Walkinshaw who nursed him and made his end bearable. Charles Stuart never returned to the islands of Scotland, where people had sacrificed so much for him in 1745 and through the sad years that followed Culloden. Apart from that brief note written before he left Skye, Flora MacDonald received no thanks from him – no acknowledgment of the service she had rendered him. Her life might have been very different but for that voyage from the Long Island to Skye.

Flora was not bitter: she was old and frail, yet she remembered it all as vividly as if it had happened only the day before. The following year she retold the story to an old friend and fellow Sgiathanach (Skyeman), Sir John MacPherson, at his request.[26] Sir John, the son of the minister of Sleat, had had a very chequered career in India during which he fell out with the powerful East India Company, yet succeeded Warren Hastings as governor general. He was now living in England where he was a Member of Parliament and asked Flora to set down her story, possibly in the hope that he might be able to persuade the powers in London to help her financially. If that was his reason it did not succeed, for soon afterwards Sir John lost his seat on trumped up charges of bribery and corruption.

Flora was too ill to write the long memorandum herself, so this and an accompanying letter were both written by someone else and she merely signed the letter. Flora set out the facts of her journey to Skye with the Prince as well as her adventures in America. The first was a fuller, more graphic description of the journey than that given to Dr Burton and Bishop Forbes in 1747, and it made clear that her stepfather, Hugh of Armadale, had been deeply involved in the escape. The second part of the note, covering the period from her emigration in 1774 to her return to London in 1779, revealed Flora's terrible fear for the safety of Allan and her boys after the Battle of Moore's Creek, and the awful experiences that followed. The note vividly portrays a brave woman, stoic about her own misfortunes, but now reduced by pain to a pitiable old woman. She told Sir John:

> The cast in both my arms are liveing monuments of my sufferings and distressis. And the long goal confinement which my husband underwent has brought on such disorders that he has totally lost the use of his legs; so that I may fairly say we both have suffered in our person, family and interest, as much as if not more than any two going under the name of Refugees or loyalists, without the smallest recompence.[27]

It was the first time in her long life that Flora MacDonald had shown any self-pity over the way in which she had suffered without recognition.

Flora was beyond help from Sir John or anyone on earth: just a few months later she died at Penduin on 4 March 1790. She was attended during this time by old Dr John MacLean, the surgeon who had sheltered Donald Roy after the '45 and dressed his injured foot, and who had drawn up the marriage contract between Flora and Allan. The doctor wrote to his son soon after, 'Nothing has occurred since I wrote you except the death of the famous Mrs Flora MacDonald, sometime of Kingsburgh. She suffered much distress for a long time in my neighbourhood at Penduin.'

The *Scots Magazine* recorded her death without reference to her heroic life, saying simply:

> March 4 1790. At Isle of Skye, Flora Macdonald, spouse to Captain Allan Macdonald, late of Kingsburgh.[28]

By a strange coincidence on the very same page the death was reported of Richard Caswell, Governor of North Carolina, the man who had defeated the Highland army at Moore's Creek.

Flora was buried in the Kingsburgh plot at Kilmuir Cemetery on the North Skye coast, less than two miles north of the point at which she and the Prince landed that summer Sunday in 1746. It was her intention to be buried in one of the sheets on which Prince Charlie had slept at Kingsburgh House that night after his escape, but it seems impossible that the sheet could have survived Flora's adventures in Britain and America. She would certainly have taken the sheet to North Carolina because she never intended to return, but she lost everything in the American Revolution – her silver, her furniture, her books, all her treasures. No mention of the Prince's sheet is made in Allan's claims or in any letters known to survive. There is, however, a fascinating shred of the Flora legend to be found in the graveyard at Hackett's Cove, St Margaret's Bay, Nova Scotia. There, according to local tradition, a woman named Jannet McDonald, an exact contemporary of Flora and said to have been related to her, was buried in 1789 wrapped in a sheet on which Prince Charlie slept during his flight. It is tempting to believe that Flora carried the sheet on which the Prince slept all through her adventures in Skye, North Carolina and New York, but left it behind in Nova Scotia, and that certainly would fit in with the kind of ill luck that dogged Flora through life. More likely it is merely another piece of fiction woven from a strand of Flora's story.

Skye gave Flora the best funeral the island could offer. In Edinburgh in 1835 the Reverend Alexander MacGregor met a man called John Macdonald, who had been present and described it in detail. According to this eyewitness Flora's body was taken from Penduin to Kingsburgh in the midst of a terrible storm of rain, thunder and lightning and it lay there until the day of the burial. 'The funeral cortege was immense – more than a mile in length – consisting of several thousands of every rank in Skye and the adjacent Isles', MacGregor was told:

> Flora's marriage and funeral, between which there was an interval of forty years, were the most numerously attended of any of which there is any record as having taken place in the Western Isles. Notwithstanding the vast assemblage present, all were liberally supplied with every variety of refreshment. Of genuine 'mountain dew' alone upwards of three hundred gallons were served. About a dozen of pipers from the MacCrimmon and MacArthur colleges in Skye, and from other quarters, simultaneously played the 'Coronach,' the usual melancholy lament for departed greatness.[29]

Three hundred gallons of whisky made it a Highland funeral to surpass all others.

Even in America she was mourned. When news of Flora's death reached North Carolina the congregation of Barbecue Church, which she had attended after her arrival, held a funeral service for her. Two decades had changed her from a despised Highlander to a legend in America.

It was a pity that Flora was not spared just a few months more, for 1790 brought her MacDonald kin more closely together. In 1789 General MacLeod returned to Dunvegan from India, forcing Alexander and Anne to seek somewhere else to live. They were given the lease of Waternish. Then William MacLeod's lease of Kingsburgh expired and it was passed on to Annabella and her husband, Cuidreach. In 1790 the family ties were further strengthened when Cuidreach's son, Donald, the young man who arrived in Carolina at Christmas in 1774, married Flora's daughter, Fanny.

Annabella offered Allan a home in his old family house at Kingsburgh and he left Penduin to live out the last two-and-a-half years of his life in the house in which he had grown up. Allan died at Kingsburgh, where he had spent so much of his life and where he had seen most of the little unclouded happiness he had ever known, on 20 September 1792. The *Scots Magazine* reported the news as briefly as it had recorded Flora's passing:

> At Kingsburgh, in the isle of Sky, Capt. Allan Macdonnell, late of the 84th foot.[30]

Johnnie returned from India in 1801, his fortune made, and ordered a memorial stone to be erected over his parents' grave. He chose a marble slab set within freestone and on it had carved the words:

> In the family mausoleum at Kilmuir lie interred the remains of the following members of the Kingsburgh family, viz:- Alexander Macdonald of Kingsburgh, his son Allan, his sons, Charles and James, his son John and two daughters; and of Flora Macdonald, who died in March, 1790, aged 68 – a name that will be mentioned in history, and, if courage and fidelity be virtues, mentioned with honour. 'She was a woman of middle stature, soft features, gentle manners, and elegant presence.' So wrote Dr Johnson.

Soon every fragment of this stone was carried away by visitors – not people from the far corners of the world like those who climb the low hill to the tomb today, but Scots men and women who decided, without the prompting of history books, that this gentle, loyal, brave woman was a heroine.

A new and more imposing memorial was set up in November 1871, a Celtic cross on a tall, slender marble stem which looked too frail to withstand the wild winds that blow over Trotternish. And so it proved. Just two years later, in December 1873, a great storm swept across Skye and blew down the Iona cross, shattering it and the memorial tablet to Flora. Like Flora herself, those who cherished her memory refused to be beaten, and a second Iona cross – equally slender – was erected in 1880, but with a strong iron stay to buttress it.

Visitors come to Kilmuir from every part of the world, but especially from North Carolina and Nova Scotia, to pay tribute to this woman who made her mark among men on two continents – the Highland heroine whose legend belongs to the whole world.

CHAPTER SIXTEEN

Heirs to the Legend

Now forced from my home and my dark halls away,
The son of the strangers has made them a prey;
My family and friends to extremity driven,
Contending for life both with earth and with heaven.

James Hogg's poem, 'The Emigrant'[1]

Flora MacDonald died surrounded by many members of her family to whom she was devoted, and doubly blessed to be mourned by the great extended family of her clan and generation. Four of her children were with her again: Charles, James, Anne and Fanny. Only John was missing, but the comfort in which she spent her last years bore testimony to his success. Of course, Sandy and Ranald had both gone before her, taken by the sea that she disliked so intensely but which had always been a part of her life, as indeed it has to be for any islander.

By the graveside at Kilmuir she received her reward at last for a life that had brought little material wealth and much suffering, both physical and of the mind. She was a legend in her lifetime in the ranks of her enemies as well as among her friends, yet she came to be honoured less in her own islands and among her closest kinsmen than in Lowland Scotland and beyond.

Visitors to Skye flock to Kilmuir in coachloads and by car, and the tourist industry makes much of her legend, but the average Sgiathanach can tell you little or nothing of her life or fame. One is likely to hear more of boatman Donald MacLeod of Galtergill, or Donald Roy MacDonald, who fought at Culloden and helped the Prince on the island. On South Uist Flora's fellow islanders seldom talk about her unless asked, and when they do it is not with hero-worship in their voices. There, people also speak more enthusiastically of other participants in the Jacobite saga, particularly of Neil MacEachain who is a hero there.

Oral tradition of the Islands has taken little notice of Flora over two centuries. A heroic adventure like the escape to Skye under cover of the short Hebridean midsummer night might be expected to recur as the subject of countless stories, poems and songs to be handed down from generation to generation in true Hebridean fashion, but Flora MacDonald features only infrequently in contemporary Gaelic and Scots folklore.

The story of the heroic Highland girl who saved Prince Charlie quickly spread through the Lowlands and England – Dr Johnson's visit saw to that – and the burgeoning romantic image of the fading Jacobite Cause fostered it further.

As time passed, carrying away Flora's contemporaries, sentiment for her strengthened, and the facts began to disappear under a mass of half-truths and fiction. James Hogg, the Ettrick Shepherd, was moved by her story, but let his Jacobite sympathies carry him far from the truth when he wrote his *Lament of Flora MacDonald* in which he depicted Flora as keening for her lost Prince beside corries 'singing to the sea'. Flora's feelings for the Prince, as described by Hogg, are pure sentimentality and fiction. The *Lament* is no more than a rather sweet little poem, which would have embarrassed its heroine and probably made her furious. Flora would have suggested that the over-sentimental shepherd from the Scottish Borders might have chosen someone else as his subject; after all, there were plenty of other women ready to swoon for Charlie.

> Far over yon hills of the heather so green,
>   And down by the corrie that sings to the sea,
> The bonny young Flora sat sighing her lane,
>   The dew on her plaid, and the tear in her e'e.
> She looked at a boat which the breezes had swung
>   Away on the waves, like a bird of the main;
> And aye as it lessened, she sighed and she sung,
>   'Fareweel to the lad I shall ne'er see again!
> Fareweel to my hero, the gallant and young!
>   Fareweel to the lad I shall ne'er see again!'

How it would have pleased the Hanoverians to have had a James Hogg around in 1746! As it was they did their best to turn the flight of Flora and Charles Edward into an unsavoury love affair in the hope of damaging the Prince's reputation, but that failed, as it was bound to, since it was utterly false. It was obvious to anyone that Charles Edward Stuart had other things on his mind in 1745 and was not particularly interested in women at that time, yet Whig pamphleteers of the period tried hard to endow him with a wild reputation in order to turn opinion against him. They made the most of his brief meeting with Clementina Walkinshaw early in 1746 and tried to suggest that he had an affair with Jenny Cameron of Glendessary. There is no evidence that Prince Charlie had a sexual relationship with any woman, or even the mildest of flirtations with the staid Flora, during the Rising and its aftermath, although he did take mistresses later, including his cousin, Louise, Duchesse de Montbazon, the Princesse de Talmont and Clementina Walkinshaw, who bore him a daughter. His relationships with all of these women were stormy to say the least, but there can be no doubt that, while no gentle ladies' man at home or in bed, Charles was interested in women in his own peculiar, uncouth way. Flora MacDonald was not one of these conquests.

Women played an important role in Prince Charlie's Cause for, while their husbands were showing faintheartedness or rushing for security under the coat tails of the Hanoverians, their wives and daughters were sporting the white cockade of the Stuarts. The wives of the two MacDonald chiefs, Sleat and Clanranald, both worked for the Prince while their husbands kept in the background, and, at the time of Charles's arrival in Edinburgh, it was said that two-thirds of men in the capital were Whigs, but the women were nearly all Jacobites.

Plenty of romantic stories were created around these female supporters of the Cause. Isabella Lumisden only agreed to marry Robert Strange, the Edinburgh engraver, on condition that he 'came out' for the Prince, and Sir Walter Scott told of meeting a woman who had been struck by a bullet accidentally discharged by a jubilant Highlander marching into Edinburgh after the battle of Prestonpans. 'Thank God the accident happened to me whose principles are known,' she said. 'Had it befallen a Whig, they would have said it was done on purpose.'[2]

The epitome of these fervent Jacobite ladies was 'Colonel Anne' Mackintosh. As soon as her husband, the Mackintosh Chief, left to raise a militia company for King George, she rode out dressed all in tartan and clansman's blue bonnet to rally her own regiment for Prince Charlie. Her bold action was matched only by that of Flora MacDonald, but the difference was that Flora 'came out' for the Cause by chance while 'Colonel Anne' was spurred on by burning devotion to the Jacobites.[3]

It is strange that neither 'Colonel Anne' nor Flora attracted much attention, especially among the growing band of female Jacobite supporters, during the latter part of the eighteenth century when Charles's hopes had been safely laid to rest. Flora, it has to be admitted, was taken up by many important people during her imprisonment, especially by Lady Primrose who raised the subscription for her, but nowhere in Jacobite legend or song of the time did she rate a mention. Lady Nairne ignored the heroine who was obvious material for a song in support of the Cause, and one must pose the question: Was this because other females were just a little jealous of her?

While those most able to foster the legend were ignoring her, Flora was becoming the popular heroine of a legend that just refused to die. People beat a path to her door in Skye just to meet her and in the hope of hearing her story. They usually left disappointed, for Flora seldom talked about the Prince's escape. In spite of this the legend of the journey over the sea to Skye continued to gain strength throughout Britain and across the ocean to every country where Scots were settled.

Following Hogg's tartan-tinged *Lament* the Victorians impressed their own peculiar stamp of romance on the Flora legend with lavishly sentimental biographies, paintings, poems and statues in her honour. But all of this only masked Flora's true image and obscured the real woman behind the legend. Fact was totally lost in a morass of half-truth and fiction.

Flora's granddaughter, Flora Frances Wylde, and the Reverend Alexander MacGregor meant well when they produced biographies of the heroine. MacGregor's *The Life of Flora MacDonald*, although claiming to be based on first-hand information given to him by Flora's daughter, Anne, is a succession of obvious inaccuracies that could easily have been checked at the time.[4] *The Autobiography of Flora MacDonald*, published by William Nimmo in Edinburgh in 1870, was no better. Readers were told that the book had been written by Flora in response to a request from her granddaughter, who had edited it. The granddaughter, Mrs Wylde, was a daughter of Flora's son, John, and her work was so full of fancy and errors of fact that it should not have been taken seriously even at the time,[5] but, alas, it was. These two works presented a picture of the heroine that its subject would hardly have recognized. Worse still, they blazed a trail that other writers followed blindly, accepting uncritically and repeating every detail, however improbable. As a result, Flora's story, as it became known to the world, did not do justice to the heroine.

At Inverness, the capital of the Highlands, a statue was erected in 1899 to honour Flora and it still stands there depicting the heroine gazing westward towards the islands, her faithful dog at her feet and a raised hand shielding her eyes from the setting sun – a romantic white rose of the Jacobite Cause.

On Skye a stained-glass window in Portree Episcopal Church commemorates Flora's life and achievement, although even this manages to record the place of her marriage and date of her death incorrectly. The window was dedicated in 1896 by one of Flora's great-granddaughters, Fanny Charlotte Hay. Flora's memory seems to be beset by error. The Iona cross over her grave at Kilmuir also contains an error in its inscription. It states that she died at Kingsburgh, whereas Dr John MacLean, the doctor who attended her at her deathbed, wrote a letter to his son soon afterwards making it clear that she died at Penduin.

The Celtic cross at Kilmuir, the window in Portree, the Inverness statue and the many pictures the Victorians painted or engraved may have etched the legend more deeply into the world's mind, but they did little to discover the real Flora MacDonald. The boat trip over the sea to Skye in their representations became a romantic Sunday outing instead of the grim flight of a hunted man across the Minch. The Flora they depicted was a dewy-eyed maiden deeply in love, rather than the strong-willed Highland woman we now know her to be, doing what she considered to be her duty. No wonder half the world came to believe that she and the Prince were in love.

The nineteenth-century poet William Edmistoun Aytoun[6] transposed the sentiment of love to the Prince:

> Give me back my trusty comrades
> Give me back my Highland maid!
> Nowhere beats the heart so kindly
> As beneath the tartan plaid!

The journey over the sea to Skye has been immortalized more surely in popular mythology by 'The Skye Boat Song' than by all the words of other writers. This song began from an old tune that Annie Campbell MacLeod heard sung by oarsmen as they rowed her from the island of Soay, off the south-west coast of Skye, to Loch Coruisk one day in 1879. As the sea became rough the men hoisted a sail, singing a kind of chant as they did so. Back at the inn where she was staying, Miss MacLeod played the sailors' chant over on the piano that evening and worked it into a refrain for a song. Several years later Harold Boulton heard it while on a visit to Scotland where he was working with Miss MacLeod to compile a book of songs. As they were being rowed up Loch Ailort they sang a song based on Annie MacLeod's tune. The words (using the names of the two oarsmen) went 'Row us along, Donald and John, over the sea to Roshven'. Boulton was so taken with the air that he wrote afterwards:

> With the tune ringing in my head I conceived the idea of making it the basis of a Jacobite song for our book. I originated the catchword, 'Over the sea to Skye', wrote the rest of the words, and called it 'The Skye Boat Song'. As such the tune and words were first published in 'Songs of the North'.[7]

Boulton's song is not an account of the Prince's voyage with Flora, but a firm avowal of the Jacobite view of the '45 and its aftermath. It makes no more than a passing reference to Flora and certainly suggests no romance between her and the Prince:

> Speed, bonnie boat, like a bird on the wing,
>   'Onward', the sailors cry:
> Carry the lad that's born to be king
>   Over the sea to Skye.
>
> Loud the winds howl, loud the waves roar,
>   Thunderclaps rend the air;
> Baffled our foes stand by the shore,
>   Follow they will not dare.
>
> Though the waves leap, soft shall ye sleep,
>   Ocean's a royal bed,
> Rocked in the deep Flora will keep
>   Watch by your weary head.
>
> Many's the lad fought on that day
>   Well the claymore could wield,
> When the night came silently lay
>   Dead on Culloden field.
>
> Burned are our homes, exile and death
>   Scatter the loyal men;
> Yet, ere the sword cool in the sheath,
>   Charlie will come again.

Robert Louis Stevenson, thinking the song was a genuine ancient folk tune, decided to try his hand at bettering the words. The result was his 'Sing me a song of the lad that is gone', and it is interesting that he too used the phrase 'Over the sea to Skye':

> Sing me a song of a lad that is gone,
>   Say, could that lad be I?
> Merry of soul he sailed on a day
>   Over the sea to Skye.

Both Stevenson and Boulton resisted the temptation to make Flora the focus of their songs, yet 'The Skye Boat Song' has become absorbed into the Flora MacDonald myth.

While Flora was becoming a part of Jacobite mythology in Scotland, she was also becoming a part of the folklore of those Highlanders who were forced to emigrate from their homeland. Even in North Carolina, where she and her kinsfolk had been reviled and treated so cruelly, the Americans at last came to terms with Highlanders. Many Highlanders stayed on in North Carolina in spite of all the repressive laws and injustices perpetrated against them during and after the War of Independence, but almost within Flora's lifetime they were being joined by waves of new immigrants, driven off their land in Scotland by the Highland Clearances which grew to become the great scourge of the nineteenth century. Among these were many of Flora's kinsmen.

Scottish names proliferated in the tightly entwined Highland community that flourished in the Carolinas. Skye and other Island surnames are still numerous: Bethune, MacAskill, MacCutcheon, MacDonald, MacEachern, MacInnis, MacIntyre, MacKinnon, MacLean, MacLeod, MacNeill, MacQueen, MacRimmon (as Carolina MacCrimmons spell the name), Martin, Morrison and Nicolson. Mainland Highland names are common too, among them: Campbell, MacColl, MacCormick, MacLaurin, MacRae and Stewart.

There are no direct descendants of Flora and Allan MacDonald in the Carolinas today, but James MacQueen, a son of Flora's half-sister, Florence, settled there to establish the MacQueens of Queensdale, a family that has contributed much to the community through the generations as ministers, lawyers, bankers, teachers, army officers and at least one state governor. Their descendants still live there.[8]

It was inevitable that the Flora legend should flourish in Carolina, and that it should be well larded with fiction just as has happened in Scotland, for Flora was as ill served by her nineteenth-century followers in America as she was at home. They added the tales of her fiery review of the troops setting out for Moore's Creek Bridge, and that terrible slander of the smothering of the old manservant.

North Carolina became the most Scottish of all the states of the USA, and this kinship with the Highlands has grown stronger with age until today it is hard to escape from Flora and her legend anywhere in the state.

The twin fires of religion and learning burned wherever Scots settled around the globe, so it was natural for the Cape Fear River Highlanders to establish a school near Centre Presbyterian Church, outside Maxton, in North Carolina in 1841. This school, named Floral College, was remarkable in that it was the first in the state to grant diplomas to women. Floral College flourished until it was forced to close during the Civil War. When peace was restored to the south it reopened, but from then on it declined and closed its doors finally in 1878.

Eighteen years on, in 1896, a new college opened at Red Springs under the inspired leadership of the Reverend Charles G. Vardell, and this continued under various names until James A. MacDonald, Editor of the *Toronto Globe*, who admired the college greatly, hit upon the appropriate and happy name of Flora MacDonald College. Time again brought change when Flora MacDonald College merged with another school in 1961 and was relocated to Laurinburg in Scotland County.

The heroine's great-great grandson, Reginald MacDonald of Kingsburgh, then residing at Pittsburgh in Pennsylvania, travelled to North Carolina to ask the trustees of the relocated college to give the new institution a Scottish name – a name that would reflect its early origins. The name 'St Andrews' was suggested by the Dean of Women at Flora MacDonald College, Mrs Sadie McCain, and by Donald F. MacDonald, one of the descendants of the MacQueens of Queensdale. The proposal was accepted and the newly formed college was named after Scotland's patron saint, but with one concession to Scottish Presbyterian reservation about saints and their veneration: it was called St Andrews Presbyterian College. St Andrews today preserves its Scots traditions through its Scottish Heritage Center for Scottish Studies which has been established in the college.

Flora MacDonald College cherished the closest links with Flora and Scotland. One of Flora's descendants presented the school with a locket that had once belonged to Flora and contained a lock of her hair and a lock of the Prince's hair. To strengthen Scottish–Carolina ties, King George V sent the college a block of granite from Balmoral which was placed proudly beside the principal building of the college, Vardell Hall. A link with Flora and Scotland that is even more prized is the marble tablet from the original Iona cross memorial which was blown down in 1873. Dr Vardell visited Scotland for the bicentenary of Flora's birth in 1922, and, while in Skye, he asked for and was given the tablet which had been badly broken when the earlier cross was blown down. He took the fragments back to North Carolina, where they were reassembled, and the tablet now rests over the graves of two unnamed children, traditionally supposed to have been Flora's, who died in America.

Once again legend has insinuated itself into truth to confuse the story of Flora MacDonald. These bodies lay for a century and a half in unmarked graves in Richmond County, but North Carolina tradition whispered insistently that the children were Flora's. Scottish-Americans wanted to believe such a romantic story, and in 1937 they had the two bodies exhumed and reinterred in the grounds of the Flora MacDonald College. Amid great pageantry the coffins were carried to their new resting place by four young women, each named Flora MacDonald, and over the graves a tablet was set with the inscription:

HERE RESTS

THE REMAINS

OF

TWO CHILDREN

OF

FLORA MACDONALD

INTERRED

RICHMOND CO. N.C.

1777

REINTERRED

APRIL 28, 1937

Alongside was placed the marble plaque from Kilmuir, proclaiming Dr Johnson's words about the heroine:

THE PRESERVER

OF

CHARLES EDWARD STUART

WILL BE MENTIONED IN HISTORY
AND, IF COURAGE AND FIDELITY
BE VIRTUES,
MENTIONED WITH HONOUR

Perhaps a clue to the truth of the story lies in the fact that, in 1937, it was possible to find four girls named Flora MacDonald in North Carolina to carry these children's coffins. Flora was a popular name in Carolina in the 1770s, just as it was common in the 1930s. So was MacDonald. The unfortunate children may well have belonged to a Flora MacDonald, but not to the heroine of the journey over the sea to Skye.

The Flora MacDonald name still remains at Red Springs. A new school, established in 1973, took over the buildings of the former Flora MacDonald College and, although this school's official name is Robeson County Day School, it has adopted the name Flora MacDonald Academy. This is a private school for boys and girls from kindergarten to college or university level, and outside it the granite from Balmoral still stands. In the grounds lie the two nameless children, serving as a memorial to the woman who was not their mother.

The story of St Andrews College demonstrates how the exiles clung to their traditions and to their Presbyterian religion in their new world. Gaelic continued to be spoken in North Carolina until comparatively recently, and today there is renewed interest in it and in other traditions. Hearts remain as loyally Highland as ever. In fact, the more American the Highland settlers have become, the more they cherish their Highland roots. A few clans, like the MacLeods and the MacNeills, have long had clan organizations in the state and held gatherings, but Flora's Clan Donald had nothing until the 1950s.

Then a strange thing happened: the second half of the century brought a dramatic upsurge in interest in things Scottish among Carolinians. Many second-, third- and even fourth-generation American-Highlanders have become caught up in the spell of their heritage: men like Donald F. MacDonald, who was one of the proposers of the name St Andrews for the merged Flora MacDonald College. Donald MacDonald did more than dream about his roots after he visited Scotland in 1954 and saw the Braemar Highland Gathering. That was something different from anything he had experienced back home, so he returned to North Carolina determined to ignite new fires of clanship there. The following year he assisted Flora's descendant, Reginald MacDonald of Kingsburgh, in founding Clan Donald in America. The first branch was in the Carolinas and was established in April 1955 at a rally, held – appropriately – at Flora MacDonald College.

It was only a step from there to Highland Games. Along with a Scottish-American clanswoman, Agnes MacRae Morton, Donald began to organize games in the state in 1956. The event was to be run by the book – the programme of the Braemar Gathering and a set of rules. As he remembers it himself:[9]

> Armed with my Braemar souvenir programme and set of rules, we set about designing and staging 'an American Braemar'. I selected 19 August as the date, because it commemorated Glenfinnan and the raising of the Prince's standard, which was primarily the start of the downfall of the Highlands and Islands, and caused our people to go to North Carolina in the first place.

Because the 'Scotch country' of eastern North Carolina is intensely hot in August, the first games were held in the western part of the state, high in the cool heights of the Blue Ridge Mountains at Grandfather Mountain, near Linville. There were problems, but all were overcome – the nearest available pipe band had to be brought in from Washington, DC, and a seemingly insurmountable difficulty arose when it was discovered that there were three prizes and three contestants for the Highland dancing, but the Braemar rules laid down that there must be more contestants for any event than the number of prizes offered. Donald recalled:

> We were in a quandary. In those days I could do a reasonable Highland Fling and a not-so-bad Sword Dance, so I joined in the contest just so that our 'Braemar rules' would be met. The three girls who had entered as solo competitors duly won the prizes and were each awarded a medal by Flora's great great grandson, who was guest of honour.

One of the winners, Marilyn MacQueen, was a direct descendant of Flora's half-sister, Florence. Another winner could boast the proud name of Flora Ragnhilt MacDonald. Her home, near Olivia, was only a short distance from Barbecue Church and Cameron's Hill (the present-day name of Mount Pleasant). Her middle name harked all the way back to the twelfth century and to the Norwegian princess, Ragnhilt, wife of the Clan Donald's great warrior-king, Somerled.

A further difficulty in the Presbyterian heart of the Carolinas lay in the fact that, to enable participants to travel the long distances from the 'Scotch Country' to Grandfather Mountain, the most convenient day to hold the games was a Sunday – the Sabbath when no self-respecting Highlander in Scotland or America would organize any entertainment. Again Donald MacDonald would not accept defeat:

> I figured the Lord might strike us dead unless we did something for Him, so I suggested to the co-founder that we start the day with outdoor worship in that incomparably beautiful mountain setting. We tried all over the Eastern United States but could find no Scottish minister who was free to preach at our Games, so I had to preach a 'sermonette' in between attempts at tossing the caber, wrestling, dancing the Highland Fling and serving as *fear-an-taighe* (master of ceremonies).

Donald continued as President of the Grandfather Mountain Highland Games for six years, helping to build them, in 1961, into a two-day event. Many other places have emulated Grandfather Mountain, and Highland Games are now held throughout the Eastern states of America. Several start with a religious service and are held on a Sunday or over a weekend. The organizers apparently believe that they are following a custom from the old country, without realizing that in Calvinistic Scotland no Highland Games would ever have been held on the Sabbath!

Today the Grandfather Mountain Games are held over a long weekend each July and form the focus of the Highland year in North Carolina. For a brief moment each summer this beautiful spot becomes a gathering place of the clans, calling to it men and women to share their common kinship as well as to enjoy all the entertainments of Highland games. This could almost be anywhere from Royal Braemar to proud little Morar on Scotland's silver western shore, except that it is more stridently Scottish, more gaudily draped in tartan and more vociferous in proclaiming kinship among clansmen and women. For these few days each July these magnificent blue mountains and wooded glens become part of the Highland homeland. In charge of the pre-games ceilidhs have been two Flora MacDonalds, mother and daughter.

When the roll of the clans is called at Grandfather Mountain the list is as long and the response as strong as might be heard anywhere in the Highlands or Islands of Scotland. The MacRaes answer 'Here'. The

MacQueens, MacColls, MacKinnons, MacCrimmons, MacLaurins, MacNeills and MacLeans, too. Then follow many who may not have a 'Mac' to their name, but are as Scottish as the Royal Stewarts themselves: the Campbells, Morrisons, Nicolsons, Martins, Frasers, Beatons and many more. And of course, Clan Donald, the greatest Scottish clan of all, answers the call for, as we have seen, it is powerful in this part of America.

At Grandfather Mountain people dress up in any tartan to which they can lay claim (and many to which they have no title at all); they listen to stirring speeches (often asking for money to preserve some clan seat) by visiting chiefs, whose ancestors probably were the very men who drove their forebears out of Scotland, and they sing sentimental songs about the 'auld country'.

When Donald MacDonald, co-founder and first President of Grandfather Mountain Games, could finally resist the call of Scotland no longer and emigrated in the reverse direction to that which his ancestors had taken, a new President of Grandfather Mountain Games took over. Nestor J. MacDonald became Chief of the Games and as a theme tune chose a favourite of his own to be sung each year at Grandfather Mountain. It is a modern Scottish song, which encapsulates that sentimental streak that brings a tear to the eye of Scots wherever they are when talk turns to 'hame'. As a nation we can feel homesick even while sitting in the shadow of Edinburgh Castle listening to 'My Grannie's Hieland Hame' as it pours out from amplifiers at the bandstand in Princes Street Gardens.

Year by year, until his death in 1991, Nestor led the singing of 'These are my Mountains':

> For these are my mountains and this is my glen,
> The braes of my childhood will know me again.
> No land's ever claimed me tho' far I did roam.
> For these are my mountains and I'm going home.

The song may be pure modern music hall, the mountains the Blue Ridge of North Carolina rather than the Cuillins of Skye, and few will ever 'go home' to Scotland, yet these people are expressing a genuine sense of clan kinship which has withstood hardship and misfortune, and still endures even in today's prosperity and contentment. At Grandfather Mountain hearts are as Highland as those of their forebears were the day they sailed from Skye, Kintyre, Appin, Islay or Wester Ross, two centuries or longer ago.

It is hard to believe that these happy, prosperous people revelling in a sea of tartan at Grandfather Mountain are descended from Scots who, over several centuries, have made a speciality of supporting lost causes on both sides of the Atlantic since long before Flora's time, and have suffered for being on the losing side in one momentous event after another. The Jacobite Risings and American Revolution were only a start: in Scotland there followed the Highland Clearances, the destruction of the Highland way of life and the discouragement of the Gaelic language and tradition. In America's south the Carolina Highlanders suffered badly in the American Civil War. In these circumstances it can hardly be surprising that Flora MacDonald is their heroine and that many want to claim MacDonald descent – preferably descent from Flora.

The Grandfather Mountain Games were just a beginning. Red Springs now has its own Flora MacDonald Highland Games, and there are gatherings at Waxhaw and Charleston in the Carolinas, and at Stone Mountain and Savannah in Georgia, as well as others in Florida, Kentucky, Virginia, Alabama, Tennessee, Texas and in the more northerly states. Renewed interest in the Gaelic tongue has followed. At the request of Donald F. MacDonald, through his nephew, Jamie, and with the support of Lewis-born Catriona MacIver Parsons, an annual Gaelic Mod was begun in 1988 at Alexandria, Virginia. The organizers included Joan MacWilliams Weiss, Elaine Ackerson, Maria Adams, Mary Gillies Swope, Liam Cassidy and Hank Campbell-Ickes, all of them enthusiasts from *An Comunn Gaidhealach Ameireaga* (The Highland Society of America). They were assisted by Mod Gold Medallist Kitty MacLeod.

Nova Scotia has treated Flora kindly: her brief stay there has been absorbed into the Scottish-Canadian tradition as one would expect in an area that has long attracted Scottish settlers. At the end of the War of Independence many families came north to settle, and, but for the British Government's meanness, Allan and Flora MacDonald might have been among them. The flood of immigrants from the Scottish Highlands continued throughout the nineteenth and early twentieth centuries, so that Nova Scotia became a strongly Scottish community.

Throughout the province, but especially in the most Scottish areas of Antigonish and Cape Breton, there is much interest in Gaelic and Highland culture, and Flora is firmly a part of that tradition. At Fort Edward, Allan's 84th Highland Emigrants Regiment has been re-created by a group of military history enthusiasts who dress in the uniform of the period, parade, play their music and re-enact battles at gatherings and outdoor events throughout the province and in New England. It is a well-deserved tribute to Allan's service there.

In the Western Isles, where Flora spent most of her life, it is sometimes hard to discover the heroine. Here the visitor might be forgiven for assuming that she is not considered the heroine that the rest of the world holds her to be. On Uist and Skye, the places where she was born, lived her life and died are not pointed out with pride.

The house on South Uist in which she was born decayed and fell into ruin more than a century-and-a-half ago, and cows shelter in the lee of the cairn that marks its location, if indeed this is its site at all. One islander who was present at the unveiling explained to me that the house actually stood in a dip a few yards from the site of the cairn. 'They put the cairn on high ground so that it would be easier seen', he said. In spite of all this care Flora's cairn, on its low eminence amid undulating country, can be missed very easily on the drive across South Uist.

On Skye, Flora's memory has fared little better. Kingsburgh, to which she brought the Prince and where she herself lived after her marriage to the tacksman's son, is a ruin; Flodigarry, her first home with Allan, is prettily modernized and has been added to; only the walls remain of the Chief of Sleat's house at Monkstadt, since its roof timbers were pulled off only a couple of generations ago; and little is left, except part of the walls, of her last home at Penduin. Now an effort is being made to restore Monkstadt, but this will take many years and much money.

The majority of visitors who make the ferry journey from Lochmaddy in North Uist to Uig in Skye are unaware that they are following the very course that Flora's small boat took, and they are never told. As they near Uig, few realize that the Prince's landing place lies only a short distance up the coast. From the land side it has neither easy access nor a sign to mark it. The present High Chief of Clan Donald, Lord Macdonald of Macdonald, now lives in the south of the island, at Kinloch, not far from Armadale, where Flora's stepfather once held the tack. There are two centres on Skye that deal with Clan Donald history. The Skye Heritage Centre, opened at Portree in 1993, tells vividly the story of Prince Charlie's escape over the sea to Skye and Flora's part in it. Thanks to the generosity of clansmen throughout the world a Clan Donald Centre has been established at Armadale, but here, where MacDonald clansmen gather from the four corners of the globe, Flora is just a small part of the greater Clan MacDonald story. The fact that the MacDonald chief in Skye did not call out his clan to fight for Prince Charlie in 1745 was a great blow to many members of Clan Donald: it was left to individual tacksmen or clansmen and women to rally to the Prince, and many did so without pausing to consider the risk. Even today, two-and-a-half centuries on, a feeling still lingers that their bravery showed up the faintheartedness of their leaders.

By tenaciously holding to the principles of Highland honour when called upon, Flora MacDonald epitomizes the spirit of clan kinship more than any other person in the clan story. The '45 Rising created a great cleavage in many clans, including Clan Donald, and Flora is almost the only person who has the power to heal that division. She, more than even the clan's founder, the great Somerled himself, has united her kinsmen. Clan Donald owes her a great debt.

The landscape and way of life in the Hebrides may change, but the spirit of the island people is eternal. Neither Flora nor the Prince would feel strangers there: they would even glimpse something familiar in today's island way of life. Men still go to sea in small boats open to those sudden storms of wind and rain that scour the Minch even in high summer, and where mists come swirling in just as they did that Sunday morning in 1746. Crofters still tend their cattle and crops, by more modern methods it is true, but their work remains their way of life. Perhaps we should not be surprised at this apparent neglect of the buildings in which Flora lived, for life has always been precarious in the Islands. In Flora's time survival often hung on the slenderest of threads: a timely spring, good seed, a generous harvest or a chief's greed. With every scrap of energy needed to win a bare living from a barren land, history counted for little. As the clan system withered, new values came into the clansmen's lives: they could no longer depend on the chief for protection, and money rather than barter became the means of obtaining the necessities of life. The islands themselves bear testimony to Flora MacDonald's life and achievement, and it is easy to conjure up her ghost without artefacts of wood and stone.

The one place where Flora MacDonald's memory is best preserved is the little graveyard at Kilmuir, which is her resting place. From her memorial on a low windswept hillside the view is unmistakably Hebridean: the foreground is filled with the expanse of Loch Snizort on the far shore of which Waternish Peninsula hides MacLeod territory, where the soldier fired on the Prince's boat, while the middle distance is the Minch, across which Flora and Betty Burke sailed. Along the far horizon runs the pale heather-purple line of the Long Island – Harris, North Uist and Benbecula can all be seen, but South Uist lies out of sight behind Waternish.

This is a restless landscape, changing hour by hour, minute by minute, just as it did that night of the voyage over the sea to Skye. A day that starts with sunlight burnishing Waternish cliffs can change quickly to a fearsome black storm that blots out the Long Island. Squalls sweep across the Minch, only to die away as quickly as they came and leave a rainbow arch linking Skye with the Long Island. This changing scene mirrors Flora's life when lost causes caught her up and carried her before them – time after time she saw life turn against her as swiftly and as violently as any Hebridean storm.

Life never recompensed Flora MacDonald – that was left to posterity and was due in no small measure to her own strong character, her plain common sense, and those qualities of courage and fidelity that Dr Johnson noted when he met her. An accident of history may have turned Flora MacDonald into a heroine, but she herself created the legend which has endured through two-and-a-half centuries.

Notes

ABBREVIATIONS

NLS: National Library of Scotland
PRO: Public Record Office, London
SRO: Scottish Record Office, Edinburgh

CHAPTER ONE: THE LADY OF THE LEGEND

1 The best-known portraits of Flora are Richard Wilson's of 1747 in the National Portrait Gallery, London, and Scottish National Portrait Gallery, Edinburgh, Allan Ramsay's of 1749 in the Ashmolean Museum, Oxford, and W. Robertson's of 1750 in the Kelvingrove Art Gallery, Glasgow.

2 Percentage of Western Isles school-leavers entering further and higher education: 1988–9, 52.1%; 1989–90, 42.86%; 1990–1, 52.76%. Borders Region came second: 35.83%; 40.89%; and 43.14% respectively. Figures from The Scottish School Leaver statistics produced annually by the Standing Committee of Careers Officers in Scotland.

3 Revd Angus MacDonald's mother was a sister of Ranald MacDonald's father, thus Flora's grandfather and father were cousins. Allan Reginald MacDonald, *The Truth about Flora MacDonald*. p. 4, n. 3.

4 Information from Donald F. MacDonald, Edinburgh.

5 Revd Robert Forbes, *The Lyon in Mourning*, 3 Vols.

6 F.F. Wylde, *The Autobiography of Flora MacDonald*, pp. 18–26.

7 Forbes, *The Lyon in Mourning*, Vol. 1, p. 117.

8 Letter from Lady Margaret MacDonald to John Mackenzie of Delvine, 1 July 1744, NLS 1309/14.

9 Letter from John Mackenzie of Delvine to Sir Alexander MacDonald of Sleat, 19 June 1740, NLS 1136/117.

10 Letter from Mackenzie of Delvine to Sir Alexander MacDonald of Sleat, 28 August 1746, NLS 1136/150.

11 Letter from Sir Alexander MacDonald of Sleat to Earl of Morton, 29 December 1739, NLS 3142/21.

12 Letter from Mackenzie of Delvine to Sir Alexander MacDonald of Sleat, 9 December 1739, NLS 1136/105.

13 Letter from Lady Margaret MacDonald to Dowager Countess of Pembroke, 30 December

1739, NLS 3142/24.

14   Letter from Sir Alexander MacDonald of Sleat to Earl of Morton, 29 December 1739, NLS 3142/21.

15   Revd A. MacGregor, *Life of Flora, MacDonald*, 5th edn, 1932, p. 51.

16   MacDonald, *Truth About Flora*, p. 2.

17   MacGregor, *Life of Flora*, pp. 63–7.

18   Forbes, *Lyon in Mourning*, Vol. 1, p. 116.

19   *Ibid.*, p. 117.

CHAPTER TWO: MEETING AT MIDNIGHT

1   Forbes, *Lyon in Mourning*, Vol. 2, p. 360.

2   *Ibid.*, Vol. 1, p. 304.

3   *Ibid.*

4   Letter from Sir Alexander MacDonald of Sleat to MacLeod of Dunvegan, 23 September 1745. Duncan Warrand (ed.), *More Culloden Papers*, Vol. 4, p. 63.

5   The fullest account of Neil MacEachain's life is given in Alasdair MacLean, *A MacDonald for the Prince*.

6   W.B. Blaikie, *Origins of the '45*, p. 243.

7   Letter from Flora MacDonald to Sir John MacPherson, 21 October 1789, NLS 2618.

8   The manuscript of Neil MacEachain's account was lost in France at the time of the Revolution. It reappeared in the possession of a Paris hairdresser and was published in the *New Monthly Magazine* in 1840, and in Blaikie's *Origins* in 1916, pp. 227–66. Felix O'Neil's account comes from Forbes's *Lyon in Mourning*, Vol. 1, pp. 102–8.

9   Forbes, *Lyon in Mourning*, Vol. 1, pp. 106, 371.

10   Blaikie, *Origins*, p. 251.

11   Forbes, *Lyon in Mourning*, Vol. 1, p. 296.

12   Letter from Flora MacDonald to Sir John MacPherson, 21 October 1789, NLS 2618.

13   Forbes, *Lyon in Mourning*, Vol. 1, p. 106.

14   *Ibid*, p. 110.

15   *Ibid.*, p. 106.

16   *Ibid.*, p. 296.

17   Blaikie, *Origins*, p. 251.

18   Forbes, *Lyon in Mourning*, Vol. 1, p. 107.

19   *Ibid.*, pp. 107, 327.

20   *Ibid.*, pp. 124, 297, 330.

21   *Ibid.*, p. 297.

22   Blaikie, *Origins*, p. 260.

23   Forbes, *Lyon in Mourning*, Vol. 2, pp. 32, 46.

24   *Ibid.*, Vol. 1, p. 111.

25   Blaikie, *Origins*, p. 260.

26   *Ibid.*

CHAPTER THREE: 'I OWE YOU A CROWN

1 Forbes, *Lyon in Mourning*, Vol. 2, p. 31.
2 *Ibid.*, Vol. 1, p. 299.
3 *Ibid.*, pp. 111, 299.
4 Flora's version comes from Forbes's *Lyon in Mourning*, Vol. 1, pp. 111, 297–300.
5 Blaikie, *Origins*, p. 261.
6 *Ibid.*, p. 261.
7 *Ibid.*, p. 262.
8 *Ibid.*, pp. 262–3.
9 J. MacKinnon and J. Morrison, *The MacLeods: Genealogy of a Clan (1968–77)*, Vol. 3, p. 36.
10 Forbes, *Lyon in Mourning*, Vol. 2, p. 13.
11 Blaikie, *Origins*, p. 264.
12 Forbes, *Lyon in Mourning*, Vol. 1, p. 77.
13 An account of Flora's stay at Kingsburgh is given in *ibid.*, pp. 117–21.
14 *Ibid.*, pp. 301–2.
15 *Ibid.*, p. 121.
16 *Ibid.*, p. 75.
17 *Ibid.*, Vol. 2, p. 21.
18 *Ibid.*, p. 22.
19 *Ibid.*, pp. 24–5.
20 *Ibid.*, p. 25.
21 *Ibid.*, p. 26.
22 *Ibid.*
23 *Ibid.*, Vol. 1, p. 114.
24 *Ibid.*, Vol. 2, p. 31.
25 *Ibid.*, Vol. 1, p. 298.
26 Letter from David Campbell to Mr Maule, 21 July 1746, quoted in E.G. Vining, *Flora MacDonald*, p. 50.
27 Forbes, *Lyon in Mourning*, Vol. 1, p. 123.
28 Letter from David Campbell to General John Campbell, 11 July 1746, NLS 3736/422.
29 *Ibid.*
30 Forbes, *Lyon in Mourning*, Vol. 1, p. 303.

CHAPTER FOUR: FLORA – INNOCENT OR GUILTY?

1 Forbes, *Lyon in Mourning*, Vol. 2, p. 100.
2 *Ibid.*, Vol. 1, pp. 110–11.
3 MacGregor, *Life of Flora*, p. 117.
4 Blaikie, *Origins*, p. 245.
5 Forbes, *Lyon in Mourning*, Vol. 2, p. 98.
6 Letter from Flora MacDonald to Sir John MacPherson, 21 October 1789, NLS 2618.
7 Blaikie, *Origins*, pp. 249–50.
8 Letter from General Campbell to Lord Cromartie, 24 July 1746, NLS 3736/447.
9 Forbes, *Lyon in Mourning*, Vol. 1, p. 267.

10 E.M. Barron, *Prince Charlie's Pilot*, p. 116.
11 Blaikie, *Origins*, p. 254.
12 *Ibid.*, p. 243.
13 *Ibid.*, p. 245.
14 Forbes, *Lyon in Mourning*, Vol. 2, p. 102.
15 *Ibid.*, pp. 24–5.
16 *Ibid.*, Vol. 1, p. 331.
17 Blaikie, *Origins*, p. 263.
18 Forbes, *Lyon in Mourning*, Vol. 1, p. 30, Vol. 2, p. 170 [author's italics].
19 *Ibid.*, Vol. 2, p. 13.

CHAPTER FIVE: CONFESSIONS AND ACCUSATIONS

1   J.S. Gibson, *Ships of the '45*, p. 154. I am indebted to John Gibson for background information on the ships involved in the search for the Prince.
2   Forbes, *Lyon in Mourning*, Vol. 2, p. 253.
3   *New Statistical Account of Scotland*, Vol. 14, p. 316.
4   Forbes, *Lyon in Mourning.*, Vol. 2, p. 253.
5   *Ibid.*, Vol. 1, p. 374.
6   *Ibid.*, p. 374.
7   Flora's deposition at Applecross, 12 July 1746, PRO SP54, Bundle 32/49, and another version in NLS 3736/432.
8   Forbes, *Lyon in Mourning*, Vol. 1, p. 120.
9   Kingsburgh's deposition to General Campbell, NLS 3736/427.
10 James Boswell, *Journal of a Tour to the Hebrides with Samuel Johnson*, Sunday 26 September 1773, Penguin Classics edition, 1984, p. 316.
11 Letter from Duke of Cumberland to General Campbell, 18 August 1746, NLS 3736/440.
12 PRO SP54, Bundle 32/49.
13 Forbes, *Lyon in Mourning*, Vol. 3, pp. 190–1.
14 *Ibid.*, Vol. 1, p. 113.
15 *Ibid.*
16 *Ibid.*, p. 114.
17 *Ibid.*
18 Sir Charles Petrie, *The Jacobite Movement*, 3rd edn, 1958, p. 394.
19 Henrietta Tayler, *History of Rebellion in 1745 and 1746*, pp. 133–4.
20 Letter from Horace Walpole to Sir Horace Mann, 1 August 1747, quoted in Speck, *The Butcher*, p. 162.
21 Forbes, *Lyon in Mourning*, Vol. 1, p. 78.
22 *Ibid.*, p. 115.
23 *Ibid.*, p. 79.
24 Letter from Lady Margaret MacDonald to Lord President Duncan Forbes, 24 July 1746, Duncan Forbes, *Culloden Papers*, pp. 290–2.
25 Letter from Sir Alexander MacDonald of Sleat to Duncan Forbes, 29 July 1746, Duncan Forbes, *Culloden Papers*, p. 292.
26 Letter from Sir Alexander MacDonald of Sleat to John MacKenzie of Delvine, 29 August

Log house similar to that in which many North Carolina settlers lived (from God's Frontiersmen, *courtesy Rory Fitzpatrick)*

Flora MacDonald's silver, comprising tray with the initials F McD, jug, sauce boat and ladle (Courtesy North Carolina Department of Cultural Resources)

Marker at Cameron's Hill, Harnett County, North Carolina, for the site of Mount Pleasant, the home of Flora's half-sister, Annabella (Courtesy D.F. MacDonald)

Marker for Barbecue Church, where Flora worshipped (Courtesy D.F. MacDonald)

Diorama depicting the battle of Moore's Creek (Courtesy US National Park Service)

Philadelphia was bustling with excitement over the signing of the Declaration of Independence at the time of Allan's arrival in the city as a prisoner (Courtesy the Historical Society of Pennsylvania)

few Cows last Summer, means very soon to return back to
but this money to carry on his improvements which he
was obliged to give up last October for want of Cash.

To my travelling expences from the Highland settlement in Anson County in North Carolina, to Fort Johnston on the River Cape fear (being fourteen days from home) to settle the plan of raising the Highlanders with Governor Martin who was at that time in the Fort	23 .. ..
To the Value of 9 Stand of Arms purchased from Messrs. Marshall and George Miller both Merchants of Cross Creek at £3..10..0 each	31. 10.
To a Silver mounted Riffle bot. of Mr. George Miller	9. 9
To Caleb Tulishtons Riffle	7.
To a Cask of Rum from Mr. Gillis of Cross Creek for the use of the Highlanders on the Expedition	7. 10.
To the Value of five horses taken from me and two Sons when made prisoners after the Engagement the Highlanders had with General Caswell at Moores Creek with two Baff Horses included	85. 10.
To my own Family Arms, Including my three Indented Servants Arms	42. 9. 6
To Blankets, shoes and Shirts purchased and given to the Common Highlanders	18. 9. 4
To my own and Two Sons Baggage with Sadles &c. being robed of every thing but barely as we stood	58. .. ..
To Expences at different Meetings with the Regulators and Highlanders &c. and money given to different Express	11. 13. 1
	299. 12. 11

Your Memorialist therefore prays that
his Case may be taken into your Consideration
And your Memorialist as in duty
bound will ever pray.

London 8th February 1785

Allen McDonald

Allan's claim for the money he spent raising the Highlanders to fight for King George (Courtesy the Public Record Office)

Letter written by Allan MacDonald from prison at Reading, Pennsylvania, to a merchant in Philadelphia ordering material for new waistcoats and breeches (Courtesy the Historical Society of Pennsylvania)

Charles, Flora's eldest son (from MacInnes's Brave Sons of Skye*)*

James, Flora's fourth son (from MacInnes's
Brave Sons of Skye*)*

John, Flora's fifth son (from MacInnes's
Brave Sons of Skye)

Alexander MacLeod of Glendale, Flora's
son-in-law (from MacInnes's Brave Sons
of Skye)

Sir Banastre Tarleton, by Francis Reynolds after Reynolds. The MacDonald boys fought with Tarleton's notorious BritishLegion in the campaign to retake the Carolinas (Courtesy Walker Art Gallery, National Museums and Galleries on Merseyside)

The Battle of Cowpens, *by Frederick Kemmelmeyer, at which Flora's son, Charles, fought for Tarleton (Courtesy Yale University Art Gallery, Mabel Brady Garvan Collection)*

Fort Edward, Nova Scotia, and the officers' quarters where Flora probably lived. The building was burnt down in June 1922 and only the Fort remains (Courtesy Canadian Parks Service)

Nova Scotian military history enthusiasts today re-enact the exploits of Allan's 2nd Battalion of the 84th Regiment (Courtesy 84th of Foot 2nd Battalion Regimental Association)

Killcups on the Kentycook (Kennetcook) River, by J.E. Woolford, close to the site of Allan's Nova Scotia land grant (Courtesy the Nova Scotia Museum)

A sleigh leaving Windsor, Nova Scotia, by Robert Petley. Although it dates from 1837 this demonstrates the difficulty of Flora's journey from Halifax to Windsor (Courtesy The Art Gallery of Nova Scotia)

The ship, Ville de Paris, *on which Ranald served, foundering in the Atlantic Ocean (Courtesy National Maritime Museum, London)*

Sir John MacPherson, by Sir Joshua Reynolds. (Courtesy the Scottish National Portrait Gallery)

Long-leaf pines frame the Flora MacDonald Academy's main building at Red Springs, North Carolina, formerly occupied by Flora MacDonald College until it became St Andrew's Presbyterian College (Courtesy D.F. MacDonald)

Four Flora MacDonalds acted as pall bearers when the remains of two nameless children, wrongly believed to have been Flora's, were re-interred in the grounds of Flora MacDonald College in 1937. The marble tablet from the memorial at Kilmuir, Skye, which was blown down in 1873, stands on the grave (Courtesy D.F. MacDonald)

Prince Charles Edward's name is still commemorated in Fayetteville, North Carolina, where a hotel is named after him (Courtesy D.F. MacDonald)

At MacRae Meadows in the shadow of Grandfather Mountain, North Carolina, Highland Games are held annually (Courtesy Hugh Morton)

Flora's memorial bears Dr Johnson's words: 'Her name will be mentioned in history and if courage and fidelity be virtues, mentioned with honour'

The Celtic cross set up over Flora's grave in 1871 was blown down two years later and replaced in 1880 (Courtesy Illustrated London News)

The unveiling of the Flora MacDonald statue at Inverness in 1899 (Courtesy Aberdeen Journals)

Flora MacDonald, by W. Robertson (Courtesy Glasgow Museums, Art Gallery & Museum, Kelvingrove)

1746, NLS 1308/199.

27 Letter from Lady Margaret MacDonald to MacKenzie of Delvine, 24 July 1746, NLS 1309/29.

28 Forbes, *Lyon in Mourning,* Vol. 1, p. 115.

29 MacGregor, *Life of Flora,* p. 144–60.

30 *The Scots Magazine,* January 1774, p.54.

CHAPTER SIX: THE ENVIED PRISONER

1 Forbes, *Lyon in Mourning,* Vol. 1, p. 112.

2 *Ibid.,* p. 116.

3 *Ibid.*

4 *Ibid.,* pp. 126–7.

5 *Ibid.,* p. 112.

6 *Ibid.,* pp. 116–7.

7 *Ibid.,* p. 117.

8 *Ibid.,* Preface, pp. xii–xiii.

9 *Ibid.,* Vol. 1, pp. 116–7.

10 *Ibid.,* p. 112.

11 *Ibid.*

12 *Ibid.,* p. 114.

13 *Ibid.,* Vol. 2, pp. 106–8.

14 William Anne Keppel, 2nd Earl of Albemarle, *Albemarle Papers,* Vol. 1, p. 237.

15 HMS *Bridgewater* Log, PRO ADM 51/114.

16 Letter from Lady Margaret to MacKenzie, 1 September 1746, NLS 1309/30.

17 Letter from Sir Alexander MacDonald of Sleat to MacKenzie of Delvine, 29 July 1746, NLS 1308/199.

18 Letter from Sir Alexander MacDonald of Sleat to MacKenzie of Delvine, 21 September 1746, NLS 1308/203.

19 Letter from Lady Margaret MacDonald to MacKenzie of Delvine, 1 September 1746, NLS 1309/30.

20 Letter from Allan MacDonald to Duncan Forbes, 27 November 1746, Forbes, *Culloden Papers,* Vol. V, p. 140.

21 Forbes, *Lyon in Mourning,* Vol. 1, p. 239.

22 Letter from Sir Alexander MacDonald of Sleat to MacKenzie of Delvine, 19 August 1746, NLS 1308/202.

23 Keppel, *Albemarle Papers,* Vol. I, p. 326.

24 Letter from Captain Knowler, possibly to Commodore Smith, 30 November 1746, NLS 3736/511.

25 Alistair Tayler and Henrietta Tayler, *Prisoners of the '45,* Vol. 1, p. 158.

26 Letter from Lord Albemarle to Lord Newcastle, Keppel, *Albemarle Papers,* Vol. 1, p. 297.

27 E.G. Vining, *Life of Flora MacDonald,* p. 67.

28 Forbes, *Lyon in Mourning,* Vol. 1, p. 296.

29 MacGregor, *Life of Flora,* p. 149.

30 Forbes, *Lyon in Mourning,* Vol. 1, p. 283.

31   MacGregor, *Life of Flora*, p. 150.
32   Boswell, *Tour to the Hebrides*, Monday 13 September 1773, p. 277.

CHAPTER SEVEN: HOME TO A HUSBAND

1   Forbes, *Lyon in Mourning*, Vol. 3, p. 82.
2   MacDonald, *Truth About Flora*, p. 67.
3   W. Forbes Gray, in *The Scotsman*, 6 January 1927, quoted in MacDonald, *Truth About Flora*, p. 67, p. 71 note.
4   Forbes, *Lyon in Mourning*, Vol. 1, p. 151.
5   *Ibid.*, p. 152.
6   *Ibid.*, pp. 294, 296–306.
7   *Ibid.*, Vol. 2, p. 17n.
8   *Ibid.*, p. 46.
9   MacGregor, *Life of Flora*, pp. 158-9
10   Forbes, *Lyon in Mourning*, Vol. 2, p. 180.
11   MacGregor, *Life of Flora*, pp. 154–7.
12   *Ibid.*, p. 155.
13   *Ibid.*, p. 156.
14   Forbes, *Lyon in Mourning*, Vol. 2, p. 178.
15   *Ibid.*, p. 181.
16   *Ibid.*
17   *Ibid.*
18   MacGregor, *Life of Flora*, pp. 158–9n.
19   Forbes, *Lyon in Mourning*, Vol. 2, p. 324.
20   *Ibid.*, Vol. 3, pp. 21–2. Flora gave the names as John MacDonald (helmsman, later drowned on a voyage to Long Island), Duncan Campbell, MacMerry and Alexander MacDonald.
21   *Ibid.*, p. 62.
22   Letter from Lady Margaret MacDonald to Duncan Forbes, Warrand, *More Culloden Papers*, Vol. 5, pp. 189–90.
23   MacGregor, *Life of Flora*, p. 159.
24   MacDonald, *Truth About Flora*, pp. 123–6. The marriage contract can be seen at Sir Walter Scott's House, Abbotsford, Melrose. Although the contract assesses Flora's fortune as £700, she actually had rather more of Lady Primrose's gift left.
25   *The Scots Magazine*, 1750, p. 556.
26   Forbes, *Lyon in Mourning*, Vol. 3, pp. 80–1.
27   *Ibid.*, p. 81.
28   *Ibid.*, p. 82.

CHAPTER EIGHT: THE TACKSMAN'S WIFE

1   Boswell, *Tour to the Hebrides*, Sunday 12 September 1773, p. 265.
2   Forbes, *Lyon in Mourning*, Vol. 3, p. 80.

3 Revds A. and A. MacDonald, *The Clan Donald*, Vol. 3, p. 560.

4 Letter from Alexander MacDonald of Kingsburgh to MacKenzie of Delvine, 14 August 1751, NLS 1306/52.

5 Boswell, *Tour to the Hebrides*, Tuesday 7 September 1773, p. 249..

6 *Ibid.*, 6 September 1773, p. 247.

7 *The Scots Magazine*, 1759, p. 159.

8 Revds A. and A. MacDonald, *The Clan Donald*, Vol. 3, p. 560.

9 Letter from Allan MacDonald to MacKenzie of Delvine, 18 November 1763, NLS 1306/59.

10 Letter from Sir James MacDonald to MacKenzie of Delvine, 14 July 1763, NLS 1309/228.

11 Letter from Sir James MacDonald to MacKenzie of Delvine, 30 July 1763, NLS 1309/231.

12 Letter from Lady Margaret MacDonald to MacKenzie of Delvine, 3 November 1763, NLS 1309/141.

13 Letter from Allan MacDonald to MacKenzie of Delvine, 22 October 1763, NLS 1306/58.

14 Letter from Sir James MacDonald to MacKenzie of Delvine, 16 October 1763, NLS 1309/252.

15 Letter from Allan MacDonald to MacKenzie of Delvine, 15 July 1763, NLS 1306/57.

16 *Ibid*, 22 October 1763, NLS 1306/58.

17 *Ibid.*, 18 November 1763, NLS 1306/59.

18 *Ibid.*

19 Boswell, *Tour to the Hebrides*, 5 September 1773, p. 224.

20 *Ibid.*

21 Letter from Allan MacDonald to MacKenzie of Delvine, 22 January 1767, quoted in MacDonald, *Truth About Flora*, pp. 107–9.

CHAPTER NINE: A WAKE FOR SKYE

1 Letter from Alexander McAllister, North Carolina, to Angus McCuaig, Islay, 29 November 1770, in McAllister Papers, University of North Carolina Library, Chapel Hill, NC.

2 Boswell, *Tour to the Hebrides*, 5 September, p. 245.

3 Letter from Lady Margaret MacDonald to MacKenzie of Delvine, 9 December 1776, NLS 1309/146.

4 *Ibid.*

5 Thomas Pennant, *Tour in Scotland and Voyage to the Hebrides 1772*, p. 305.

6 *Ibid*, p. 306.

7 *Ibid.*, p. 300.

8 *Ibid.*, pp. 307–10.

9 William L. Saunders, *Colonial Records of North Carolina*, Vol. 4, pp. 489–90. *Argyll Colony Plus Magazine*, published in Fort Worth, Texas, is devoted to these colonists.

10 Letter from Flora MacDonald to Duke of Atholl, 23 April 1774, quoted in MacDonald, *Truth About Flora*, pp. 110–11.

11 I am indebted to the Royal Marines Museum, Southsea, for information on Ranald's career.

12 Letter from Alexander MacDonald of Kingsburgh to MacKenzie of Delvine, 30 April 1771, NLS 1306/54.

13   Letter from Edmund MacQueen to MacKenzie of Delvine, 2 October 1771, NLS 1306/78.

14   Specimen of handwriting, NLS 1306/79. *Ars non habet inimicum nisi ignorantem, Home Book of Quotations.*

15   Letter from Flora MacDonald to MacKenzie of Delvine, 12 August 1772, NLS 1306/72.

16   Allan MacDonald to MacKenzie of Delvine, 30 November 1772, NLS 1306/65.

17   *The Scots Magazine,* July 1771, p. 325.

18   Scotus Americanus, *Information concerning the Province of North Carolina addressed to emigrants from the Highlands and Western Isles of Scotland.* The pamphlet was published in Glasgow, 1773.

19   Letter from Alexander Campbell of Balole to Lachlan MacKinnon Corriechatachain. Papers of Dugald Gilchrist of Ospisdale, SRO GD 153/51/71/12. I am indebted to the article by Alexander Murdoch in the *North Carolina Historical Review,* Vol. 67, No. 4, October 1990, for this reference.

20   *The Scots Magazine,* 1772, p. 111.

21   Forbes, *Lyon in Mourning,* Vol. 3, p. 262.

22   Pennant, *Tour in Scotland,* p. 345.

23   Letter from Flora MacDonald to MacKenzie of Delvine, 12 August 1772, NLS 1306/72.

24   Letter from Allan MacDonald to MacKenzie of Delvine, 2 March 1773, NLS 1306/68.

25   Pennant, *Tour in Scotland,* p. 306.

26   Boswell, *Tour to the Hebrides,* pp. 169, 235, 241, 262, 265, 279–80, 300, 312, 327.

27   *Ibid.,* 1 September 1773, p. 138.

28   *Ibid.,* 2 September 1773, p. 241.

29   *Ibid.,* 4 September 1773, p. 242.

30   *Ibid.,* 8 September 1773, p. 250.

31   Letter from Lord MacDonald to James Boswell, 26 November 1785, Boswell Papers, Yale University. *The Private Papers of James Boswell from Malahide Castle in the collection of Lt.-Col. Ralph Heyward Isham,* Vol. xvi, p. 234, quoted in F.A. Pottle and C.H. Bennett (eds.), 1963, *Boswell: Journal of a Tour to the Hebrides with Samuel Johnson,* p. 154 n.

32   Boswell, *Tour to the Hebrides,* 6 September 1773, p. 247.

33   *Ibid.,* 12 September 1773, p. 262.

34   *Ibid.,* 22 September 1773, p. 300.

35   *Ibid.,* 24 September 1773, p. 312.

36   *Ibid.,* 12 September 1773, p. 265.

37   *Ibid.,* 13 September 1773, pp. 266–77.

38   *Ibid.,* p. 279.

39   *Ibid.,* p. 280.

40   Samuel Johnson, *Works,* [12 vols., 1823], Vol. 9, pp. 391–2.

41   Boswell, *Tour to the Hebrides,* 2 October 1773, p. 327.

42   Letter from Flora MacDonald to Duke of Atholl, 23 April 1774, quoted in MacDonald, *Truth About Flora,* pp. 110–11.

43   *Ibid.*

44   *Ibid.*

45   MacDonald, *Truth About Flora,* p. 97.

46   D. Whyte, *Dictionary of Scots Emigrants to the USA,* pp. 263–4.

47   James Banks, *The Life and Character of Flora MacDonald,* p. 19.

48   Allan MacDonald's Claim, Loyalist Papers, PRO AO13, Bundles 87 and 122.

49 McAllister Family Papers, Wilson Library, University of North Carolina.

50 William Dry's Record Book, Department of Archives and History, Raleigh, North Carolina.

51 Janet Schaw, *Journal of a Lady of Quality*, E.W. Andrews and C.M. Andrews (eds), contains a description of a voyage from Scotland to North Carolina at the time Flora made the journey.

52 Schaw, *Lady of Quality*, p. 53.

53 *Ibid.*, pp. 52–3.

54 *The Scots Magazine*, 1774, quoted in Meyer's, *The Highland Scots of North Carolina*, p. 64.

CHAPTER TEN: LAIRDS OF AMERICA

1   Charles W. Dunn, *A North Carolina Gaelic Bard*, quoted in H.H. Merrens, *Colonial North Carolina in the 18th Century*, p. 220.

2   Schaw, *Lady of Quality*, p. 141.

3   *Ibid.*, p. 145.

4   I.C.C. Graham, *Colonists from Scotland*, p. 108.

5   Meyer, *Highland Scots*, p. 120.

6   MacGregor, *Life of Flora*, pp. 164–5.

7   J.P. MacLean, *Flora MacDonald in America*, p. 32.

8   Schaw, *Lady of Quality*, p. 155.

9   W.B. Beacroft & M.A. Smale, *The Making of America: from Wilderness to World Power*, p. 38.

10 Schaw, *Lady of Quality*, p. 149.

11 *Ibid.*, p. 177.

12 *Ibid.*, p. 158.

13 *Ibid.*, p. 175.

14 Alexander MacDonald's Claim, Loyalist Papers, PRO AO13, Bundles 100 and 115.

15 William H. Foote, *Sketches of North Carolina*, pp. 155–6.

16 Letter from R.R. MacMillan to Revd William Black, 1908, *Argyll Colony Plus*, 1991.

17 Schaw, *Lady of Quality*, p. 281.

18 Charles Woodmason, *The Carolina Back Country On the Eve of the Revolution: Journal and other writings of Charles Woodmason, Anglican Itinerant*, p. 59. Schaw, *Lady of Quality*, p. 179.

19 *History of North America 1776* pp. 187–9. Schaw, *Lady of Quality*, pp. 146, 174–7, 200. John Brickell, *The Natural History of North Carolina*, pp. 46–51. William Bartram, *Travels Through North and South Carolina*, etc, 1791. Meyer, *Highland Scots*, pp. 104–9. Letters from Sandy Allen, Raleigh, NC, to author.

20 Woodmason, *Carolina Back Country*, p. 11.

21 Schaw, *Lady of Quality*, p. 153.

22 Allan MacDonald's Claim, Loyalist Papers, PRO AO13, Bundles 87 and 122.

23 Letter from Dr Donald MacKinnon to Rassie Wicker, *c.* 1953, quoted by Eloise Wicker Wright in *Argyll Colony Plus*, 1990.

24 Letter from Flora MacDonald to Sir John MacPherson, 21 October 1789, NLS 2618.

25 *The State Magazine*, North Carolina, 2 January 1954, p. 6.

26 Allan MacDonald's Claim, Loyalist Papers, PRO AO13, Bundles 87 and 122.

27 Rassie Wicker, *Miscellaneous Ancient Records in Moore County*, typescript (supplied courtesy of Eloise W. Knight), p. 342.

CHAPTER ELEVEN: LOYAL TO WHOM?

1   Letter from Governor Martin to the Earl of Dartmouth, 30 June 1775, W.L. Saunders (ed.), *Colonial Records of North Carolina*, W.L. Saunders (ed.), Vol. 10, p. 47.

2   Wicker, *Ancient Records*, pp. 338–9, 515.

3   Letter from Governor Martin to the Earl of Dartmouth, 12 November 1775, Saunders, *Colonial Records*, Vol. 10, p. 326.

4   *Ibid.*, pp. 324-8. Meyer, *Highland Scots*, p. 155.

5   Saunders, *Colonial Records*, Vol. 9, p. iv.

6   *Ibid.*, pp. 160–2.

7   *Ibid.*, p. 69.

8   Letter from Flora MacDonald to Sir John MacPherson, 21 October 1789, NLS 2618.

9   *Clan Donald Magazine*, Vol. 9, 1981, p. 83.

10   *Clan Donald Magazine*, Vol. 4, 1968, pp. 60–1.

11   *Ibid.*

12   Letter from Governor Martin to his secretary, text from Dr Donald MacKinnon, published in *Argyll Colony Plus*. Martin also said he planned to spend part of the summer of 1775 at Allan's plantation.

13   Schaw, *Lady of Quality*, p. 193 and Miss Schaw sent a letter with them to be forwarded to Britain by the Governor.

14   Allan MacDonald's Claim, Loyalist Papers, PRO AO13, Bundles 87 and 122.

15   Saunders, Colonial Records, Vol. 10, pp. 125–6.

16   Letter from Governor Martin to the Earl of Dartmouth, 30 June 1775, Saunders, *Colonial Records*, Vol. 10, pp. 46–7. Sent by the Lady of Quality's brother, Alexander Schaw, in early July: Schaw, *Lady of Quality*, p. 196.

17   Letter from Governor Martin to the Earl of Dartmouth, 20 July 1775, Saunders, *Colonial Records*, Vol. 10, pp. 108–9. Schaw, *Lady of Quality*, p. 205.

18   Proceedings of the Committee of Safety, 3 July 1775. Saunders, *Colonial Records*, Vol. 10, p. 65.

19   Governor Martin's 'fiery' Proclamation, 8 August 1775. Saunders, *Colonial Records*, Vol. 10, pp. 141–51.

20   Proceedings of the Provincial Congress, 25 August 1775. *Ibid.*, Vol. 10, p. 180.

21   *Ibid.*, 23 August 1775. Saunders, *Colonial Records*, Vol. 10, pp. 173–4.

22   Letter from Governor Martin to the Earl of Dartmouth, 5 July 1775. Saunders, *Colonial Records*, Vol. 10, pp. 247–8.

23   Rankin, *The Moore's Creek Bridge Campaign*, p. 11.

24   Letter from Governor Martin to the Earl of Dartmouth, 16 October 1775. *Ibid.*, Vol. 10, pp. 274–8.

25   Governor Martin's Proclamation, 10 January 1776. Saunders, *Colonial Records*, Vol .10, pp. 397, 441–2.

CHAPTER TWELVE: A SECOND CULLODEN

1   Margaret Wheeler Willard (ed.), *Letters on the American Revolution 1774–1776*, pp. 314–5.
2   Order from General Martin to General MacDonald, 10 January 1776. Saunders, *Colonial Records*, Vol. 10, pp. 441–2.
3   Letter from Flora MacDonald to Sir John MacPherson, 21 October 1789, NLS 2618.
4   Manifesto to General MacDonald, 5 February 1776. Saunders, *Colonial Records*, Vol. 10, p. 443.
5   Adelaide L. Fries (ed.), *Records of the Moravians in North Carolina*, Vol. 3, p. 1026. Rankin, *Moore's Creek*, p. 13.
6   *Narravtive of a Body of Loyalists*, quoted in Wicker, *Ancient Records*, p. 435.
7   Thomas Rutherford's manifesto, 13 February 1776. Saunders, *Colonial Records*, Vol. 10, p. 452.
8   *Narrative of a Body of Loyalists*, quoted in Wicker, *Ancient Records*, p. 436.
9   Allan MacDonald's Claim, Loyalist Papers, PRO AO13, Bundles 87 and 122.
10 Letter from Professor Moore of Boston, *Clan Donald Journal*, Vol. 1, No. 8, August 1896, pp. 61–2.
11 *Ibid.*
12 Wicker, *Ancient Records*, p. 436.
13 *Ibid.*
14 Rankin, *Moore's Creek*, pp. 18–36. Wicker, *Ancient Records*, pp. 436–7.
15 Wicker, *Ancient Records*, p. 340.
16 *American Archives Series 5*, Vol. 2, p. 192.
17 Letter from Flora MacDonald to Sir John MacPherson, 21 October 1789, NLS 2618.

CHAPTER THIRTEEN: THE YEARS OF FEAR

1   Letter from Allan MacDonald to Continental Congress, 18 July 1777, *Papers of Continental Congress*, No. 78, Vol. 15, f. 231, quoted in J.P. MacLean, *Flora in America*, p. 69.
2   Letter from Flora MacDonald to Sir John MacPherson, 21 October 1789, NLS 2618.
3   *Ibid.*
4   R.O. DeMond, *Loyalists in North Carolina*, p. 119.
5   Letter from Captain MacDonald to Allan MacDonald, 31 December 1777. *Letterbook of Captain Alexander MacDonald*: (New York Historical Society), p. 387.
6   Letter from Flora MacDonald to Sir John MacPherson, 21 October 1789, NLS 2618.
7   *Ibid.*
8   *The Quince Silver*, typescript, Lower Cape Fear Historical Society.
9   Wicker, *Ancient Records*, p. 343.
10 Alexander MacLeod's Claim, *Loyalist Papers*, PRO AO13, Bundles 100 and 115.
11 Alexander MacDonald's Claim *Loyalist Papers*, PRO AO13, Bundle 121.
12 Eli Washington Caruthers, *Interesting Revolutionary Incidents and Sketches of Character, Chiefly in the Old North State*.
13 Saunders, *Colonial Records*, Vol. 2, pp. 295–6.
14 *Ibid.*, Vol. 10, p. 509.
15 *Ibid.*, Vol. 2, p. 295–6.

16 W .C. Ford, *Journals of the Continental Congress 1774–1789*, Vol. 10, p. 385.

17 Petition of Allan MacDonald of Kingsburgh, April 5 1777, *Papers of Continental Congress*, No. 42, Vol. 5, f. 41.

18 Letter from Allan MacDonald to Alexander Bartram, Library of Pennsylvania Historical Society.

19 *Papers of Continental Congress*, No. 78, Vol. 15, f. 231.

20 MacLean, *Flora in America*, pp. 67–70.

CHAPTER FOURTEEN: FREEDOM AT LAST

1 Letter from Captain MacDonald to Allan MacDonald, 31 December 1777. *Letterbook of Captain Alexander MacDonald*, p. 387.

2 *Ibid.*

3 *Ibid.*, p. 378.

4 Allan MacDonald's Claim, *Loyalist Papers*, PRO AO13, Bundles 87 and 122.

5 Letter from Captain MacDonald to Allan MacDonald, 31 December 1777. *Letterbook of Captain Alexander MacDonald*, p. 387.

6 I*bid.*, p. 389.

7 *Ibid.*, p. 388.

8 Letter from Captain MacDonald to Allan MacDonald, 12 January 1778. *Ibid.*, p. 394.

9 Letter from Captain MacDonald to Allan MacDonald, 19 February 1778. *Ibid.*, p. 401.

10 *Ibid.*, pp. 401–2.

11 *Ibid.*, p. 402.

12 Letter from Flora MacDonald to Sir John MacPherson, 21 October 1789, NLS 2618.

13 Walter Clark (ed.), *State Records of North Carolina*, Vol. 13, p. 64.

14 *Ibid.*, Vol .13, pp. 64–5.

15 Donald MacDonald's Claim, *Loyalist Papers*, PRO AO13, Bundle 121.

16 Letter from Flora MacDonald to Sir John MacPherson, 21 October 1789, NLS 2618.

17 Letter from Captain MacDonald to William McAdam, 10 June 1778. *Letterbook of Captain Alexander MacDonald*, p. 420.

18 Letter from Captain MacDonald to James Loudin, 9 June 1778. *Ibid.*, p. 416.

19 Letter from Captain MacDonald to John Ogilvie, 30 June 1778. *Ibid.*, p. 423.

20 Letter from Captain MacDonald to William McAdam, 21 April 1778. *Ibid.*, p. 441.

21 Letter from Flora MacDonald to Sir John MacPherson, 21 October 1789, NLS 2618.

22 *Ibid.*

23 *Ibid.*

24 Letter from Captain MacDonald to Mr Reily, Staten Island, 14 January 1777, and to Gilbert Meyer, 16 October 1777. *Letterbook of Captain Alexander MacDonald*, pp. 328, 377.

25 Letter from Captain MacDonald to unknown correspondent, 5 December 1778. *Ibid.*, p. 475.

26 Letter from Captain MacDonald to General Francis McLean, 17 December 1778. *Ibid.*, pp. 484–5.

27 Letter from Captain MacDonald to William McAdam, 19 January 1779. *Ibid.*, p. 496.

28 MacGregor, *Life of Flora*, p. 169.

29 F.F. Wylde, *Autobiography of Flora*, p. 138.

30 Letter from Flora MacDonald to Sir John MacPherson, 21 October 1789, NLS 2618.

CHAPTER FIFTEEN: HOME TO THE ISLANDS

1   Letter from Flora MacDonald to Sir John MacPherson, 21 October 1789, NLS 2618.

2   *Ibid.*

3   MacDonald, *Truth about Flora*, p. 95.

4   Letter from Flora MacDonald to Donald MacDonald, 17 May 1780, MacDonald: *Truth about Flora*, pp. 111–2.

5   Letter from Flora MacDonald to Mrs John MacKenzie, 12 July 1780. MacGregor, *Life of Flora*, p. 171.

6   *Ibid.*

7   *Ibid.*

8   *Ibid.*

9   Letter from Allan MacDonald to MacDonald of Balranald, 25 November 1781, Chevalier de Johnstone, *Memorials of the Rebellion in 1745 and 1746*, p. iii.

10   Allan MacDonald's Claim, *Loyalist Papers*, PRO AO13, Bundles 87 and 122.

11   'Per Mare Per Terram', by Donald J. MacDonald of Castleton, *Clan Donald Magazine*, Vol. 9, 1981, pp. 79–86.

12   Letter from Flora MacDonald to Donald MacDonald of Balranald, 10 December 1781, NLS 1707/43.

13   Letter from Flora MacDonald to Mrs MacKenzie of Delvine, undated; MacGregor, *Life of Flora*, pp. 171–2.

14   *Ibid.*

15   *Ibid.*

16   *Ibid.*

17   Letter from Flora MacDonald to Sir John MacPherson, 21 October 1789, NLS 2618.

18   Allan MacDonald's Claim, *Loyalist Papers*, PRO AO13, Bundles 87 and 122.

19   *Clan Donald Magazine*, Vol. 9, 1981, pp. 82–5. Letter from E. Bartholemew, Royal Marines Museum, to author, 10 February 1993.

20   Information from John V. Duncanson, Falmouth, Nova Scotia.

21   Allan MacDonald's Claim, *Loyalist Papers*, PRO AO13, Bundles 87 and 122.

22   *Ibid.*

23   Letter from John MacDonald to Flora MacDonald, 5 May 1787. MacDonald, *Truth about Flora*, p. 112.

24   *Ibid.*

25   *Fasti Ecclesiastiae Scoticanae*, Vol. 7, p. 170.

26   Letter from Flora MacDonald to Sir John MacPherson, 21 October 1789, NLS 2618.

27   *Ibid.*

28   *The Scots Magazine*, 1790, p. 205.

29   MacGregor, *Life of Flora*, p. 176.

30   *The Scots Magazine*, 1792, p. 518.

CHAPTER SIXTEEN: HEIRS TO THE LEGEND

1   James Hogg, *Jacobite Relics of Scotland*, Vol. 2, p. 426, Song XXII.

2   Hugh Douglas, *Charles Edward Stuart*, p. 106.

3 Fitzroy MacLean, *Bonnie Prince Charlie*, pp. 220–1.

4 MacGregor's *Life of Flora* was first published in 1882 and ran into many editions.

5 Wylde's *Autobiography of Flora* was published in 1870. Wylde could not have known Flora.

6 William Edmistoun Aytoun, 1813–65.

7 Letter from General Sir Patrick Palmer to *The Times*, 4 June 1991.

8 I am indebted to Donald F. MacDonald and James MacDonald of North Carolina and Edinburgh for information on their family who are descended on their maternal side through the MacQueens from Flora's half-sister.

9 Letters from Donald F. MacDonald to the author, 8 July 1989, 28 January 1990, 10 February 1990.

Bibliography

Alexis, or *The Young Adventurer*. London, 1746.

Ashe, Samuel A'Court, *History of North Carolina*. Greensborough, 1908.

Banks, James, *The Life and Character of Flora MacDonald*. Fayetteville, 1857.

Barron, E.M., *Prince Charlie's Pilot*. Inverness, 1913.

Bartram, William, *Travels Through North and South Carolina, etc.* Dublin, 1791.

Bass, Robert D., *The Green Dragoon: Life of Sir Banastre Tarleton*. New York, 1957.

Beacroft, W.B. and Smale, M.A., *The Making of America: from Wilderness to World Power*. London, 1982.

Blaikie, Walter B., *Itinerary of Charles Edward Stuart*. Edinburgh, Scottish Historical Society, 1897.

Blaikie, Walter B. (ed.), *Origins of the Forty-Five and Other Papers Relating to the Rising*. Scottish Historical Society, 1916.

Boatner, Mark Mayo, *Encyclopedia of the American Revolution*. New York, 1969.

Boswell, James, *Journal of a Tour to the Hebrides with Samuel Johnson*. Penguin Classics Edition: London, 1984.

Brickell, John, *The Natural History of North Carolina*. London, 1743.

Brown, Wallace, *The King's Friends*. Providence, 1965.

Butler, Lindley S., *North Carolina and the Coming of the Revolution, 1763-1776*. Raleigh, 1976.

Cameron, Alexander, *History and Traditions of Isle of Skye*. Inverness, 1871.

Carruth, Revd J.A., *Flora MacDonald the Highland Heroine*. Norwich, 1973.

Caruthers, Eli Washington, *Interesting Revolutionary Incidents: and Sketches of Character, Chiefly in the Old North State*, 1st Series. Philadelphia, 1854.

Chambers, Robert, *History of the Rebellion 1745–6*. Edinburgh, 1829.

Chambers, Robert, *Traditions of Edinburgh*. Edinburgh, 1868.

Clan Donald Journal. 1896.

Clan Donald Magazine. 1953 and 1968.

Clark, Murtrie Jane, *Loyalists in the Southern Campaign of the Revolution*. Baltimore, MD, 1981.

Clark, Walter (ed.), *State Records of North Carolina*, See Saunders, W.L.

Clinton, Sir Henry, *The American Rebellion*. Wm. B. Willcox (ed.). New Haven, 1954.

Clowes, William Laird, *The Royal Navy: a History*, Vol. 3. London, 1898.

DeMond, Robert O., *Loyalists in North Carolina During the Revolution*. Baltimore, MD, 1979.

Dill, Alonzo Thomas, *Governor Tryon and his Palace*. Chapel Hill, 1955.

Doran, J., *London in Jacobite Times*, 2 Vols. London, 1877.

Douglas, Hugh, *Charles Edward Stuart*. London, 1975.

Drummond, J., *The Female Rebels, Being Some Remarkable Incidents of the Lives, Characters and Families of the Titular Duke and Duchess of Perth, the Lord and Lady Ogilvy and of Miss Flora MacDonald*. London, 1747.

Fletcher, Inglis, *The Scotswoman*. Indianapolis, 1954.

Foote, W.H., *Sketches of North Carolina*. New York, 1846.

Forbes, Duncan, *Culloden Papers: Comprising an extensive and interesting correspondence from the year 1625 to 1748, including numerous letters from the unfortunate Lord Lovat and other distinguished persons of the time; With occasional State papers*. The whole published from the originals in the possession of D.G. Forbes of Culloden. London, 1815.

Forbes, Revd Robert, *The Lyon In Mourning*, 3 Vols, Henry Paton (ed.). Scottish Historical Society, Edinburgh, 1895–1896.

Force, Peter (ed.), *American Archives*. Washington, 1837–46.

Ford, W.C. (ed.), *Journals of the Continental Congress 1774–1789*. Washington, 1823.

Fries, Adelaide L. (ed.), *Records of the Moravians in North Carolina*, Vols. 1–3. Raleigh, 1922, 1925, 1926.

Gibson, John S., *Ships of The Forty-Five*. London, 1967.

Graham, I.C.C., *Colonists from Scotland*. American Historical Association, Ithaca, 1956.

Grant, Anne, *Letters Written by Mrs Grant of Laggan covering Highland Affairs and Persons Connected with the Stuart Cause in the 18th Century*, J.R.N. MacPhail (ed.). Scottish Historical Society, 1896.

Grant, I.F., *The Clan MacLeod*. Edinburgh, 1953.

Green, Paul, *The Highland Call*. Chapel Hill, 1941.

Hawks, Francis L., David L. Swan and Wm. A. Graham, *A Revolutionary History of North Carolina, in Three Lectures*. Wm. D. Cooke (compiler). Raleigh, 1853.

History of North Carolina, Vols 1–6, Chicago, n.d.

History of North America. London, 1776.

Hooker, Richard J. (ed.), *Journal and other Writings of Charles Woodmason, Anglican Itinerant*. Chapel Hill, 1953.

Johnson, Samuel, *Journey to the Western Isles of Scotland*, J.D. Fleeman (ed.). Oxford, 1985.

Johnstone, Chevalier de, *Memorials of the Rebellion in 1745 and 1746*. London, 1820.

Jolly, William, *Flora MacDonald in Uist*. Stirling, 1932.

Keppel (2nd Earl of Albemarle), William Anne, *Albemarle Papers*, Charles Sanford Terry (ed.). New Spalding Club, Aberdeen, 1902.

Lang, Andrew (ed.), *Highlands of Scotland in 1750*: Ms 104, King's Library, British Museum. Edinburgh, 1896.

Lang, Andrew, *Prince Charles Edward Stuart, the Young Chevalier*. London, 1903.

Lenman, Bruce, *The Jacobite Risings in Britain 1689–1746*. London, 1980.

Lenman, Bruce, *Jacobite Cause*. London, 1986.

Lewis, W.S., Hunting Smith, W. and Lam, G.L. (eds), *Horace Walpole's Correspondence with Sir Horace Mann, etc.* (London, 1967).

Linklater, Eric, *The Prince in the Heather*. London, 1976.

Logan, G. Murray, *Scottish Highlanders and the American Revolution*. Halifax , 1976.

Logan, Robert A., *Flora MacDonald's Husband in North America*. Typescript, Public Archives of Nova Scotia, 1964.

Love, A. Richardson, Jnr, 'North Carolina's Highland Scots Cultural Continuity and Change in 18th Century Scotland and Colonial America'. Unpublished thesis, University of North Carolina. Chapel Hill, 1981.

MacBean, Alexander, (Minister of Inverness 1746), *Memorial Concerning the Highlands, 1746*. Scottish Historical Society, 1916.

MacDonald, Revd A., *Memorials of the 45*. Inverness, 1930.

MacDonald, Captain Alexander, *Letterbook of Captain Alex MacDonald*. New York History Society Collection, New York, 1882.

MacDonald, Allan Reginald, *The Truth about Flora MacDonald*. Inverness, 1938.

MacDonald, Revds Angus and Archibald, *The Clan Donald*, 3 vols. Inverness, 1896, 1900, 1904.

MacDonald, Donald J. of Castleton, *Clan Donald*. Loanhead, 1978.

MacDonald, James Alexander, *Flora MacDonald: a History and a Message from James A. MacDonald*. Washington , 1916.

MacEachern, Leora. H and Williams, Isabel M. (ed.), *Wilmington-New Hanover Safety Committee Minutes 1774–1776*. Wilmington, 1974.

MacGregor, Alexander, *The Life of Flora MacDonald*. Stirling, 1882.

MacInnes, John, *Brave Sons of Skye*. London, 1899.

MacLean, Alasdair, *A MacDonald for the Prince*. Stornoway, 1982.

MacLean, Angus Wilton, *Highland Scots Settlements in North Carolina*. Ms, National Library of Scotland.

MacLean, Fitzroy, *Bonnie Prince Charlie*. London, 1988.

MacLean, J.P., *Flora MacDonald in America*. Lumberton, 1909. (Reprinted Morgantown, 1984).

Mackenzie, Alexander, *History of the MacDonalds*. Inverness, 1881.

MacKinnon, J. and Morrison, J., *The MacLeods: Genealogy of a Clan (1968–77)*. Edinburgh, 1967–77.

McLynn, Frank, *The Jacobites*. London, 1985.

Merrens, H.H., *Colonial North Carolina in the 18th Century: a Study in Historical Geography*. Chapel Hill, 1964.

Meyer, Duane, *The Highland Scots of North Carolina 1732–1776*. Chapel Hill, 1961.

Middlekauff, Robert L., *The Glorious Cause: The American Revolution 1763–1789*. New York, 1982.

Murray, C. de B., *Forbes of Culloden*. London, 1936.

New Statistical Account of Scotland 1845, Vol. 14, Inverness-shire. Edinburgh, 1845.

Nicolson, Alexander, *History of Skye*. Glasgow, 1930.

'A Narrative of the Proceedings of a Body of Loyalists in North Carolina.' In General Howe's letter of 25 April 1776. Colonial Office Records 1776. (Included In Wicker, *Miscellaneous Ancient Records of Moore County.*)

North Carolina Handbook, 1893.

North Carolina Historical Review, Vol. 67, No. 4, October 1990.

Pennant, Thomas, *A Tour of Scotland and Voyage to the Hebrides: 1772*. London, 1774.

The Quince Silver. Typescript, Lower Cape Fear Historical Society.

Quynn, Dorothy Mackay, 'Flora MacDonald in History', *North Carolina Historical Review*, Vol. XVIII, No. 3, 1941.

Rankin, Hugh F., *The Moore's Creek Bridge Campaign, 1776*. Burgaw, 1986.

Rose, Duncan, *Flora MacDonald and the Scottish Highlanders in America*. American Historical Register, Boston, 1897.

Roy, James A., *The Scot In Canada*. Toronto, 1947.

Sabine, Lorenzo, *Biographical Sketches of Loyalists of the American Revolution*. Boston, 1865 (Reprinted Baltimore, 1979).

Saunders, William L. (ed.), *Colonial Records of North Carolina*, Vols 1–10. Continued as *State Records of North Carolina*, Vols 11–30, Walter Clark (ed.). Raleigh & Goldsboro, NC.

1880–1905. Reprinted New York, 1967—1970.

Schaw, Janet, *Journal of a Lady of Quality*, Evangeline Walker Andrews and Charles MacLean Andrews (eds). New Haven, 1921.

Scobie, Major J.A. Mackay, *The Highland Independent Companies of 1745–1747*. Society of Army Historical Research, 1941.

Seton, Sir Bruce and Arnot, J.G. (eds.), *Prisoners of the '45*, 3 vols. Edinburgh, 1938–9.

Speck, W.A., *The Butcher: The Duke of Cumberland and the Suppression of the '45*. Oxford, 1981, p. 162.

The Scots Magazine.

The State Magazine NC, 1954.

Tayler, Alistair and Tayler, Henrietta, *1745 and After*. London, 1938.

Tayler, Alistair and Tayler, Henrietta, *History of the Rebellion 1745-46*. Roxburghe Club, 1944.

Tayler, Alistair and Tayler, Henrietta, *A Jacobite Miscellany*. Roxburghe Club, 1948.

Tayler, Henrietta, *Jacobite Epilogue*. London, 1941.

Troxler, Carole Watterson, *The Loyalist Experience in North Carolina*. Raleigh, 1976.

Vining, Elizabeth Gray, *Flora MacDonald: Her Life in the Highlands and America*. Philadelphia, 1966 and London, 1967.

Waddell, Alfred Moore, *A History of New Hanover County and the Lower Cape Fear Region*. 1909.

Warrand, Duncan (ed.), *More Culloden Papers*. Inverness, 1930.

Wicker, Rassie E., *Miscellaneous Ancient Records in Moore County*. Typescript.

Willard, Margaret Wheeler (ed.), *Letters on the American Revolution 1774–1776*. Boston, 1925.

Wylde, F.F., *The Autobiography of Flora MacDonald*. Edinburgh, 1870.

Whyte, Donald, *Dictionary of Scottish Emigrants to the USA*. Baltimore, 1972.

Woodmason, Charles, *The Carolina Backcountry on the Eve of the Revolution: Journal and other Writings of Charles Woodmason, Anglican Itinerant*, Richard J. Hooker (ed.). Chapel Hill, 1953).

Index

Abbreviations

NC - North Carolina
SC - South Carolina
NS - Nova Scotia

Jacobite
SPY WARS
H U G H   D O U G L A S

The Jacobite story is more than the tale of Bonnie Prince Charlie, his unlucky father and grandfather, and a handful of battles – the Boyne, Sheriffmuir, Preston, Prestonpans, Falkirk and Culloden. It is also one of history's longest-running spy sagas, the story of the dark underbelly of the Jacobite years, of spies and counter-spies, treachery and manipulation.

The Jacobite Movement began with the Glorious Revolution of 1688 when James II of England and VII of Scotland fled and his daughter, Mary, and her husband, William of Orange, took over the thrones. It ended in 1788 with the death of Prince Charlie who ruled as 'King over the Water'. Although destroyed several times – in the defeats of the risings of 1715, 1719 and 1745, and with the wrecking of several invasion attempts by France and Spain – in an intelligence war that drew in people from Sussex smugglers to Highland clansmen, the Jacobites proved remarkably able to haunt the Hanoverian government.

Across Europe 'moles' dug for secrets at every court, and kings, ambassadors, soldiers, cardinals and royal mistresses all took part, from the great Duke of Marlborough to Madame de Pompadour and the devious King Louis XV. Even young Glengarry, heir to a highland chieftainship, sold himself to Prince Charlie's enemies. Sir Robert Walpole proved a compulsive master mole-catcher, Baron Philip von Stosch combined art with spying, and the Irish adventurer, pimp and card-sharper, Dudley Bradstreet, claimed with justification to have wrecked Prince Charlie's 1745 rising.

As for the prince, in his character lurked all the makings of a great spy and the defects of a bad one. He was a master of disguise and intrigue, which fooled his enemies, yet his arrogance and impetuosity contributed greatly to the Jacobites' eventual defeat in the espionage war. In the final analysis all the battles won and lost during the Jacobite century do not account for the failure of the Stuarts to be restored to the kingdoms they lost at the Glorious Revolution: ultimate defeat lay in their failure to win the intelligence war.

Hbk ISBN 0 7509 1425 4   UK £19.9 US $34.95

The Private Passions of

BONNIE PRINCE CHARLIE

HUGH DOUGLAS

'a sympathetic account'
The Daily Telegraph

'entertaining and well-researched . . .'
The Sunday Telegraph

Charles Edward Stuart lives on as a romantic hero of legend yet, behind that image, history shows him to be a charismatic self-seeker who loved only himself and his cause. But is this true or fair? In this book, now available in a revised paperback edition, Hugh Douglas shows that Bonnie Prince Charlie was also a man capable of love, and of passionate love at that. Here is a re-examination of the Scottish hero whose flawed character and lack of success in matters of the heart influenced his relations with the royal courts of Europe and played an important part in his role in the history of Scotland and England – perhaps contributing as much to the defeat of the Jacobite cause as 'Butcher' Cumberland's musket fire at Culloden. As well as the torrid affair with the young Duchesse de Montbazon in Paris and the tragic tale of Clementine Walkinshaw, which resulted in a child, the author looks at the Prince's other relationships with women, from the formative one with his mother, to his disastrous late dynastic marriage to Louise de Stolberg, in which he was left a lonely, elderly cuckold, comforted by his daughter in his last years. Here is revealed another side to this always fascinating, sometimes cruel, but deeply passionate man.

Pbk ISBN 0 7509 1902 7   UK £11.99 US $19.95

ROBERT BURNS

The Tinder Heart

HUGH DOUGLAS

'Hugh Douglas has marvellously outlined Burns's life in the light of his chief enthusiasms: women and song.'

MURIEL SPARK, The Sunday Times

'a balanced study of the poet whose joyful sex-life outraged "guid folk" . . . Douglas has rare meat to chew upon, but gives much more in perceptive biographical writing. . . . discerning.'

MOIRA SHEARER, The Daily Telegraph

Though the catalyst for much of his poetry, Robert Burns' sex life has often been denied, glossed over, even bowdlerized out of recognition. How could a man who revelled so unashamedly in earthy, unending sexual adventures write so tenderly about women and love? How could he father eight illegitimate children, yet conceive that timeless song of faithfulness 'John Anderson my Jo'? Was Robert Burns 'not so much a conspicuous sinner as a man who sinned conspicuously'?

Hugh Douglas seeks out the truth about Burns to show a man who was much less secure than his actions suggest, one for whom sex was an act of rebellion as well as love. His peasant background was a shaping force in his attitude to women. Though amorous love was the impulse which drove him to verse, his love for his children usually transcended that for their mothers. Burns called himself 'an extravagant prodigal of affection' and Hugh Douglas here examines the extravagance which shaped Burns' life and poetry anew, tracing his relationships with women from a loving apprenticeship at his mother's knee to Jean Armour, his loyal, supportive wife. He also examines Burns' many amorous adventures: Nelly Kilpatrick, his harvest-field partner, who first inspired him to write; Highland Mary Campbell; the enigma of 'E'; Peggy Chalmers, who rejected him; Clarinda, who always held back; and Maria Riddell, who came nearest to being his intellectual equal.

Pbk ISBN 0 7509 1903 5   UK £9.99 US $17.95